Holy Day, Holiday

Holy Day, Holiday

The American Sunday

Alexis McCrossen

CORNELL UNIVERSITY PRESS

ITHACA AND LONDON

First published 2000 by Cornell University Press

Printed in the United States of America

Library of Congress Cataloging-in-Publication Data

McCrossen, Alexis.
    Holy day, holiday : the American Sunday / Alexis McCrossen.
        p.   cm.
    Includes bibliographical references (p.) and index.
    ISBN 0-8014-3417-3 (cloth)
        1. Sunday—History of doctrines—19th century.   2. Weekly rest-day—
United States—History—19th century.   3. Rest—Religious aspects—
Christianity—History of doctrines—19th century.   4. Sunday—History of
doctrines—20th century.   5. Weekly rest-day—United States—History—
20th century.   6. Rest—Religious aspects—Christianity—History of
doctrines—20th century.   I. Title.

BV111.M35   2000
263'.3'0973—dc21   99-055042

Cornell University Press strives to use environmentally responsible suppliers and materials to the fullest extent possible in the publishing of its books. Such materials include vegetable-based, low-VOC inks and acid-free papers that are recycled, totally chlorine-free, or partly composed of nonwood fibers. Books that bear the logo of the FSC (Forest Stewardship Council) use paper taken from forests that have been inspected and certified as meeting the highest standards for environmental and social responsibility. For further information, visit our website at www.cornellpress.cornell.edu.

Cloth printing   10   9   8   7   6   5   4   3   2

To my parents

Preston G. McCrossen

and

Macon McCrossen,

with love

Contents

Illustrations

Acknowledgments

I thank the teachers, friends, relatives, colleagues, librarians, and institutions that supported me while I wrote this book.

David D. Hall and Stephan Thernstrom expertly guided me through the first stages of this project, assuring me all along that it would one day be a book. I appreciate the interest, dedication, and patience they extended over the years. I also am grateful to the following teachers, peers, and friends: Cynthia Blair, Thomas Cripps, Juliana DiGiosia, Amy Dillingham, Jessica Dorman, Ellen Fitzpatrick, Becky Gould, R. Marie Griffith, Linda Hammett, Patrick Kelley, Kimerer LaMothe, Susan Lively, Christine McFadden, Charles McGovern, John McGreevy, Michael McNally, John O'Keefe, Eric Pakula, Kate Phillips, Juliet Schor, Tracy K. Smith, Andrew Walsh, and Ron Yanosky. During the initial stages of research and writing, I received generous financial support from Harvard University's History of American Civilization program, the Lilly Foundation, Radcliffe College, and the Whiting Foundation, for which I am thankful.

During the later stages, I received further support, advice, and encouragement from Sarah Barnes, William R. Hutchison, and Winton Solberg, who each provided me with extremely helpful critiques of the manuscript. I deeply appreciate the enthusiasm of my editor at Cornell University Press, Peter Agree, and the care Kay Scheuer took with the manuscript. Richard R. John shared documents, citations, and ideas that have substantially improved this book. Richard W. Fox generously shared a collection of sources concerning Sunday which he had been gathering over the years for his study of liberal Protestantism. I owe a special debt to David D. Hall, who with his unerring eye read the manuscript in its final stages and who has been the best mentor imaginable.

The comments of scholars and friends at conferences and in correspondence have also been invaluable. I want especially to thank Gail Bederman, Marie Bolton, Anne Boylan, Mark Chaves, Walter H. Conser, Richard Doyle, Ken Fones-Wolf, Allen C. Guelzo, William Hutchinson, Linda Kahn, Jackson Lears, David Lowenthal, Colleen McDannell, Roy Rosenzweig, Louise L. Stevenson, and Peter J. Thuesen. The members of the American Religious History Colloquium and the American Civilization Colloquium at Harvard University, the National Endowment for the Humanities 1996 summer workshop "Grace, Fortune, and Luck" at Rutgers University, and the Dallas Area Social History Group were generous with praise, criticism, and enthusiasm for this project. I thank the organizers and participants.

I am grateful for the financial and institutional support I received for the later stages of the work. At Southern Methodist University the Sharpe Fund of the Clements Department of History, Dedman College, and the University Research Council each funded travel to archives as well as other research and publication expenses. A Littleton-Griswold grant from the American Historical Association allowed me to spend several weeks at the South Carolina Historical Society with the Aaron Solomon papers to learn more about the constitutional challenge to Sunday laws during the 1960s. The summer faculty fellowship program of the Louisville Institute generously funded a summer in New York City, where I was able to write substantial portions of the book and do critical research in area archives.

I thank the administrators of the Clements Department of History, Brenda Cooper, Judy Mason, and Mildred Pinkston, and my colleagues in the department. At Southern Methodist University and in Dallas, colleagues, students, and friends lent their help through the many stages of the project: Stephanie Cole, Ed Countryman, Melissa Dowling, David Doyle, Jane Elder, David Farmer, Margaret Garcia-Davidson, Donna Ginther, Kenneth Imo, Tom Knock, Alison Parker, Carol Payne, Martha Selby, Willard Spiegelman, and Kathleen Wellman. Research on both coasts would not have been possible, or fun, without the hospitality of Elizabeth Cohen and Teal Eich in New York City; Kit and Jan Cammermeyer, Bill and Liz Foster, Kristin Majeska, Tamara Helen Mc-Crossen, and Nate Orr in Washington, D.C.; and David and Nathalie Cowan and Chris and Molly Gales in San Francisco.

I have made use of the Aaron Solomon Collection and the Allston-Pringle Collection (South Carolina Historical Society), the holdings of the University of California's Bancroft Library, diaries in the Joseph

Downs Collection of Manuscripts and Ephemera (Winterthur Museum and Library), the Sam DeVincent Collection of Illustrated Sheet Music Covers (Archives Center, National Museum of American History, the Smithsonian Institution), the resources of the Museum of Radio and Television Broadcasting (New York City), the collections in the Library of Congress, and the Black Women Oral History Project (Schlesinger Library, Radcliffe College). I thank each institution for permission to quote passages and reproduce illustrations from the collections.

Several people deserve special thanks for putting up with me and this project for so long: my sister, Tamara Helen McCrossen, and dear friends Amy Amend, Tom Augst, Sarah Barnes, and Amy Greenberg. I offer special thanks to Adam Herring.

I dedicate this book to my parents, partly because that is what grateful children do, and mostly because I love them. I have enjoyed preparing this book, above all the conversations with strangers and friends about their Sundays, my Sundays, and Sunday in general.

Introduction:
A Method of Reckoning Time

Julian West, a man of the nineteenth century who unexpectedly re-
turns to life in the year 2000 in Edward Bellamy's utopian novel *Looking Backward*, is surprised to find that "the method of reckoning time"
has not changed, that the days are not "counted in lots of five, ten or fifteen," and that the twentieth century still had "Sundays and sermons."
In his time there were "prophets who foretold" that "the world would
have dispensed with both."[1] But the world did not. In West's twentieth
century, as in ours, Sunday remains a vital institution and a symbol of
the division of time between work, rest, and leisure in the United
States.

The irreversibility of time—and, within the calendar of Christian culture in the modern world, the inevitability of Sundays—must not hide
from us the changing historical use of this, the most distinctive day of
the week. In addition to telling a version of Sunday's history (complete
with blue laws, Sabbatarians, Sabbath breakers, and such), in this book
I map out a cultural history of rest within American culture. The cate-
gories of work and rest frame my version of Sunday's history. I delineate
how conflict, negotiation, and accommodation over the meaning of
Sunday complicated, broadened, and eventually depleted American
meanings for rest.

Although historians have studied blue laws, Sabbatarianism, and
local disputes over Sunday sports and movies, Sunday itself has been
marginal in the analyses and narratives.[2] But nineteenth-century Americans, even if they lost track on other days of the week, always knew

when it was Sunday. As all days do, Sunday in the nineteenth century came in winter and spring, summer and fall; sometimes it was rainy and cold, at other times "the very elements seemed to know it was a holy day" and, in the words of one diarist, "wished to favor its observance." Not uncommon in accounts of the day are reflections on the tribute paid by the weather to Sunday: "the air itself was purer and more wholesome than on weekdays"; "the sun shines with unusual brilliancy."[3] One mid-century diarist reveals a deep awareness of the day: "The first and last day of this year falls on Sunday, and there are 53 Sundays in the year, an unusual occurrence." After experiencing a loss of religious faith in 1880, another diarist ceased to note the day of the week, although he had been doing so for nearly twenty years. Indeed, the day still held meaning midway through the twentieth century: many oral histories concerning the bombing of Pearl Harbor begin, "It was Sunday."[4]

The attentive reader will realize that this book is mostly a history of Sunday during the long nineteenth century, for it is during this time that Sunday took its enduring forms. Any person's experience might demonstrate that Sunday is irreducible to a single interpretive framework. Nevertheless, I have crafted a narrative that imposes a chronological history on a recurring "event." There were turning points in Sunday's history, and it is these that I highlight. Sunday was never an empty vessel, but I am primarily concerned with the meanings that have accumulated since 1800. Apart from several significant, but numerically small groups, Americans of disparate backgrounds have had this in common—they have agreed to cease working each Sunday except under the direst necessity. Shifting attention from work to rest opened up spaces of time for Americans to devote to religion, family, learning, and fun. I separate these developments from each other for close analysis, but it is important to note that change in all spheres of social life was simultaneous, contingent, and overlapping. Religious meanings for Sunday vied for power in the antebellum period; domestic and didactic ones ascended at mid century; and values associated with the consumer culture—pleasure, amusement, fun, diversion, recreation—spread around the start of the twentieth century. In sum, disputes over the meaning of rest, due to the growth of competing religious traditions, changes in the shape and function of families, and the expansion of opportunities for learning and amusement shaped Sunday during the last two centuries.

Through its exploration of the rudimentary meanings for *the* day of rest, Chapter 1 frames the history of Sunday within a world view that divided daily life into work and rest. In it I recount the origins of Sunday, estimate how many Americans performed wage labor on

Sittin' Around on Sunday [1935]. Sam DeVincent Collection of Illustrated Sheet Music Covers, Archives Center, National Museum of American History, Smithsonian Institution.

A middle-aged man in his pajamas and slippers epitomizes rest's most subversive meaning—idleness. Throughout the nineteenth century Sunday promised the kind of rest that could be quarantined from the contaminating effects of idleness. But as the fear of idleness diminished, there became more room within mainstream culture to indulge in rising late, reading funnies, and even drinking from a straw. As the song's lyrics state: "Call it lazy but it's lovely."

Sunday, and propose that Sunday be studied as a symbol and as an institution. In doing so I set aside the often discussed competition between the sacred and the secular, as well as questions concerning de-Christianization that have preoccupied so many sociologists and social critics over the last century. My emphasis in this chapter on the centrality of work, rest, and leisure to the history of Sunday runs through the entire book, displacing a more conventional framework that invokes "sacred" and "secular."

Chapters 2, 3, and 4 establish the signal place of Sunday in American debates over work, rest, and culture. Chapter 2 concerns the antebellum controversy about transporting and delivering the United States mails on Sunday. Between 1810 and 1830 Sabbatarianism (a long-lived movement devoted to institutionalizing Sunday as the Sabbath) first took an organized form in the United States. During the 1830s and 1840s Sabbatarians and their opponents articulated religious meanings for Sunday that resonated throughout their century and ours. Although the protest against transporting and delivering the mail on Sunday failed, it did strengthen awareness of the day as the primary site in the new nation for religious activity. During the same decades nostalgia for the "Puritan Sabbath" generated enough momentum that what came to be known as the "traditional Sabbath" took shape in American literature and memory.

The third chapter describes Sunday on the frontier, in cities, and during the Civil War. In all three sites new meanings for and practices on Sunday emerged. Sundays on the frontier and in the city gave rise to a second wave of Sabbatarian activity in the late 1850s, which swept up millions of followers after the war. The war's own disruptive effect on American culture extended to its Sundays, during which soldiers fought battles, medics attended to the wounded and dying, and trains and supplies moved continually.

Demographic, technological, and civic developments between 1840 and 1870—such as the large-scale Irish and German immigration, the expansion of the system of railroads, and the rise of the public library—set in motion factors that would remake Sunday into "man's day" rather than God's during the last three decades of the nineteenth century. Chapter 4 discusses the relationship between culture and democracy, debates over which informed new hopes for Sunday. It then details how liberal Protestants countered Sabbatarian meanings for the day through their insistence that the Boston Public Library—at the time the nation's flagship public library—be open on Sunday. Liberal Protestants accepted a variety of individual wants and needs; their toleration aided the expansion of Sunday's horizons.

Chapters 5, 6, 7, and 8 explore what these new horizons encompassed, as well as the problems that took shape in these new confines. By the end of the nineteenth century, extensive visiting and socializing characterized urban and rural Sundays; mothers and wives spent considerable energy making the day into a "family day"; Sunday newspapers became widely available; libraries, museums, fairs, and other didactic institutions opened; parks, seaside resorts, amusement parks, and other recreational sites teemed with visitors; and freight and passenger trains ran continuously in nearly every part of the nation. The means for experiencing Sunday and getting rest had dilated considerably, as had the potential for missing out on them altogether.

American leisure, situated within the home, cultural institutions, and commercial recreations, came to material and ideological life on the innumerable Sundays between 1870 and 1930. The fifth chapter explains how "apostles of culture," inspired by religious liberalism, fashioned Sunday into a vestibule for "Culture." Believing that "Culture" could lift immigrants and the native-born out of degradation, reformers hoped to turn Sunday into, as Jane Addams described it, "a life-saving station for the higher life." A librarian captured the essence of the Sunday-opening movement when she reasoned that "there is a large class of people who will not go to church and who will not read the Bible, who could be reached by the means of grace afforded by a library."[5] Sunday could enable people of all stations in life, who had no other free time, to educate themselves. To do so, Americans needed libraries, museums, and world's fairs—central vehicles of education until the 1920s—to open each Sunday. Chapters 6 and 7 detail how excursions, spectacles, and commerce became part of the ideal Sunday and central to American leisure. The mark of the dollar has altered the day considerably: large profits are made by providing the kinds of services—transportation, entertainment, and sales—that transformed a day of rest into one of leisure. Chapter 8 describes the social spaces and activities that Sunday provided for families. It addresses in particular the arrival of newspapers, radio, and television in all but a few American dwellings, a process that changed everyday life, Sunday, and above all, rest.

Shortly after the turn of the century a Sabbatarian suggested that "even in heaven, it would appear, there is a recognition of the value of the pause, the lull, the quiescent period, the rest."[6] During the last two centuries, Sunday gained power from its status as *the* day of rest. Sunday remains meaningful in our time because of the continued effort of Americans to gain satisfaction and meaning from their work and from their rest, and to seek such satisfaction in activities germane to both

THE BULLETIN

of the

NEW YORK SABBATH COMMITTEE

31 Bible House, New York City.

| Vol. 1. | NOVEMBER, 1914 | No. 5 |

DON'T KILL THE TREE THAT SHADES YOU

"Don't Kill the Tree That Shades You". General Research Division, The New York Public Library, Astor, Lenox and Tilden Foundations.

The Sabbath, this illustration implies, assures rest for all people. The bearded older man represents the Sabbatarian commitment to banning work on Sunday through means both persuasive and coercive. He protects "Sabbath Rest" from the laborer's ax-strokes, explaining that it shelters workingmen and future generations from relentless toil.

holy days and holidays. The book's closing chapter considers changing strategies for obtaining rest, including resorting to times of the week other than Sunday. It contends, as does the entire book, that conflict over work, rest, and leisure best explains the continuities and changes in meanings for and practices on Sunday.

1 What Is a Day of Rest?

What is a day of rest? To one man, the attendance upon church brings restfulness to the wearied mind; to another, some other form of occupation would determine the character of the day of rest, but to the man whose muscles have been strained to their utmost tension for six days and for ten hours each day, whose nervous force has been largely drawn upon through the action of speeded machinery, and who has had no time during the week for reading, for recreation, and for many of the amenities which come to people of different callings, a day of rest may be entirely another affair.

—CARROLL D. WRIGHT, *Sunday Labor* (1885)

"What is a day of rest?" asked pioneering labor analyst Carroll D. Wright in one of the few studies of Sunday labor ever published. In an industrializing society still dependent on armies of agricultural laborers, Sunday stood in opposition to relentless work for the majority of nineteenth-century Americans.[1] The six working days blended into one unit—the workweek—in contrast to Sunday, the day of rest. Americans disagreed about what constituted rest rather than idleness, dissipation, or work. Conflicts over these distinctions mark Sunday's history; through the course of the century an array of practices designated as restful emerged, some in concert, some in conflict. When Americans contrasted holy day and holiday, they activated different definitions of work and rest. Thus these spheres are the most useful way to frame Sunday's history.

I begin this chapter by briefly surveying Sunday's long relationship with Christianity. Through the nineteenth century rest, as the opposite of work, signaled a shift of energy from the duties of this world to those of another, radically different kind, and so consensus held that churches provided the proper setting and Sundays the proper time for rest. Yet, as important as rest was, most Americans have been more concerned with work, especially where to find it and how to keep it. I detail how an increasing proportion of them after the Civil War found it on Sunday.

Chapters 2–7 suggest that this did not necessarily destroy Sunday's status as a day of rest; much of the work enabled the expansion of practices associated with rest and with religion. It is because of this complication that I cannot tell Sunday's history as if it were about secularization—that is, as if it followed a trajectory from holy day to holiday. Instead, the day was a realm where holy day and holiday vied for power. It provided Americans with symbolic and institutional parameters within which the meanings of work and rest were negotiated.

Origins: Sunday before 1800

The history of Sunday is perplexing, more a story of overlays and fluidity than of sharp and well-defined changes. Since Sunday entered the weekly calendar, sometime between 100 B.C. and A.D. 150, there have been moments when it was redefined in a clear manner, as when Constantine decreed the Sunday-Sabbath in A.D. 321, or when the religious importance of Sunday receded, as during the Middle Ages. The Protestant Reformation's reappraisal of Sunday as the Sabbath, spurring Puritan efforts in England and the Low Countries to remodel the liturgical calendar around the weekly Sabbath day, was one of the most highly charged moments in the history of Sunday. This revival of the Sunday-Sabbath altered the rhythms of the Christian year, replacing numerous but intermittent saints' days with a weekly holy day.[2]

The term "Sabbath" itself has a contested history. The Book of Exodus identifies the seventh day of the week—Saturday—as the day on which God rested, which is why He made it the Sabbath for the Jews. For a number of reasons, early Christians sought to transfer their day of worship from Saturday to Sunday. They continued, nonetheless, to observe the Jewish Sabbath, and thus were inclined to call Sunday "the Lord's Day." When sixteenth- and seventeenth-century Puritans and related sectarian groups became committed to an Old Testament emphasis for Christianity, they began to refer to Sunday as the Sabbath, a practice that spread among later Protestants. No small number of Americans were taught, as was the New England mill-girl Lucy Larcom, "that it was heathenish to call the day Sunday." Still, the record suggests that Americans referred to the day as Sunday at times, as the Sabbath at others. A gold miner's mid-century diary, for instance, records "there is no work done Saturday afternoons or Sunday on the Sabbath." A diary replete with rich entries concerning Sunday at sea in 1849 also mixes the terms Sunday and Sabbath: the entry for May 27 begins "Today, being Sunday, we had preaching." The next Sunday's entry opens "A more beautiful Sabbath morning I never saw." A week later, the entry reads "Sunday morning, bright and pleasant."[3] Sabbath was one meaning—a powerful one—for Sunday. When Sunday arrived none argued whether it was Sunday; some, however, disputed whether it was the Sabbath.

The American Sunday is best understood within an Anglo-American context, with roots in both Puritan and Anglican traditions. Conflicts over Sunday in sixteenth- and seventeenth-century England revolved around Anglican and Puritan modes of observing the day. Medieval English Sundays were so riotous—with ales, wakes, feasts, dances, and fairs taking place in churchyards—that some lamented that Sunday in England better served the devil than did any other day of the week. Near the beginning of the seventeenth century, the Puritans began to practice strict Sabbath observance within the Church of England. Although no friend of the Puritans, James I issued *The Book of Sports* in 1617. It enumerated lawful Sunday recreations and banned ales, wakes, and bear baiting among other ceremonies of misrule. Around the same time, English Puritans and Anglicans began to reconsider the relationship between sports and labor. Puritans suggested that since sports were types of bodily labor, they detracted from bodily rest and from service to God: therefore, they should be banned on Sunday. There were many who considered moderate sport beneficial, but even Anglican bishops began to agree that recreation "belongs not to rest, but to labor."[4] Nevertheless, a core of the English population remained committed to a version of Sunday observance that allowed for, at the very least, sporting, drinking, and visiting after morning services. In 1647, owing to the persistence of Sunday recreation, the Parliament (under Puritan influence) designated the second Tuesday of each month as the day for recreation.[5] Despite the provision of a time for recreation apart from Sunday, the English population continued to mix rest and recreation in varying degrees, perhaps because Puritans had also eliminated all holy days, including Christmas, except Sunday. Over the following decades conflict over Sunday in England veered between Puritan and Anglican strictures.[6]

This conflict would continue across the Atlantic. Along with many other long-lived customs, the Puritans brought a strict form of Sunday observance to the New World that influenced how the other British North American colonies developed their own blend of Sunday regulation. Sunday laws—known as "blue laws" because of the supposed color of paper on which they were published in colonial Connecticut—emerged out of widely shared respect for Sunday. Both law and custom set the day apart from the rest of the week; even Quakers (who were suspicious of civil laws regarding religious belief and observance) passed

Anti-Blue Law Magazine, cover (1921). General Research Division, The New York Public Library, Astor, Lenox and Tilden Foundations.

The designation "blue laws," which colloquially refers to those laws that regulate morality, suggests Puritan and Pilgrim influence. Sometime during the first part of the nineteenth century, many Americans came to believe that "tradition" included abstinence from alcohol, strict Sunday observance, and rigid separation of the sexes, and either rejected or cleaved to these imagined traditions. The association of strict Sunday observance with Puritanism persists to this day.

a Sabbath Law in 1705 in Pennsylvania, and Catholic-dominated Maryland did so shortly thereafter. By no means was Sunday observance uniform—Virginians raced and gambled on horses, the enslaved in North and South tended their own plots and went to market in nearby towns, and fishermen in Marblehead, Massachusetts, repaired to taverns rather than church. It was, however, common.[7]

The relationship between work, recreation, and rest prior to and after the eighteenth century significantly influenced Sundays as well. Before the 1730s, one historian tells us, "work and recreations did not yet constitute separate realms of experience." In this context, the day of rest stood in contrast all other days, whether they were spent in labor or in leisure or in a fluid combination of the two. The few who made up the elite in England, Europe, and the American colonies were the first to consider labor and leisure as "separable—but not yet separate and certainly not opposite or oppositional—spheres of life." For them, leisure was time spent in "necessary and productive activities," many of which were found in "less physical forms of work" and recreation. Rest and leisure, then, shared little common purpose. The conviction that physical discomfort was an essential part of worship, which other descendants of the Puritans expressed in late eighteenth-century conflicts over heating their meeting houses on Sundays, further illuminates the contrast that once held between rest and leisure. Starting in the 1750s Americans of all ranks began to recognize distinct times and places where leisure activities dominated, and it is out of this recognition as well as out of changing patterns of work—such as the rise of the daily and hourly wage—that the separation of labor and leisure that characterizes modern life emerged.[8] Work and rest remained in opposition until after the end of the nineteenth century, but as leisure matured into a separate sphere, its distinction from rest lost clarity. If leisure was not work, was it rest? The conflicts over Sunday observance, then, reveal a great deal about the emergence of labor and leisure as separate spheres.

Working on Sunday

The seemingly insatiable, but unpredictable, demand for labor that characterized mercantile and industrial capitalism, even in their early stages, exercised tremendous influence as Americans sought to make Sunday the day of rest. Before the Civil War few Americans worked on Sunday. Slaves were an exception. Although slave labor in fields, foundries, and workshops was normally suspended on Sundays, it is impossible to call Sunday a day of rest for enslaved Americans. Many slaves used the day to supplement their diets—by hunting, fishing, gathering, and gardening—and others were engaged in household duties, their own and those of their owners.[9] The frontier was another area of exception. Consensus and law mandated that Sunday was the rest day, but not all work stopped. A miner described the streets of Sacramento one Sunday during the Gold Rush as "just as busy as on week days, scores of people buying and selling . . . carpenters all at work on building." It was so much like a week day that he "was not aware it was Sunday till late in the afternoon." A decade or so later, a farmer confessed to his diary: "Another breach in my Sunday resolve not to work, by killing the hog." Near the end of the 1880s, a businessman and farm owner wrote to his wife that he and his son "worked hard all day Sunday picking up, burning, cleaning chicken houses, until everything was as neat as a pin."[10]

During the antebellum period the widespread refusal of servants to work on Sundays highlights the ubiquity of Sunday's status as the day of rest and how limited were the prevailing meanings of rest. After the Civil War, employers were able to require at least a half-day's labor from their domestic servants, especially their cooks, because the supply of labor was no longer as scant as it once had been. Lucy Salmon, who investigated conditions in domestic service in the 1890s, noted that "Sunday in a private family is usually anything but a day of rest to the domestic." Guests "to dinner or tea or both," meant "extra work."[11] As the century passed, the idealization of the "domestic Sabbath" also created more work for nonservant women each Sunday. Images of "idle womanhood" that served to isolate women from the salutary effects of the work ethic also prevented them from claiming the right to rest on Sunday.[12] Their job—making the home restful—was never-ending, especially as the definition of rest expanded. Families that relied on the wage labor of husband and wife often did household chores on Sundays. In the 1870s a carpenter described going to church in the morning and then having "little things to do at home on Sundays to make it comfortable and happy; things that we can't do on other days."[13] The extent and nature of labor done in many homes on Sunday suggests that even though some members of a family may have ceased working, the day was anything but restful for wives, mothers, and domestic servants.

It was, however, increasing instances of farm and factory labor after the Civil War, rather than household labor, that first alarmed Americans concerning the status of their day of rest. Snapshots from Sundays in rural areas, where a majority of the American population lived until 1920, might picture rest, but more likely would reveal farmers milking cows, feeding hogs, gathering eggs, picking cotton, or threshing wheat. Some farm work had always been done on Sunday regardless of religious strictures, and there were times and seasons when continuous labor was necessary, as during critical periods of the harvest. A farmer turned minister explained that "God Almighty didn't construct a six-day cow, and the hogs are none the less hungry because it is a holy day." It was particularly difficult to accommodate large-scale farm production to a six-day workweek. In the 1860s, for instance, cheese factories in upstate New York began to run on Sundays in response to increased supplies of milk and demands for cheese. Not only were operatives forced to work, but farmers delivered milk once, and many times twice, a day to the factories, disrupting church services with "the rattling of milk carts" and otherwise "interfering with the devotions of the closet and the family and the sanctuary." As farming turned corporate during the late decades of the nineteenth century, Sunday labor on the farm became less evenly distributed. Mechanical milking devices, automatic sprinklers, cold storage, and other developments allowed prosperous farmers to take Sunday as a day of rest, while older habits continued to characterize the Sundays of their laborers, tenant farmers, and sharecroppers.[14]

Within the world of industrial labor a different pattern emerged. During the first part of the century, few people worked, since there was little demand, owing to the absence of continuous manufacturing industries and the small number of transportation lines. The number of Americans working on Sunday increased sharply with the outbreak of the Civil War and continued even when peace came. With the development of continuous manufacture, the integration of production processes, and the expansion of the transportation network during the last third of the nineteenth century, the demand for Sunday labor increased. By the turn of the century nearly a third of all steel workers (mostly the unskilled) endured twelve-hour shifts seven days a week. Mining, oil drilling, canning, and other industrial processes also became seven-day-a-week occupations. Railroad workers spent Sunday in the yards doing repairs or on the rails running the countless passenger, freight, and mail trains. Such a work schedule undoubtedly contributed to high rates of mortality on and off the job. Sunday was the day when steel and other industrial workers took "the long turn" (two twelve-hour shifts in a row), perhaps because it was the first day in the new week, and therefore the start of a new shift schedule and pay period.[15] As such, it came to stand for more than simply a violation of the day of rest; it represented the relentlessness of the machine-driven economy. Continuous manufacture stole rest from many. Additionally, its visibility mocked Sunday's status as the day of rest. Clouds of smoke and steam marked many a horizon, while men and women in work clothes and with exhausted faces trudged through the streets, perhaps pleased to have another day's work in an uncertain economy, but themselves a symbol of Sunday's tenuous status as the day of rest.

The increase was most apparent in the service sector. New ways to rest required more services, which in turn required that more people work on Sunday inside and outside the home. Barber shops, bakeries, drug stores, train depots, and restaurants were already open on Sundays in antebellum cities. After the Civil War, small shopkeepers stayed open, librarians handed out reading materials, bartenders poured drinks, and streetcar conductors ran their routes on Sundays. By the turn of the twentieth century, millions were laboring each Sunday. The average number of hours worked per week had decreased across the board by the 1920s, but more Americans than ever before were working on Sunday. With incomes rising and the world of goods and services expanding, why would individuals prefer having all services rendered exclusively between Monday and Saturday? Sunday was the day when services could be most deeply savored. With this in mind, one can see how the availability of services enhanced Sunday's status, especially as Americans came to attribute more and more value to what could be bought and sold in the marketplace. The irony was that the rest day required, and still requires, work. As one New Yorker recently declared: "Cooking anything is out. On my perfect Sunday, others toil for me."[16]

Secularization?

Declension models—tracing the fall from high to low or holy to profane—characterize many of the narratives about the history of American culture and society. Some historians of late, however, have highlighted the interdependency of "high" and "low" culture, and few today consider either as belonging to a separate, hierarchical sphere. Great nineteenth-century American authors like Walt Whitman and Henry James read the penny press, attended vaudeville theatricals, and took part in various fads; they also incorporated themes and materials from commercial culture into their canonical poems, stories, essays, and novels. Here, as in many other places, high and low were mixed. It is and was only critics who would separate them. Contemporary scholars and critics who treat "sacred" and "secular" in an oppositional manner do so following similar assumptions that informed the study of culture for so long. Were I to accept a scholastic quarantine of the sacred from the secular, the holy from the profane, this world from the next, I would greatly miscast the history of Sunday.

This book's title disavows secularization. A model of secularization that depicts a transformation of sacred *into* profane, religious *into* secular, or holy day *into* holiday provides a classic declension narrative that might allow a history of Sunday to be written with more ease and clarity than I have experienced or accomplished. I argue, instead, that through various processes—some negotiated, others inevitable—groups and individuals shifted the boundaries delimiting Sunday's meanings. In making and remaking Sunday, Americans have invoked holy day and holiday not as antitheses but as part of a continuum. Its parameters always contained elements sacred and profane, but far more important were the poles of work and rest. Secularization theories have their uses, but in a book such as this one they obscure salient questions.

Throughout the nineteenth century, the teachings of Christian churches shaped the ways that Americans observed Sunday, the laws that legislatures wrote to protect Sunday, and the central meanings of the day. By the twentieth century, progressive reformers, amusement proprietors, and sporting enthusiasts gained substantial influence over the meanings and uses of the day. Yet although the authority to speak to and for spiritual well-being had expanded well beyond the pulpit, Christian assumptions and goals were not abandoned. Some social theorists have called the expansion of initiatives and responsibilities beyond the reach of clergy and church "secularization"; others call it "de-Christianization."[17] I find that both terms suggest an absence of sacred or Christian purpose, which the evidence concerning Sunday in the United States does not support. Domestic, didactic, and commercial meanings for Sunday *joined* rather than replaced religious meanings. In doing so they bridged the gap between rest and leisure.

Clearly Christianity plays a significant part in the history of Sunday. The intricate and numerous developments within American religious history are a backdrop to the history of Sunday. Theological disputes that took place in churches, religious periodicals, and meeting halls directly shaped the ways that millions of Americans spent their Sundays. Several biblical texts address the Sabbath; American Protestants who believed that Sunday was the Sabbath read them carefully. In addition to the fourth commandment, the following texts became the basis of a great deal of exegesis and debate:

> Isaiah 58:13–14 "If thou turn away thy foot from the sabbath, from doing thy pleasure on my holy day . . . Then shalt thou delight thyself in the Lord."

Romans 14:5 "One man esteemeth one day above another; another esteemeth every day alike. Let every man be fully persuaded in his own mind."

Colossians 2:16–17 "Let no man therefore judge you in meat, or in drink, or in respect of a holyday, or of the new moon, or of the sabbath days . . ."

Ephesians 5:15–16 "See then that ye walk circumspectly, not as fools, but as wise men, redeeming the time, because the days are evil."

Ezekiel 22:8 "Thou hast despised mine holy things, and hast profaned my Sabbaths."

Mark 2:27 "The sabbath was made for man, not man for the sabbath."

Each of these precepts invokes the divide between work and rest, although none mandates what characterizes either state. This necessity— of distinguishing between work and rest—frames the history of Sunday in the United States.

Rest and Leisure

The blurry boundaries between work, rest, and leisure owe much to Christian traditions. One of Sunday's most resonant symbolic meanings, which emerged out of Christian tradition, was as a marker of time. Nineteenth-century Protestants characterized Sunday as "God's Timepiece for Eternity" and believed it made the week and time itself. At mid century a Presbyterian warned that without "the Sabbath, we should all be carried off into the fathomless abyss." Although some worried about the disappearance of Sunday as awareness of "the bell, the clock and the deadline" heightened, others believed that Sunday and the clock could work in concert.[18] The wildly popular minister Henry Ward Beecher, for instance, stressed the interdependence of Sunday and the clock, the nineteenth century's two symbols of time. In one of his many fictions, he depicted a patriarch in rural New England leading family prayer. The length and solemnity of the ritual made Sunday's silence conspicuous. "Out in the wide hall could be heard in the stillness the old clock, that now lifted up its voice with unwonted emphasis, as if, unnoticed through the bustling week, Sunday was its vantage ground, to proclaim to mortals the swift flight of time."[19] In Beecher's world, the suffusion of Sunday with religious and eternal time underscored the difference between rest and leisure. Setting Sunday aside also underscored mundane time: it divided work from rest days and distinguished one week from the next. As such, it mandated "civilized" rhythms of work and rest.[20]

Sunday affected most Americans, even those who observed another day of worship. With schools, offices, stores, and streets quieted, it was obvious that the United States followed Christian rhythms, and for the few who did not do so, primarily Americans who were Jewish, "the lonely days were Sundays," as one noted.[21] The prevalence of a commercial calendar that banned trade, commerce, and most labor on Sunday prompted Reform Jews to shift their Sabbath observances to Sunday in the late decades of the century. The embrace of Sunday, which they never considered as the Sabbath, waned after several decades, but its initial success and the very experiment itself reveal Sunday's potency as a symbol and site of religion.[22] Seventh-Day Adventists and Seventh-Day Baptists defied the hegemonic rhythm of work and rest; they believed that God had proclaimed the seventh day (Saturday) the Sabbath and meant for it to be observed as such by all groups, not just the Israelites.[23] Other Baptists and Catholics chafed against Sunday laws, even though they considered Sunday a day of worship and devotion. Yet regardless of whether they believed Sunday was the Sabbath, most Americans did not work on Sunday.

During the closing decades of the nineteenth century, when the work ethic underwent revisions, the meanings of rest also expanded. It was at this time that mass leisure emerged, a result in part of technological, economic, and demographic forces, and in part of changing meanings for work and rest. Until the 1930s, most Americans had little free time other than Sunday morning, afternoon, and evening. Throughout the 1800s, Americans incorporated leisure activities into Sunday observances, which exacerbated political and religious leaders' worries that the day would cease to be one of rest. In their view, rest and leisure were incompatible.[24] Over the course of the nineteenth century, however, Americans invested leisure with the same power for good and evil that they had imposed on Sunday for centuries. Just as the right use of Sunday was construed as essential to the vitality of the republic in the nineteenth century, so did the right use of leisure become an issue of national security by the twentieth. The National Education Association's 1933 publication *Leisure and National Security* made the relationship between leisure and the nation's health explicit and picked up on the same themes that those concerned with Sunday observance had been sounding for centuries.[25] Today, rather than fret about Sunday, critics assess the nation's religious, economic, and cultural health by evaluating the quantity and quality of its leisure. Carroll D. Wright and his nineteenth-century contemporaries asked how and if Americans rested; twentieth-century investigators turned to leisure, something for which there are industries and budgets. The current crises concerning the overworked, materialistic, and uncouth American have much in common

THE BULLETIN
of the
NEW YORK SABBATH COMMITTEE
31 Bible House, New York City.

Vol. 1.   AUGUST, 1914   No. 4

The Bible—

—The Constitution

The Four Outlooks upon life's relations and duties to which the Holy Sabbath lifts man up:
—1. Toward our God, the holy and eternal
2. Toward our State and our Christian Citizenship
3. Toward our home and our neighbors
4. Toward our own hearts and the interests of our immortal souls

The four sides of the foundation are the four scriptural uses of the Holy Sabbath:
1. Rest
2. Worship
3. Works of Mercy
4. Works of Necessity

WORSHIP   REST

SABBATH   SABBATH

TIME BEGAN IN THE INSTITUTION OF THE SABBATH

Drawn by M.S.Logan

Liberty's only secure foundation is the Holy Sabbath

"Where there is no Christian Sabbath, there is no Christian morality; and without this free institutions can not long be sustained."—Justice McLean of the Supreme Court of the United States

"Liberty's Only Secure Foundation Is in the Holy Sabbath." Cover, *New York Sabbath Committee Bulletin* (1914). General Research Division, The New York Public Library, Astor, Lenox and Tilden Foundations.

Oft repeated throughout the nineteenth century was the conviction that Sunday observed as the Christian Sabbath was an important national institution. As such it guaranteed the health of the church, the home, and the state. In this view, time "began in the institution of the Sabbath," therefore the rhythms of work and rest that it mandated were inviolable. Many Americans venerated Sunday, the flag, and the Statue of Liberty as national symbols.

with earlier anxieties about the relationship between Sunday observance and character.

To this day Sunday can be a trial, a reminder of what one writer called
"the awkwardness of failure, of badly managed time."[26] But it can also
be a time when, regardless of constraints, renewal occurs. Americans
continue to resist treating Sunday as part of the work sphere. As leisure
and rest came to be synonymous, the day changed. Sunday's history reveals how individuals and institutions negotiated and revised the
boundaries between work, leisure, and rest. In 1800 it was easy for
Americans to claim that Sunday was a day of rest. Nearly two hundred
years later, leisure has obscured the distinct meanings for rest that once
held, and so when asked, most Americans no longer know what is a day
of rest.

2 A Sermon, Three Hundred Miles Long

> In the language of a traveler, this line of stages was like a sermon, three hundred miles long, preaching to the inhabitants and to strangers, exhorting them to obey the precept, *Remember the Sabbath-day, to keep it holy.*
>
> —LEWIS TAPPAN (1831)

In the early years of the republic, mail stages moved between towns on Sunday; occasionally postmasters opened their offices (usually after church services) to sort and dispense the mail. No single policy governed this practice. All the states had laws against Sunday travel, however, so when it became apparent that by default the post office, and therefore the national government, endorsed the running of stages and ships on Sundays, a crisis concerning the sovereignty of federal law erupted. This early conflict concerning the power of the central government prompted groups and individuals to formulate and express meanings for the day that supported broader views about the regulation of public life, the relationship between church and state, and the rhythms of work and rest in a market economy.

Shortly after the official formation of the nation many began to fear for its health and vitality, and the perceived disarray of the American Sunday came to preoccupy some people, especially those caught up in the fervor of evangelical Christianity. Few worked on Sundays, but reformers pinpointed traveling, drinking, and "laying about in idleness" as detrimental to good citizenship, and therefore to the nation's health. Profanation of the Sabbath headed compendia of the "evils of the times," which included drinking and swearing. The gradual disestablishment of the church precluded such attempts to control the public's Sunday habits as fining those who skipped church services. Local and state laws regulating Sunday observance remained on the books, however, and it was when the post office, one of the few bureaucratic arms of the newly formed nation, challenged these laws that those committed to making and keeping Sunday the Christian Sabbath were compelled to seek new ways to influence both meaning and practice.

Tactics to shape and control the meanings of Sunday during the first part of the century varied. When evangelical businessmen decided to open a stage line in upstate New York, the "Pioneer Line," that would cease operations each Sunday, they believed that the new enterprise was delivering "a sermon, three hundred miles long."[1] By observing Sunday as the Sabbath the owners hoped to impose onto the day a particular set of religious meanings. Leaders emerging out of other religious traditions or with a stake in the separation of church and state understood the day and its place in American life differently. Despite congressional refusal to prohibit the transportation and delivery of mails on Sunday, it was religious meanings—in all their variety and contradiction—that prevailed.

Around the same time that sectarian and denominational competition produced multiple sets of meanings for Sunday, some of the nation's most prominent authors reimagined and reworked the "Puritan Sabbath." Their concoction, "the traditional Sabbath," exerted pressure on religious and civic meanings for Sunday well into the twentieth century. The conflation of the Puritans' religious convictions concerning Sunday with the nation's heritage—that is, with the invented tradition of European settlers—made religious meanings for Sunday safe for a nation whose constitution so proudly proclaimed a separation between church and state.

Sunday Mails

The Sunday mails crisis began in 1808 when the Presbyterian church in western Pennsylvania excluded Hugh Wylie from membership; as local postmaster he had been opening the post office on Sunday, and was thus guilty of violating the fourth commandment mandating Sabbath observance. Wylie appealed to the postmaster general and to his pastor, who took the case to the Ohio Presbytery, the Pittsburgh synod, and eventually the Presbyterian General Assembly. The postmaster general ordered Wylie to continue distributing the mail whenever it arrived (including on Sunday), yet the General Assembly upheld his exclusion. So, Wylie had to choose between his job and his church. Wylie's dilemma, and that of other local postmasters facing similar choices, spurred the United States Congress to pass an act in 1810 requiring the transportation and delivery of mails on all days of the week.[2]

The *"Holy Alliance" or Satan's Legions at Sabbath Pranks.* Engraving by James Aiken (1829). Courtesy, American Antiquarian Society.

Aiken's engraving mocks the efforts to stop Sunday mails, showing protesters to be little other than ineffectual men in frock coats urged on by a crowd of women with petitions in hand. It highlights the suspicion that evangelical innovations (such as Sunday schools, tract societies, and Sabbatarian organizations) would subvert the separation of church and state.

Presbyterian and Congregational churches and individuals were surprised and alarmed that the federal government would interfere in what was considered a local affair. For years they petitioned Congress to repeal the law. During this period, a few "good morals" organizations included the Sabbath among their interests. Lyman Beecher's New Haven, Connecticut, church, for instance, founded a society "For Suppression of Vice and the Promotion of Good Morals" in 1812 that included among its goals improving Sabbath observance. Other congregations and communities followed suit over the next few years, and the first society solely dedicated to improving Sabbath observance formed in Massachusetts in 1814. Presbyterians and Congregationalists led these early Sabbatarian societies. Across the Atlantic, where evangelical revivals that would shape nineteenth-century Britain were well underway, those committed to keeping Sunday as the Sabbath were also active as founders of Sabbatarian organizations. Nevertheless, by 1817 the first phase of the protest against Sunday mails had fizzled. A congressman from Northampton, Massachusetts, put the issue to rest with his argument that "only if every state banned all forms of public conveyance on the Sabbath" would Congress be justified in repealing the 1810 law. Otherwise, he argued, private couriers would step in to fill the breach, which would further prevent the Christian Sabbath from flourishing.[3]

In the mid 1820s, at the height of the revivalist fervor known as the Second Great Awakening, protest against Sunday mails began again. This time, in addition to petitioning the federal government, evangelical laymen formed the first national Sabbatarian organization, the General Union Promoting the Observance of the Christian Sabbath, which actively pursued the repeal of the 1810 law. In addition, the Presbyterian General Assembly as well as the Connecticut General Association of Congregationalist ministers urged members to boycott on all days of the week transportation companies that ran lines on Sundays. The boycott generated a new wave of petitions to the United States Congress begging for cessation of postal activity on Sunday. Prominent clergy and laymen, including Arthur and Lewis Tappan, Josiah Bissell, Lyman Beecher, and Theodore Frelinghuysen, happy to be called Sabbatarians, led the movement. In their zeal, they tried several tactics: asking sympathizers to boycott Sabbath-breaking enterprises (and even composing a Sabbatarian pledge to this effect); financing Sabbath-keeping businesses (such as the Pioneer Line); and publishing and distributing tracts proclaiming the value of Sunday when treated as the Sabbath. The cultural work required to change hearts and minds was at once coercive and persuasive: meanings for Sunday played a powerful role in both private and public behavior, and thus were at the heart of Sabbatarian strategy. Sabbatarians tried to ensure political power, or at the very least a voice in politics, for recently disestablished churches, but above all, they sought to remind people to "remember the Sabbath day."

Opponents of Sabbatarianism also politicked and petitioned, warning that evangelical designs to build a Christian republic would subvert republican freedom. They favored the sanctification of Sunday, but believed this was possible even as the mails moved continuously throughout the young nation. An approving, though unofficial, Senate report (1829) on Sunday mail agreeably began with the generalization "that some respite from the ordinary vocations of life is an established principle. . . . One day in seven has also been determined upon as the proportion of time; and in conformity to the wishes of the great majority of citizens of this country, the first day of the week, commonly called Sunday, has been set apart to that object." The framers of the document carefully avoided religious justifications for setting Sunday apart. With reassurances that the committee did "not wish to disturb" the practice of observing Sunday as the Christian Sabbath, the report also emphasized that it did not want "to determine for any whether they shall esteem one day above another, or esteem all days alike holy." The government had no intention of interfering with custom, however. It was willing to suspend "all public business on Sunday, except in cases of absolute necessity, or of great public utility."[4]

Christians of all denominations were split over the propriety of transporting and delivering mail on Sunday. After 1832, when the controversy abated for a second time, with the opposition to Sabbatarian sentiment prevailing, absolutely no efforts were made toward the repeal of local or state blue laws. Nor were the laws broken with any more frequency than before. Many on both sides of the issue called Sunday the Sabbath, and respected it as such. Thus the conclusion of one of the leaders that "the labors of those particularly interested in the effort were not wholly ineffectual," is warranted. "The publications that were issued, and the meetings that were held, awakened attention to the subject of Sabbath desecration, and in numerous instances produced salutary reformations."[5]

Although Sabbatarians and their opponents shared assumptions about the religious nature of Sunday, they disagreed about Sunday mail because of variant beliefs about the emerging market culture. Sabbatarians—mostly merchants and clergymen on the Atlantic seaboard—were at least as committed to market values as were those less sympathetic to the cause. The separation of Sunday from the other days of the week worked in concert with the rise of industrial capitalism. Each accelerated the ongoing differentiation of time, seen in the popularity of watches, the rise of hourly wage labor, and the use of the clock to regulate labor in both the North and the South. Attention to Sunday also demarcated the time for work from that for rest. Setting it aside for worship, rest, and play was as much a part of the new orientation toward time as "punching in and out" would be toward the end of the century. As the mechanical clock, time zones, and standardized time came to regulate all aspects of American life, the importance of Sunday was heightened. Here was a day when the majority ceased working. Sabbatarianism, then, despite its reliance on archaic bans against this kind of sporting and that kind of resting, accommodated impulses toward modernization.

Initially the desire for continuous mails, as the way to meet the need for rapid movement of information, prevailed over the trend toward

highly differentiated times. Merchants on the eastern seaboard may
have supported Sabbatarianism because they had easy access to market
news, whereas those further inland relied on the mails for vital information. Those inland did not utterly disregard the Christian Sabbath;
rather, when they were forced to choose between the mail or the Sabbath, they chose the mail. Events a few decades later support such
analysis. The running of more and more mail trains through the week
and the commercialization of telegraphy both ensured faster movement
and more even distribution of market information. In response during
the 1840s and 1850s the postmaster general suspended the transportation and delivery of mail on Sundays along many routes; later, in 1912,
delivery of the mail on Sunday would cease altogether.[6] A clash within
an economy and society rooted in the market, rather than a struggle between commercial and anticommercial forces, characterizes the Sunday mails crisis. Sunday, important because it was on the cusp between
work and rest, served as a site for the reconfiguration of American culture and society as both became imbricated in a market economy.

The Sabbath Question

During the 1830s and 1840s Sabbatarians elaborated on their identification of Sunday as the Sabbath at conferences, in published tracts, and
from pulpits. A literal interpretation of the fourth commandment,
which could be read or heard in Sunday-school classes, around the
hearth, and in legislative sessions throughout the nineteenth century,
was the basis for the spreading Sabbatarian theology:

> Keep the sabbath day to sanctify it, as the Lord thy God hath com-
> manded thee. Six days shalt thou labour, and do all thy work: But the
> seventh day is the sabbath of the Lord thy God.

But if "the seventh day is the sabbath," then what was Sunday? Most
Christians agreed that Sunday (the first day of the week) was "the Lord's
day" and the day for Christian worship. Not all assented to the substitu-
tion of "Sabbath" for Sunday, the Lord's Day, and other referents, because
of the obligations its use implied. In response, Sabbatarians explained
that when Christ rose, he shifted the Sabbath of the Old Testament from
the seventh day to the first day of the week, so Christians were obliged to
observe Sunday as the Sabbath. "The Sabbath was *made* (i.e., it was *in-
stituted and set apart* by heaven)," postulated the prominent evangelical
Lyman Beecher, "for the spiritual use and benefit of man." Rather than

being made for the Jews, the Sabbath was "made for *man.*" Beecher interpreted the text from the Gospel of Mark as denoting the Sabbath's "universal necessity and perpetual obligation." He and other Sabbatarians argued that "the term *man* is generic, and includes the race of all ages and nations."[7] Americans assented to Sunday as the Sabbath, either explicitly or implicitly; the fourth commandment provided the basis as well as the language for legislating Sunday as a day of rest through the nineteenth and much of the twentieth centuries.

In the attempt to fix the biblical Sabbath as Sunday's meaning, Sabbatarians formed new organizations, including the American and Foreign Sabbath Union (1843) under the leadership of the temperance reformer Justin Edwards, the Philadelphia Sabbath Association (1840), and the Baltimore Sabbath Union (1843). Sabbatarian conventions were common: in the 1840s alone Sabbatarians hosted the "Bethel and Sabbath Convention" in Cincinnati and the National Lord's Day Convention in Baltimore, as well as twenty-four county conventions just in the state of Pennsylvania, seven state conventions, and fifteen "General Sabbath Conventions." The meeting in Baltimore featured former president John Quincy Adams committing himself in front of more than 1,700 delegates, "to give all the faculties of my soul" to propagate "opinions in favor of the sacred observance of the Sabbath."[8]

Sabbatarians established principles for regulating Sunday based on the division between work and rest. They suggested that rest was at the heart of the Sabbath, which the translation from Greek of the word itself into "rest" confirmed. In addition they argued that the fourth commandment established the proportion of weekly work and rest. An 1850s children's manual expressed this conviction in a chapter titled, "We Were Not Made to Be Idle, But to Work," which stressed that "lazy people as truly break this [the fourth] commandment as they who work or play on the Sabbath."[9] The lengthiness of the American workweek and workday remained unchanged for decades owing to reluctance to tamper with the fourth commandment's division of the week. When faced with demands for shorter workweeks and workdays, many employers cited the text of the commandment, "six days shalt thou labor," and refused reform. Six days of work, one of rest—this was the shape of the American week, reinforced by religion, culture, and law.

Throughout the antebellum period, a large majority of Americans understood abstention from work each Sunday as fundamental to observing the day as the Sabbath. But there was more to Sabbath observance than putting up one's tools; in the opinion of Sabbatarians it required public worship and private meditation. In all likelihood observing Sunday as a Sabbath was not as universal as it was in Harriet Beecher

Stowe's picture of a New England village, where "going to meeting" was "as necessary and inevitable a consequence of waking up on Sunday morning as eating one's breakfast."[10] Yet in the 1840s and into the 1850s Sabbatarians succeeded in extending acceptance of their view of the day, in hastening its circumscribed treatment as a day of rest, and in spreading what many called "the New England Sabbath" to western Pennsylvania and New York, Ohio, and Indiana. Throughout the nation, as the French visitor Alexis de Tocqueville commented in 1831, few were "permitted to go on a hunt, to dance, or even to play an instrument on Sunday." Dramatic changes in the religious landscape bolstered faith and practice: the tumultuous Second Great Awakening more than doubled church membership in the United States; the establishment of Sunday schools "trained Americans in evangelical standards, especially Sabbath keeping"; and the vast dissemination of religious literature spread Christian knowledge and sentiment.[11]

Tocqueville nonetheless intuited that there was "a great store of doubt and indifference hidden underneath these external forms" of religion. Bitter struggles over what constituted orthodox religion in the 1830s and 1840s pushed some Christians to elaborate new meanings for Sunday and for rest. The hostility of friends and sympathizers that greeted William Lloyd Garrison's claim in 1836 that there was "no Scriptural authority for the divinity of the Sabbath" suggests that they wished to avoid the Sabbath question.[12] A few years later, reformers who were moving toward liberal Protestantism frankly questioned the constriction of the meaning of Sunday to qualities associated with the term "Sabbath." In hopes of publicizing what they considered ecclesiastical tyranny, Christian pacifists and anarchists convened the 1840 Charndon Street Convention in Boston to highlight how the "Sabbath, Ministry and Church" were human inventions, without "Divine ordination." They ran out of time before they could turn to the Church and Ministry, but they did spend three days arguing about the creation and the status of the Sabbath. Tellingly, the convention failed to reach a vote on the resolution "That the first day of the week is ordained by divine authority as the Christian Sabbath." It also defeated an amendment that read "there is ordained by divine authority a weekly Sabbath, perpetually binding on man." But the assembly also ignored Garrison's call for the abolition of the day.[13] Consensus was impossible. If anything, most of these opponents of Sabbatarianism probably believed that Sunday was and should remain the Christian Sabbath.

Still, the inability of this assortment of radicals and freethinkers to cast the Sabbath as man-made, and therefore neither divinely ordained nor perpetually binding, suggests that Sabbatarian exegesis concerning the fourth commandment had wide, if not universal, currency. Apart from the inconclusive burst of rhetorical activity in Boston, unfavorable reaction to Sabbatarian activity and to the spreading custom of setting Sunday aside for rest and worship was limited. Even the radical Christian Theodore Parker maintained that the Sabbath was an institution full of promise for mankind; in no way did he question the conflation of Sunday and the Sabbath. Parker sought to stress the improvements that Christians could make in their observance of the day, such as taking a walk or indulging in cheerful conversation. He did not encourage followers to abandon the day, as Garrison had done.[14] Parker's suggestion that Americans could improve Sunday formed the core of aspirations for the day that gained power after the Civil War.

Vital to these new hopes for Sunday before mid century were Unitarians, who began to lose faith in the applicability of the fourth commandment to modern life at the same time that they fashioned the tendency that came to be known as "religious liberalism." These men and women, most of whom lived in New England, believed that Christianity provided a guide for living, rather than an avenue toward eternal life. They applied "religious principles" to social problems and moral dilemmas. As one of their twentieth-century champions explains, they "did not *confuse* religion and ethics, the secular and the sacred—they *fused* them." The liberal Protestant approach to amusements and to Sunday exemplifies such fusion.[15]

Antebellum Unitarians fostered the integration of leisure into the Christian life. "Society is the better, the safer, the more moral and religious," Henry Whitney Bellows told his wealthy congregation of New Yorkers, "for amusement." The expansion of the supply of commercial amusements in urban areas precipitated a decrease in the price of admission. Christians could either reform amusements, or watch them wreak havoc; banning them altogether was impossible. One of Bellows's fellow Unitarians penned *A Plea for Amusements* (1847), which cast art galleries, dance halls, theaters, gardens, and gymnasiums as "useful agencies in refining manners and forging bonds of unity among classes and between generations." In his view, renewal, not dissipation, could be the result of recreation. "Recreation or amusement," echoed another Unitarian leader, "are but other names for rest."[16] If they were synonymous with rest, then there was no reason to ban them on Sundays.

Not wanting to undermine Sunday's status as the day of worship, religious liberals sought "eternal ground" for Sunday observance apart from the fourth commandment. They claimed Christianity suspended the fourth commandment as it was given to the Jews. Instead, "the Sabbath was written on man's nature." Unitarians turned in particular to the Gospel of Mark 2:27, wherein Mark reports that Christ proclaimed that "the Sabbath was made for man, not man for the Sabbath." They argued that all people "need Rest and Repose." Society should allow activities on Sunday that minister to physical and spiritual needs. "To do nothing is physical rest: to be engaged in full activity is the rest of the soul." To Unitarians, Sunday had heady potential for religious experience, if only it could be "made a delight."[17]

The divide between orthodoxy and liberalism quickly deepened (mostly because of disagreement concerning an entirely different issue—biblical sanction for slavery) so that the radicals among Unitarians began to wonder if there was any scriptural basis for Sabbath observance. Biblical references to slavery upset their deep antislavery convictions to such an extent that they began to entertain historicist biblical interpretations. The abolitionist William Logan Fisher authored an antiorthodox "history of the institution of the Sabbath" in 1845, with the purpose of revealing that its origins were human, not divine (an effort similar to abolitionist critiques of slavery). Another abolitionist, Charles C. Burleigh, claimed that in their attempt to prove the Sabbatic command perpetual and universal Sabbatarians had misconstrued Christ's proclamation reported in the Gospel of Mark. Christ, he believed, "said that the Sabbath was made for man, not in distinction from its being made for a particular nation or age, but in denial of its paramount authority over man." In addition to individual efforts to reshape the theological meanings of Sunday, radical abolitionists including William Lloyd Garrison, Lucretia Mott, and Theodore Parker gathered in early 1848 to protest Sabbatarian hegemony. This time, unlike the Charndon Street Convention just eight years earlier, the Anti-Sabbath Convention unanimously branded the Sabbath a man-made institution. In doing so, it expressed the conviction that the obligation to observe the Sabbath was not universal: "the Sabbath, according to the Jewish scriptures, was given to '*the children of Israel,*'—AND TO NO OTHER PEOPLE." The meeting aimed to do more than "destroy superstition and cant," as one historian has claimed; it attempted to sever the meaning of Sunday from biblical literalism.[18]

Anti-Sabbatarians at the convention depicted the orthodoxy represented by Sabbatarianism as harmful to the spiritual life of children and adults alike. Personal experiences verified such sentiments. Several anti-Sabbatarians shared memories of the Sabbath being "pressed upon" their childhood Sundays. One recounted how his terror of breaking the Sabbath paralyzed him: although he vowed to swim on Sundays, his limbs were inert and he could not "venture out into the deep." He and others were outraged that the stultifying theology about Sunday they incorporated during childhood had wide currency.[19] The anti-Sabbatarians also complained that institutionalizing Sunday as the Sabbath differentiated time in an unreasonable manner. Garrison, for instance, denounced tying "men up to the idea that one day is more holy than another" and repeated his plea for the destruction of the Sunday Sabbath altogether. He hoped to eradicate the Sabbath as one of the cognates for Sunday. Another speaker bolstered Garrison's effort, bravely announcing, "There is no Sabbath. It is all humbug and delusion. All days are alike."[20] Paradoxically their critique of Sabbatarianism as "irrational" ran counter to the emerging centrality of differentiated time. Indeed, the pivotal meaning of Sunday—as a day of rest—came from the idea of the Sabbath. Obviously, participants in the Anti-Sabbath Convention did not seek to implement a seven-day workweek. What, then, was their goal?

When situated in the context of the abolitionist campaign, the Anti-Sabbath Convention's aims become clear. Abolitionists, focused as they were on the emancipation of the slaves, were also attempting to save themselves from all forms of slavery, including that of Christians to the church. By challenging Sabbatarianism, they called into question the church's authority over lifestyles and relationships. Rejection of clerical authority suffused every moment of the convention. Speaker after speaker pointed to orthodox Protestants' protection of a *day*. They accused Sabbatarians of respecting "the fourth commandment more than the other nine, so that in the sight of God, it is incomparably more offensive to indulge in work or recreation on the Sabbath, than it is to worship idols, to dishonor father and mother, to lie, steal, commit adultery, and murder!"[21]

The Anti-Sabbath Convention's dedication to advancing "the cause of a pure Christianity, promoting true and acceptable worship, and inculcating strict moral and religious accountability, in all concerns of life, ON ALL DAYS OF THE WEEK ALIKE" was mostly a critique of how churches nationwide acquiesced in slavery. Nevertheless, it did propose alternative religious meanings for the day. These meanings were written into the convention's many resolutions, such as Resolution 19, which read, "It is an innocent act to plough in the field, to fish in the sea, to work in the shop, to ride in the railroad car, to indulge in recreation and amusement, on the first as on any other day of the week." Another resolution needled Sabbatarians for propagating superstition about the day, describing it as an "attempt to frighten the ignorant and unenlightened into a belief that God frequently suspends the natural laws of the universe, and miraculously interferes to punish with blasting judgments such as engage in labor or recreation on the first day of the week."[22]

Anti-Sabbatarians did not want to abolish all the differences between Sunday and the other days of the week, but they wanted to diversify and improve how Americans spent their time. They encouraged the workingman to go out with his family on Sunday in steamboats and railroad cars; "in the fields and woods he might offer acceptable homage and worship to the Highest." The convention's approval of "running passenger-cars on Sunday, from city to country, and from country to city," met with the accusation in a Boston newspaper that it sought "with malignant energy to destroy that day of rest from servile labor which is the poor man's richest earthly boon, and without which he must be exposed to unremitting toil." Expecting such criticism, anti-Sabbatarians had stressed that they did not intend to abolish a weekly rest day, they simply wanted "the law of rest from labor [to] stand on its true foundation." As one speaker pleaded, "Let us establish rest-days for the sake of man, and not for the sake of theology and dogmatic religion."[23]

But desire to affix the Sabbath to Sunday was powerful in the rapidly expanding nation that knew no end of work, and so ridicule and satire shaped popular response to the Anti-Sabbath Convention. Shortly after the convention, for instance, the *Boston Post* ran a notice for an "Anti-Monday Convention" inviting all laundresses, tub makers, and soap boilers to attend a meeting concerning the "abolition of Monday from the calendar and creation."[24] In the face of widespread acceptance of the differentiation between Monday and Sunday, anti-Sabbatarians returned to other reforms, mainly the abolition of slavery. Nevertheless, they made a claim for Sunday as "man's day" that resonated loudly later in the century. Their progeny would also reject the obligations rendered by casting Sunday as the Sabbath, but they too would spin meanings for Sunday based on its difference from and superiority to the other days of the week.

In the late nineteenth century only the more radical of the inheritors of the abolitionists' mantle persisted in criticizing the differentiation of time, which Sunday so powerfully signified. The century's most famous agnostic, Robert Ingersoll, asked: "How is it possible for a space of time to be holy? Can time be moral or immoral? Can it be vicious or virtuous? Can one hour, one day be better than another? Can we divide the days into sacred and profane?" He contended that days were not property, could not "be damaged, kidnapped, starved, or oppressed." Ingersoll hoped that in a democracy individuals would be free to do as they wished with their time. In his estimation, keeping Sunday as the Sabbath was not a sign of salvation; instead it was simply an excuse to show off nice clothes. Sunday in the United States was an "outward Sabbath only." Calling it the Sabbath, and forcing people to treat it as such, turned it into "a dead day wasted in dreaming orthodox dreams of heaven," or, even worse, "a sick day passed in Orthodox dressing-gowns and slippers, piously sighing for the coming of Monday."[25] Ingersoll's reaction to Sabbatarian meanings for Sunday drew on Garrison's bold declarations earlier in the century. It points us in the direction that most anti-Sabbatarians were unwilling to follow: abolishing the Sabbath and Sunday altogether.

Jewish, Seventh-Day Adventist, and Seventh-Day Baptist doctrine and practice did reject the widespread connection between Sunday and the Sabbath. Each group believed that Saturday, as the seventh day of the week, was the "true Sabbath." Most Jews in The United States were reluctant to challenge Sunday laws aggressively during the nineteenth century because of their desire to assimilate and avoid religious controversy and persecution. But seventh-day Christians, home-grown products, were all too willing to refute claims that the Sabbath had been transferred with divine sanction to the first day of the week. They understood God's word as immutable; if the fourth commandment said rest on the seventh day, then it was advisable to do so. Because they published a great deal and were involved in controversies over Sunday observance, they influenced mainstream Protestant understandings of the Sabbath. Seventh-Day Baptists, who had been observing a Saturday Sabbath since the eighteenth century, and Adventists, who in 1860 had declared belief in the seventh-day Sabbath "co-essential with the imminent second coming," were sometimes harassed for working on Sunday. They were vociferous and contentious because Sunday laws prevented them from pursuing their normal occupations and labors, which put them at a disadvantage in an economy where continual labor—in field, factory, and home—was necessary. The subtitle of the seventh-day organ *Liberty*—"Devoted to the American Idea of Religious Liberty Exemplified in the Complete Separation of Church and State"—expressed their alarm over the apparent union of church and state. This and other publications aimed to expose the bigotry central to the enforcement of all Sunday laws.[26] Seventh-day publicists goaded adversaries with suggestions that they adopt a full-fledged Catholic Sunday if they could not return to the biblical Sabbath. They characterized the Sunday Sabbath as a fraud, warning that as long as Christians persisted in observing it the day would be plagued with unseemly behavior and other calamities. It was God's way of demonstrating His disapproval. They also warned that "we cannot leave the temporal and the eternal to be mingled in our lives haphazard. Shall we aim so to divide our days that half shall be secular and half sacred?" The Sabbath, as the bridge between the temporal and eternal, needed to be situated on the firmest foundation,—the fourth commandment.[27] In effect, seventh-day Christians hoped to undermine the conviction that the Sabbath had been transferred to Sunday, in the effort to secure for themselves the complete liberty necessary for arranging their week around Saturday worship. Seventh-day claims undermined the certainty that the Sabbath should be the basis of Sunday's meanings. One Sunday-Sabbath adherent claimed that the seventh-day believers' distributions of tracts and pamphlets "increase the desecration of the Lord's-day, but not the hallowing of Saturday."[28] Whether or not seventh-day believers' meanings for Sunday influenced practice is less important than the ways that mainstream religious authorities responded to these meanings for Sunday (and for the Sabbath). To a certain degree, anti-Sabbatarians and seventh-day Christians challenged Sunday's close association with the biblical Sabbath. Their alternative meanings contributed to the disintegration of the certainty that there was a scriptural basis for Sunday as the Sabbath, and thus allowed broader religious meanings for Sunday to accrue.

The Traditional Sabbath

Tradition, however, might supply justification for the Sunday Sabbath, and what better tradition existed for Americans than the Puritan one created in New England? During the 1830s and 1840s nostalgia for the Puritan Sabbath flourished, prompted in part by a national literature steeped in Puritan themes and images. Throughout the period of the early republic and well into the nineteenth century, a history of the young nation was recounted in which the Puritans of New England took center stage. In addition to a deluge of historical romances about Puritanism, several Puritan texts, such as Cotton Mather's *Magnalia Christi Americana* and John Winthrop's *History of New England*, were printed or reprinted during the 1820s. These texts cast Puritanism as the father of republicanism and detailed how the Puritan struggle to settle New England precipitated uniquely American characteristics.[29] Within this history were the laws, acts, and beliefs that built a foundation for the nation and for Sunday.

Nathaniel Hawthorne and Harriet Beecher Stowe each recast the Puritan Sabbath in a manner that prompted the conflation of "traditional" with "Puritan." While a student at Bowdoin College, Hawthorne was fined fifty cents for card playing and faced other strict regulations, including the warning that "they who profane the Sabbath by unnecessary business, visiting or receiving visits, or by walking abroad, or by an amusement, or in other ways, may be admonished or suspended."

Hawthorne's "ambivalence concerning his Puritan inheritance," as a biographer later put it, shaped his depiction of Sunday, found in works that include *The House of Seven Gables* and *Twice-Told Tales*.[30] "Sunday at Home," one of a set of sketches published in *Twice-Told Tales* (1837) that concern New England past and present, is at once a tribute to and dismissal of the Puritan Sabbath. It begins with the narrator (perhaps the same one who describes "Sights from the Steeple" in another of the collection's sketches) opening his curtains one Sunday morning to contemplate the local church; he focuses on the steeple housing the bell that "reminds thousands of busy individuals of their separate and most secret affairs." The narrator wonders about the steeple's "moral loneliness," which the church's "vacant pews and empty galleries, the silent organ, the voiceless pulpit" share. A "holier brightness" emanating from the "Sabbath sunshine" lit the church and the eternal time it represented, but each was a void rather than sanctified. The narrator stays at home, explaining that "my inner man goes constantly to church while many, whose bodily presence fills the accustomed seats, have left their souls at home." He then comments, "For six days more, there will be no face of man in the pews, . . . nor a voice in the pulpit, nor music in the choir." The church itself was "a desert in the heart of the town." The Sabbath, too, had become only a symbol of religious life and eternal time. Hawthorne may have designed the conclusion—"may the steeple still point heavenward, and be decked with the hallowed sunshine of the Sabbath morn"—to sweeten his otherwise bitter commentary.[31] Nostalgia such as his, sentimental and inconclusive though it was, did communicate a sense of the Sabbath as a traditional American institution, and one that was in peril.

Harriet Beecher Stowe, another author who spent her lifetime working through New England's Puritan antecedents, also devoted some of her early prose to the Puritan Sabbath. In one piece, she speculated that "nothing could be more perfect than the Puritan Sabbath." In another, she admonished, "We may rail at Blue Laws and Puritan strictness as much as we please, but certainly those communities where our fathers carried out their ideas fully had their strong points." She especially commended the "weekly union of all classes" as "a most powerful and efficient means of civilization." Part of Stowe's lifelong ambition was to connect the nation's Puritan heritage to the "American experiment" with democracy. She urged that the Puritan "Sunday habit" be adapted to modern times, as a means of promoting and nurturing democracy.[32]

Stowe also spun vivid memories of the Puritan Sabbath. One of her many narrators remembered his childhood passed in the household of an uncle for whom "Sunday was the centre of his whole worldly and religious system." Now an elderly gentleman, he wondered:

> The Puritan Sabbath—is there such a thing existing now, or has it gone with the things that were, to be looked on as a curiosity in the museum of the past? Can any one, in memory, take himself back to the unbroken stillness of that day, and recall the sense of religious awe which seemed to brood in the very atmosphere, checking the merry laugh of childhood, and chaining in unwonted stillness the tongue of volatile youth, and imparting even to the sunshine of heaven, and the unconscious notes of animals, a tone of gravity and repose?[33]

Stowe hoped to revive such Sundays, but she also advised, through parable-like stories, that the day needed modernization and adaptation, particularly for children. Her narrators recall cold dinners, tithing men who kept children from laughing in services, and stern ministers who inhabited a "Sabbath-day sphere." The Puritan Sabbath had many faults: "Its wearisome restraints and over-strictness cast a gloom on religion." "Sabbath-keeping is the iron rod of bigots."[34] Nonetheless, her remembrances—which produced "daguerreotypes of Sunday congregations" and family squabbles over the merits of the Puritan Sabbath, and depicted idealized Sabbaths—reflected and reinforced widely felt nostalgia for the Puritan Sabbath. It is no coincidence that Hawthorne and Stowe were both reworking and rethinking the meaning of the Sabbath during the middle decades of the century, for it was at that time that new meanings for Sunday gained wide currency, and that old fears associated with violation of the day returned. A jumble of impressions, memories, and convictions served to transform the Puritan Sabbath of historical and fictional narratives into the "traditional Sabbath." During the later part of the nineteenth century, antiquarians such as Henry M. Brooks, D. L. Lanisors, and Alice Morse Earle continued the cultural work— depicting the Puritan Sabbath as beneficent—that Hawthorne, Beecher, and their contemporaries began.[35]

One of the most confusing and troubling aspects of the Puritan Sabbath was that it fed superstition, both during the colonial era and after. As one historian of early America has noted: "A belief developed that a close correlation existed between abuse of the Sabbath and the calamities that befell New England," and so "superstitions regarding the use of the holy day deepened."[36] Some eighteenth-century descendants of the Puritans devoted themselves to obliterating superstition, seeing it as the remnant of pagan and popish religion. But the logic that connected calamity with Sabbath-breaking pervaded private ruminations well through the nineteenth century. In diaries at mid century, some men interpreted unfortunate events that occurred on Sunday as signs of a "displeased God." A member of a company traveling overland to California, for instance, after expressing regret that he had to travel one Sunday so as to stay with the group, then described a storm during which "a thunderbolt descended and struck two of Col. Avery's oxen dead." He connected this misfortune with the company's violation of the Sabbath: "I could not help but think it was an exhibition of the displeasure of the Almighty for this violation of his holy day." That the oxen "were only about 60 rods from the camp where we were preparing supper, when struck down," made the warning all the more ominous to the diarist. A physician passing through New Orleans who witnessed rampant "Sabbath-breaking" and gambling on the same Sunday that a fire devastated a portion of the city, interpreted the destruction as a sign: "I pray God this event may be a warning to the Sabbath breaker." Still another traveler, sailing down the California coast to Mexico, felt that God had punished him for his Sabbath-breaking. He recounts going ashore and shooting rabbits that were hiding in a cactus grove; while he retrieved the game, thorns pierced his entire body. "I was obliged to undress and pull them out, one by one, served me right for being thus engaged on a Sunday."[37]

Both the first and second phases of the movement against Sunday mails reinforced Americans' commitment to Sunday as a day of rest, even though the act mandating Sunday mails remained intact until 1912. The Sabbatarian decision to protest the federal government's sanction of Sunday mails drew national attention to the problem of Sunday, and activated fears about the extent of the federal government's sovereignty. Dissent over Sunday provoked several reactions. In the 1840s practices fell more and more into line with the orderly setting apart of one day a week for worship and rest: Sunday observance was church-oriented across almost all denominations, railroad owners voluntarily halted their trains on Sundays, towns chained their streets to prevent carriages from passing through, and many employers took care to structure the work week around Sunday. Nostalgia for the Puritan Sabbath enabled its identification as the "traditional Sabbath." But other forces were at play—migration, immigration, urbanization, and war—that would forge new meanings for Sunday and rest, as well as elicit Sabbatarian response.

3 Far from Civilized Country

> I often thought as if we all ought to go to church on this day but we
> were getting far from civilized country.
>
> —OVERLAND TRAIL diary entry (1849)

Americans struggling to find their way through the fluid social spaces
of the frontier, city, battlefield, and home front looked to Sunday for sta-
bility. Feelings about the meanings for the day, above all as a sign of civilization, flowed deep. Sabbatarians understood civilization as a place
where God's word was law; other Christians defined it more broadly.
Embedded in the latter group's notion of civilization was balance: between mind and body, intellect and emotion, beauty and morality, and
work and rest. Lifestyle mattered to them; how people lived was proof
of a nation's level of civilization. Citizens who had enough time and
freedom to rest, recreate, and acquaint themselves with the world's
finest literature, art, and music lived in bona fide civilizations. The Sabbatarian stranglehold on Sunday, in these people's view, was preventing
American civilization from full development. Americans were unsure
about where civilization could be found and nurtured. Some turned to
the middle-class home, the Protestant church, or the lyceum. Others
looked to elite enclaves such as the university, private club, or
athenaeum. Most believed that properly observed Sundays would foster
civilization. The devil was in the details—one person's propriety was
another's desecration. Fear that the United States was moving further
and further away from Christianity and civilization, in large part because of the pernicious influences of life on the frontier, in the city, and
at war, pulsed ever more strongly. It seemed clear to many observers
and some participants that such Sundays were inferior to the "traditional Sabbath." In response, Sabbatarians strove to fashion Sunday into

a site for Christian civilization, and thereby bring the American people, and the nation itself, closer to salvation.

"Every Day Is Alike": Sunday on the Frontier

A pioneer on the Overland Trail in the 1860s noted in her diary "Every day is alike to us, though we try to keep our memory right as to the time of the week, month, and year." A few entries later she lamented, "Sunday, yes just the same as every other day in the week out of civilization."[1] Just as building a church was a rite of passage most frontier settlements went through on their way to becoming "civilized," so was Sabbath observance another route toward civilization. A homesick Overlander crossing the plains during the Gold Rush longed for "the noise of the church going bell" which would "tell of civilization."[2] After studying emigrants' guides and first-hand accounts of the crossing, one historian concluded a majority intended to keep the Sabbath while traveling, but "once they entered a land where neither law nor usage imposed restraint," pioneers "lost their moral bearings." Some "heroic Sabbatarians" were able to observe the day as they would have at their distant homes. In general, however, those who did not travel on Sunday spent the day repairing wagons, washing clothes, and preparing food. Rest was rare.[3] That pioneers crossing the continent experienced different kinds of Sundays from those to which they were accustomed, or failed to experience Sunday at all, is incontestable. Most of the accounts of the journey were sent back east: so relatives and friends knew about and vicariously experienced Sundays on the frontier.

The Yankee reformer Frederick Law Olmsted, no Sabbatarian, neatly highlighted the civilized and savage potentials for Sunday in his 1857 travelogue *A Journey through Texas*. Unable to attend services in the nearby town of Crockett, assured that the saddler "didn't do work on Sundays," and unable to procure flour, butter, or fresh meat for their Sunday dinner, Olmsted and his traveling companions "occupied our day writing and reading." They also fought off the neighboring farmer's hogs, foraged for eggs and fowl, and made small repairs to their gear. Not an altogether civilized day, but, still, the travelers did write letters and read, while the sound of "two negroes all day splitting rails" echoed through the scrub. What they witnessed on the nearby trail, further cast their Sunday into stark relief.

An emigrant party from Alabama passed, having fifty negroes, and 100 head of cattle, sheep, etc., going to the Brazos, to settle. "Oh, my God!

Sunday Morning in the Mines. Painting by Charles Christian Nahl (1872). E. B. Crocker Collection, Crocker Art Museum, Sacramento, California.

Few panned for gold on Sundays during the gold rushes that punctuated the history of the mid-century American West. Pickaxes, screens, and other tools of the miner's trade lie inert in the painting's foreground. In the middleground boxing, horse racing, gambling, washing, letter writing, and reading what might be a Bible suggest a range of ways that miners rested on Sunday.

How tired I am" I heard an old negro woman exclaim. A man of powerful frame answered, "I feel like as tho' I couldn't lift my legs much longer."

Olmsted ironically captioned this description "The Day of Rest."[4]

It is tempting to conclude that traveling overland to California, making similar migrations to other parts of the continent, and settling the frontier changed Americans' view of Sunday. The symbolic resonance of the day—as a sign, above all, of civilization—suggests otherwise. Sojourners and settlers treated Sunday differently from the other days of the week, whether they engaged in more than usual gambling, drinking, and fighting, or in letter writing, introspection, and devotions. While many prospectors in mining camps drank, gambled, and raced horses, others read the Bible, wrote letters home, and attended makeshift services. One wrote his mother, "There is naught about us that tells it is the Sabbath except the suspension of work by the miners around us and the quietness of the hillside of Nature."[5] Though the circumstances of emigration and settlement often prevented consecrated Sunday observance, some managed to sanctify the day through books, letters, and reminiscences. Sunday on the frontier tended to reinforce the commitment to alternating work and rest, and connected this ideal with civilization.

City Sundays and the "Continental Sabbath"

Sundays were far from uniform in antebellum cities. Occasionally a ship or train arrived on Sunday; rarely did one leave. Ferries kept circumscribed schedules. One or two entrepreneurs sponsored excursions in July and August. But it was also true that accidents, suicides, brawls, and all manner of disorder often characterized urban Sundays. Predictably, horses and carriages were involved in accidents, such as the one caused by "two drunken rowdies" racing a horse and buggy in mid-century Brooklyn. A disproportionate number of the desperate attempted suicide on Sundays—such persons as Hannah Hawkins who in 1852 "desired to become 'food for fishes' " and jumped Sunday night "from one of the [New York City] ferry boats into the muddy waters of the East River." It was reported that "some people fished her out and took her home where she promised to bide her time." (Into the 1920s observers noted that an unusual number of suicides occurred on Sunday.) Newspapers reported assaults and burglaries: in the vicinity of Manhattan two sailors tried to murder their captain early one Sunday morning; a "gang of rowdies" assaulted and beat a man insensible one Sunday evening; soldiers chased "colored waiters" with swords and bayonets another Sunday afternoon. Men were caught breaking into apartments, pickpockets carried on their trade, and if shops were open some persons shoplifted. Gambling, disorderly conduct, and public intoxication also found their way into many a Sunday.[6]

Throughout the antebellum era private libraries, voluntary associations, and lecture societies competed with churches and saloons for the Sunday attention of urban dwellers. Most private libraries opened on Sundays, providing a place for members to relax, read newspapers, and educate themselves. The reading room of the Boston Athenaeum (organized in 1808), for instance, was open Sundays for its members, who were primarily from the city's native-born elite. Sunday-school libraries, established in the 1820s and by the 1850s numbering in the thousands, usually issued books on Sundays. YMCA libraries, founded in the 1850s, also opened as alternatives to saloons and other urban attractions. In the same vein, at mid century the reformer Charles Loring Brace opened coffee-and-reading rooms in New York City on every day of the week, including Sunday, in an effort to attract "the dangerous classes."[7]

Voluntary associations ranging from schools to fire companies provided additional gathering places and opportunities. Schools devoted to fostering literacy met on Sundays. In 1803, for instance, New York City widows began to offer adults and children, both black and white, lessons in reading and writing on Sundays. In North Carolina and Delaware, working children and the children of workers also received instruction on Sundays. By the 1820s networks of interdenominational Sunday-school societies that focused on teaching a generic kind of Protestantism, as well as denominational ones, could be found across the nation. Included among these were schools that served African Americans in Baltimore and other northern cities. Led by Rebecca Gratz, Philadelphia's Jewish population started its own Sunday school in 1838.[8] Although volunteer fire companies did not always share the same didactic impulse as did the various societies devoted to education, their houses, which characterized every antebellum city, were never empty on Sundays. Sometimes the companies even opened their doors to rivals and friends, inviting community leaders both male and female to inspect their engines and houses. In addition to fighting fires, the volunteers also paraded through various neighborhoods on Sundays; each activity meant to earn the city's admiration and ultimately its tribute.[9]

Reformers and devotees of "free religion" each sponsored Sunday discussions and lectures. In Boston these were first held in 1840 in Winchester Hall before being moved to Armory Hall, where participants "exhorted one another." The meetings, which were usually focused on religious questions, were important in the ministry of one of the nineteenth century's greatest theologians, Theodore Parker. His dedication to what he called "free speech and free thought" distinguished lectures from sermons.[10] Some readers may consider such meetings tantamount to church services, but participants were convinced that they were making better use of Sunday than those who attended church. Temperance, abolitionist, and women's rights lectures were given Sunday afternoons and evenings in Boston, Cincinnati, and other cities.

During the middle decades of the century, "the Continental Sabbath" augmented the cosmopolitan Sunday of disorder and crime, rallies and lessons, libraries and lectures. As cities swelled with German, Irish, Jewish, and French immigrants, certain neighborhoods came alive each Sunday with variety theaters and dance halls, small entrepreneurs offering chances to win prizes in games of chance, "museums" displaying midgets, Indians, or treasures from far-away places, and daguerreotype establishments where a portrait could be made. New York City's "Kleindeutschland" (Little Germany)—with hundreds of beer halls, saloons, and wine gardens—provided public space for the intensive social life of the German community. Staten Island became the home of several lager breweries, which built lavish resorts. Sundays were especially busy in these places, for it was then that entire families went to drink beer, visit with friends, listen to music, and dance, just as Germans and others did in Europe.[11] It was widely assumed that "rhine-wine is the religion of those [Germans] who can afford to pay for wine, and lager-bier of those who can't."[12] Passion for the Continental Sunday ran deep. When the New York state government introduced a police force to New York City in 1857, crowds, incited by rumors that beer would no longer be sold on Sundays, rioted. After nearly a decade of conflict over Sunday drinking, many Germans cast their ballots in favor of the Democratic Party during the elections of 1866 because Republicans had passed laws forbidding the sale of lager or liquor on Sunday.[13]

In reaction, some native-born urbanites denounced the efforts of Germans in American cities "to have our method of keeping Sunday done away with, and their method adopted in its stead." An essay titled "The Foreign Movement on the Sunday Question," published shortly before the Civil War, neatly expressed the differences between the "traditional" American and the newly imported Continental Sabbaths. It contrasted native-born Americans' regard for Sunday—"as a day of rest, of religious exercise, and of abstinence from labor and public diversions of every kind"—with that of the "natives of Continental Europe," who dared to make it "a day of pleasure, recreation, and enjoyment." Patriotic Americans were called to fight a battle against German, Irish, and French newcomers who were trying to "regulate our social life, make us open theatres on Sunday, substitute lager bier saloons for churches," and turn American cities into "German towns." It seemed as though the "holiday of despotism"—smuggled into the United States by refugees from war, tyranny, and oppression—would obliterate the "holy day of freedom".[14] The "American" Sunday deserved protection. The passage and enforcement of Sunday laws was considered the best approach to this vital task. During a fictional family discussion, one participant exclaimed that the Continental Sabbath "does not suit democratic institutions." Rest, not recreation, cultivated virtue among the citizenry. "If the Sabbath of America is simply to be a universal loafing, picnicking, dining-out day, as it is now with all our foreign populations," he argued, "we shall need what they have in Europe, the gendarmes at every turn."[15] Powerful groups of Americans believed the

"Broadway Sunday Sacred Concert in New York." *Harper's Weekly* (1859). Museum of the City of New York, Print Archives (95.50.19).

This engraving and the one that follows accompanied a five-part series in *Harper's Weekly* depicting the "Continental Sabbath" that German and Irish immigrants brought to American cities. Women who offer beer, flowers, kisses, and their bodies frame the depiction of what were decidedly not *sacred* concerts. Places such as this one, which were popular in most American cities after the 1850s, fashioned new ways to rest on Sunday.

Continental Sabbath threatened American liberty and democratic institutions.

A five-part series about the beery Sundays of New York City's German population—"Sketches of the People Who Oppose Our Sunday Laws"—published in *Harper's Weekly: A Journal of Civilization* in 1859 makes the case against the Continental Sabbath evident. The reporter began the series, "One recent Sunday evening, as I was walking alone on the undignified side of Broadway, rain began to fall with violence." Seeking shelter, he found himself at what many Americans facetiously called a "*sacred* concert." It was held in a "long smoky hall filled with men drinking cocktails," boys tending to beer, and waitresses "bewildering" the customers. At one end of the hall a stage displayed "a rural scene of peculiar qualities," including "sun-flowers blossoming from trees with green trunks and blue leaves." "A cos-

"Sunday Morning in the Fourth Ward, New York." *Harper's Weekly* (1859). Museum of the City of New York, Print Archives (54.38.34).

It was feared that Sundays spent apart from church and home would devolve into idleness. Note the open doors and windows, the female child with beer stein in hand, the woman with children in the gutter, and the crowd, some still in workday clothes, gathered at an intersection characterized by liquor stores. This kind of "Continental Sabbath" was as dangerous to the nation's and individual's well-being as no Sunday at all.

mopolitan array" of performers provided entertainment that was far from sacred, with jigs and minstrelsy headlining. The reporter contrasted "sacred concerts," the Stadt Theatre, and Jones's Woods with church services, family gatherings in the home, silence, and stillness (components of the "traditional Sabbath"). The series' closing essay, "Sunday in Chatham Street," included the native born, the working poor, the idle poor, and the indigent among Sabbath-breakers and completed the picture of city Sundays as decadent, dangerous, and deadly, not only for city dwellers, but for the nation as a whole.[16]

Saloons proliferated in nearly every American city, much to the alarm of Sabbatarians, who depicted drinking establishments as alien, drawing maps of the westward movement of saloons, beer gardens, and "sacred concerts" to the "virgin lands" of St. Louis, Detroit, Toledo, Chicago, Cincinnati, and San Francisco.[17] The Second Great Awakening fomented the conviction that saloons, second only to cities, threatened the well-being of the American family. Temperance literature was filled with warnings about how saloons and liquor destroy the family.

This connection was used to strengthen the case against the "Continental Sabbath." One Sabbatarian tract described a hard-working father who, left to his own devices for a few Sundays, wandered "through the side-door" of a saloon, and succumbed to whiskey and lager. Unable to resist the temptation, he continued visiting the saloon on Sundays, even as his family went to church. Eventually he lost his job, and so made daily visits to the saloon. Soon thereafter, his family was evicted from its home, his wife died, and the last we hear is about his orphaned children walking to church one Sunday and feeling mortified seeing him stumbling in the gutter. On the "only day which most families can spend together," Sunday, the saloon owner "tempts the husband to leave his wife sitting in solitude,—the father to become estranged from his children."[18]

It was feared that the Continental Sabbath might destroy the American Sunday. Instead, as later chapters make clear, many city residents, foreign- and native-born, were in the vanguard. It was in cities where alternatives to church and home could be found. The refusal to differentiate leisure from rest, first obvious in city populations, fundamentally altered Sunday observance, but not without decades of resistance.

"There Is No Sunday Now": Sunday during the Civil War

The Civil War disrupted almost all aspects of social life, from marriage and birth rates to rhythms of work and rest. During the war Sabbatarians and others expressed concern about the countless military maneuvers performed on Sunday, the battles fought on Sunday (including the Battle of Bull Run), and the amount of work done on Sunday. A northern tract printed early in the conflict articulated the rationale for observing Sunday: "Our soldiers need a Sabbath . . . The impolicy of this careless dealing with sacred time would seem to be obvious . . . Our final plea for restraining further violations of the Sabbath is based on the dependence of the nation and its armies on the divine favor and blessing."[19] In response to this and other appeals, in 1861 General George B. McClellan ordered the Union Army to observe the Sabbath, the commander of the Union flotilla of gunboats issued an order to "abstain from unnecessary work," and President Lincoln issued a proclamation in 1862 in favor of limiting Sunday labor and fighting.[20] A major general in the Union Army testified:

> I would appeal to the American people to save our Sabbath. If our wealth should be lost in this terrible war, it may be recovered. If our young men are killed off, others will grow up and take their places. BUT

IF OUR AMERICAN SABBATH IS LOST, IT CAN NEVER BE RESTORED, AND ALL
IS LOST.[21]

The Confederate Army's leadership shared this sentiment: Robert E.
Lee issued a general order in 1862 suspending all duties except inspec-
tion on Sunday. He reiterated his concern about "proper observance of
the Sabbath" in 1864, stressing "its importance, not only as a moral and
religious duty, but as contributing to the personal health and well being
of the troops."[22] Despite orders, however, both sides moved troops and
fought battles on Sundays.

The contrast between Sunday and other days of the week also diminished on the home front during the war. The demand for news of the
war was so insatiable that most daily newspaper publishers printed one
or two editions each Sunday, breaking with the customary five- or six-
day publication schedule. Trains ran with mail, supplies, and even
troops, and factories stayed open for military manufacture. In these and
other ways, the Civil War loosened standards regulating Sunday. For the
most part, forms of wartime measures continued even when peace returned. The Civil War itself was not responsible for the changing nature
of Sunday, but it provided an opportunity for industrial, technological,
and commercial innovations to impose themselves on Sunday.

During the war men and women on both sides noted that there was
"no Sabbath" and "no Sunday." Their laments are worth attention, if
only because they are so similar. In her youth, the reformer Dorothea
Dix held Sunday sacred in various ways—attending services, teaching
Sunday school, writing letters, and performing works of charity. At
some point during the Civil War, however, she stopped attending services, declaring "there is no Sunday now."[23] "There is Sunday in the al-
manac," wrote a private from Iowa in his journal, "but in military affairs there seems to be no sacred day." A chaplain ministering to Union
soldiers, including the wounded, while on a march through Virginia
shortly after the war's end, observed, "It has not seemed much like a
Sunday." He added that he was "too tired for much profitable reflections, besides we hav'nt much to eat." Both sides agreed that "one of
the miseries of war," as General Lee reflected in a letter to his daughter
Annie Carter Lee, "is that there is no Sabbath, and the current of work
and strife has no cessation."[24]

That some experienced the loss of Sunday during the war does not
mean that all did, however. In fact, many soldiers came to the day with
rekindled Christian sentiments. Chaplains on both sides held services
in camps and on battlefields, visited the wounded and dying in hospi-
tals, and even crossed lines to minister to those of their faith. More no-
tably, soldiers participated in revivals that may have resulted in more

than one hundred thousand conversions. In addition, reminiscences suggest that however compromised Sunday may have been, its special and sacred aspects were sometimes made manifest during the war. A Catholic chaplain for the Confederate Army recorded powerful impressions in his diary about Easter Sunday, 1863, spent near Fredericksburg, Virginia: "The snow had been falling all night and early in the morning it continued to come down so thickly that one could hardly see fifty yards distant. . . . It was edifying to see them [a large number of soldiers] standing in the snow before Mass commenced, how much more so to see them on their bended knees and with uncovered heads defying as it were the angry elements." A few Sundays later while on the picket line along one side of the Rappahannock River, he watched Yankee and Confederate soldiers send small boats back and forth "laden with tobacco and other commodities."[25] Such piety and congeniality contrasted with incidents such as the capture of Union serviceman ashore for services at the Presbyterian church of Rodney, Mississippi, or with bloody battles, or with the gathering up and burial of the dead, or with the execution of AWOL soldiers.[26]

On Sundays during the war, family members remembered one another and reflected on the transience of their lives and dreams. One letter from a Confederate soldier to his wife opens "Another Sunday has made its appearance and as it is such a beautiful day, I shall devote some part of it to my dearest one who is so far from me." That anxieties about his and his family's well-being reached a high pitch on Sunday was probably typical. Another Sunday letter to his wife, written shortly before he received a mortal wound, closes: "My dear, I constantly pray to my Father in Heaven that he may spare my life, yours, and the little ones so that we may meet on earth again and . . . that we may live happier than we did before the War. I feel as if we ought constantly to pray to our Maker . . . to stop this unholy War. Oh, that He would put a stop to it."[27]

In northern and southern churches prayers were offered pleading that lives be spared and victory granted, sermons given to rally spirits, and remembrances shared of soldiers who had been wounded or killed during the previous week. Americans found it hard to transcend their worries, fears, and heartbreak on all days, including Sundays. As the war came to an end, some in both North and South rejoiced that they might return to prewar Sundays. Bessie Allston, the young mistress of a South Carolina plantation ravaged by Sherman's army, wrote in her diary one Sunday late in the war:

> The day is bright and beautiful. Everything looks full of peace & joy—and thank Heaven there are none of the Enemy now near us—This

morning we all walked to church & got there in full time—there was not a vehicle of any sort except a mule cart at the church. Everyone looked cheerful.[28]

Sabbatarian Sentiment

Shortly before the Civil War, the New York Sabbath Committee (NYSC) first convened (1857), prompted by a religious revival that was sweeping through New York City. The title of its first tract—*The Sabbath: As It Was and As It Is*—reflects the founders' nostalgia for simpler times. The tract opens, "Our ancestors loved the Christian Sabbath"; it closes with a jeremiad warning that the "Divine Ruler" will invariably "visit rebellious cities and nations." Other NYSC publications flesh out various threats to America's Sunday, each of which stood in contrast to what Sabbatarians imagined as the Sabbath of their forefathers, both Dutch and Puritan:

> *Railroads and the Sabbath* (1858)
> *The Sabbath in Europe: The Holy Day of Freedom—The Holiday of Despotism* (1859)
> *Sunday Theatres, "Sacred Concerts," and Beer Gardens* (1860)
> *Plea for the Sabbath in War* (1861)

Here were the forces that would destroy the Puritan legacy: railroads, immigrants, war, and intemperate amusements.[29] Over the next seven decades the New York Sabbath Committee entered almost every battle over leisure activities that reconfigured American culture; saloons, excursions, newspapers, museums, baseball, motion pictures, radio, and dancing highlight the list. Along with numerous other Sabbatarian organizations that formed before the century's end, it was intent on keeping rest and leisure in separate spheres.[30]

During the decades following the Civil War, immigration, industrialization, and urbanization exacerbated nostalgia for a homogenous Protestant and agrarian nation that adhered to a single model of Sunday observance. Concern about Sunday spilled over from the Presbyterian and Congregationalist to the Methodist and Baptist camps in the North and South during the 1870s. The General Assemblies of these mainline Protestant denominations passed resolutions against Sabbath-breaking and in the 1880s and 1890s joined crusades to protect Sunday, Christianity, and American civilization. Although the Catholic Church in the United States made a case against Sunday laws in the 1870s, in the

1890s it joined mainstream Protestants in expressing concern about the manner in which Americans passed Sunday.[31] Other "purity reformers," especially temperance activists, joined Sabbatarians in the attempt to mold a Christian republic. They had powerful allies among politicians, merchants, and educators and exercised influence over local and national politics. Every president of the United States from Grant to Coolidge endorsed the Sabbatarian cause, while senators and congressmen proposed Sabbatarian measures, like closing World's Fairs and prohibiting government work on Sundays. International conferences devoted to solving "the Sunday problem" were held in conjunction with the World's Fairs that thrilled Americans in Chicago, St. Louis, and San Francisco.[32] Discussion and debate about Sunday filled the columns of the nation's newspapers, magazines, and religious periodicals.

No consensus was reached, however, and a diversity of meanings for Sunday continued to vie for power. The rise of liberal Protestantism, the arrival of millions of European immigrants, the valorization of the middle-class home, and the advances in transportation and communications technology reshaped meanings and uses for Sunday in a more lasting fashion than Sabbatarian meetings, publications, and petitions. Yet, the Sabbatarian sentiment retained uncanny power.

In 1849 Henry David Thoreau published *A Week on the Concord and Merrimack Rivers*, which detailed his journeys with his brother along two New England rivers in a canoe. The chapter titled "Sunday," rich in the kinds of metaphysics that Thoreau is famous for, provides a sense of what religious liberals hoped Sunday could be. He described a Sunday spent on a riverbank: "The stillness was intense and almost conscious, as if it were a natural Sabbath, and we fancied that the morning was the evening of a celestial day ... The world seemed decked out for some holiday." In contrast, when Thoreau later heard "the sound of the sabbath bell far away, now breaking on these shores" it did not "awaken pleasing associations, but melancholy and sombre ones rather." He mused on strict ministers, long church services replete with empty preaching, and superstitions about Sunday. Thoreau's chapter on Sunday contemplates the relationship between religion, nature, books, and poetry.[33] The holiday that Thoreau anticipated was not the Continental Sabbath found in America's cities; nor was it the austere Sabbath inherited from the Puritans; it was a day for culture.

4 The Sabbath for Man

The Sabbath was made for man, not man for the Sabbath.
—MARK 2:27

In a letter detailing his position on "the old Sunday question" Frederick Law Olmsted declared in 1871 that he belonged to "the ranks of 'the enemies of the Sabbath,' " a place that he came to "by a rational, honest & conscientious process." He contrasted the "Scotch & English Sunday" with that of the Germans and found favor with the results of the latter, which created "conscientious workmen." Here Olmsted was in accord with the general conviction that the right use of Sunday was fundamental to character, and that the misuse of the day accounted for "weak and vicious, morbid" people. But he differed from his friends and from other well-educated, genteel reformers in his elevation of the "Sunday trained conscience," which "rescued men from a sordid self-centered life," over the "Sabbath trained conscience." With the passing of each decade, more and more Americans came to share Olmsted's belief that Sundays "would be better for more real amusement—recreation & less preaching & elaborate wordy praying."[1] Central to this reevaluation was the development and spread of a liberal theology that remade Sunday into a day for culture.

After the Civil War, societies sponsoring lecture series on Sundays proliferated, with the desire "to teach knowledge, not faith." From their own vantage they were providing "a very impressive lesson of the use that may be made of Sunday, aside from its religious observance."[2] As one of the many liberal ministers who worked to situate Sunday in "Culture" explained, "the Sabbath should be used as an opportunity to lift a suffering world from its social and physical degradation."[3] With

that and other goals in mind, labor meetings, political addresses, and reform rallies were frequently held on Sunday afternoons and evenings.[4]
Political activity was one route to reform, culture was another. Religious liberals, social reformers, and the "metropolitan gentry" believed
that Sunday was the ideal site to "harmonize Christ and culture," a
process that some historians have labeled "sacralization."[5] The fusion
of religious with cultural uses for Sunday fundamentally altered the
meaning of rest; the emphasis on culture established legitimate grounds
for experiences beyond the confines of the church and opened the way
for leisure activities.

Culture and Democracy

Throughout the nineteenth century, ideals concerning the uplifting
potential of some kinds of culture circulated, but it was not until the
Sunday-opening movement that these ideals clashed with an older con-
ception of culture as beneficial to the elite but corrupting to the masses.
Inheriting from the Whigs an ambivalence about democracy, some
Americans envisioned culture as a privilege of an educated elite. But
under the influence of religious liberals and genteel reformers, others,
particularly the younger members of the Anglo-American urban elite,
embraced culture as a tool for refining and uplifting the electorate in
whose hands rested the fate of democratic politics. In cities across
America this more liberal, but well-connected, generation—the metropolitan gentry—began to put their energy and authority toward the formation of cultural institutions and to contend that opening such institutions each Sunday could expand "the means of grace."

Although the divine nature of Sunday and its status as a rest day were
central issues in the Sunday-opening movement, other questions came
up. Were libraries and museums "class institutions"? What were the relationships and obligations of these institutions to America's diverse
population? How did the question of profit figure into Sunday opening?
What was the proper relationship between cosmopolitan culture and
Sunday? By the turn of the century a range of new meanings for Sunday
and for rest—emerging out of the ideal of culture as uplifting—had
taken hold.

Culture was a set of highly differentiated activities, centered on the
consumption of poetry, prose, liquor, tea, Shakespeare, burlesque, physical prowess, painting, "nature," lectures, or any of an expanding range
of goods and experiences. During the nineteenth century, just as today,
assumptions abounded concerning the usefulness of various cultural

activities in the shaping of character—some kinds of print literature, some kinds of plastic arts, and many kinds of knowledge were uplifting, but for all but the highly educated most were degrading and dangerous. Americans had never been as suspicious of books as they were of the plastic and dramatic arts. A great many public and mercantile libraries were built before and after the Civil War, and most Americans prized their literacy. But painting, theater, dance, and the like were considered unnecessary, possibly even corrupting. According to one historian, art museums—as repositories of paintings and sculptures—were considered both "suspicious and European" well into the 1880s. Other kinds of museums, devoted to the display of oddities, dioramas, and spectacles, which multiplied in American cities from the late eighteenth century, the best known being P. T. Barnum's for-profit ventures, presented mostly sensationalist fare.[6] World's Fairs, immersed in the rhetoric of Progress and Manifest Destiny, managed to avoid much censure.

Religious liberals, the metropolitan gentry, and social reformers argued that opening cultural institutions on Sundays would uplift the entire community, promote democracy, and improve the day itself. Their opponents believed that Sunday opening, even if harmless, would lead to the ruin of Sunday: how could the difference between a library and a theater, a museum and a store, a fair and a baseball game be upheld in a democracy where all men, and therefore all passions, were equal before the law? To protect Sunday from the worst aspects of American culture, the day would have to remain off limits to all but the kind of religion found in church.

A number of developments made the last third of the nineteenth century a time of dramatic change and discontinuity. Railroads ran routes between cities near and far; bold capitalists built resorts, theaters, and amusement parks; others put together professional baseball teams, sponsored prize fights, or promoted the bicycle craze; publishers experimented with new genres such as dime novels and Sunday newspapers. Millions of immigrants arrived, seeking homes and jobs in cities large and small. They brought with them distinct customs and great desires. Southerners white and black, rich and poor, male and female, struggled against one another in manifold ways that are still not well enough understood or gauged.

Inspired by the will to harness rapid technological, economic, and social change, philanthropists, communities, and religious denominations built numerous universities, colleges, libraries, museums, and public parks during the late nineteenth century. These institutions were meant to be helpmeets to the republic: places that would nurture good citizenship and democracy. Public libraries, for instance, were

THE DEACON'S MARE.

Deacon's Mare, Getting the Word Go! Published by Currier & Ives (1879). Museum of the City of New York, The Harry T. Peters Collection (56.300.523).

A congregation of men and women representing various social classes emerge from a church just in time to witness the runaway horse, squawking rooster, barking dogs, breaking eggs, and cheering boy. The peace and quiet of the ideal Sunday are certainly absent, but whether the deacon and his wife had attended church or have been caught skipping the service to take a Sunday drive the lithograph does not tell us.

meant to continue the education begun, but rarely finished, by the common schools, and therefore to protect the nation's republican form of government. Other institutions aimed to nurture intelligent and rational citizens. Older ones, such as the church and Sunday, underwent extensive revision, partly in the attempt to adapt to changing demographics, partly to develop closer alliances with the new institutions that had captured the nation's imagination, and partly to accommodate new activities and pursuits.[7]

Through this period of unprecedented growth, change, and conflict, Sunday as an institution and as a day was imbued with greater significance than ever before, and experienced its most rapid reformulation. Two responses to the expansion in Sunday's meanings and uses warrant attention. One is the Sabbatarian response, which sought to quarantine

Sunday from the many forces remaking the United States. The other is that of a different set of reformers, those who sought to adapt these forces to accomplish Sunday's highest purposes. Sabbatarians and conservative Protestants wished to uphold the distinction between rest and leisure; liberal Protestants did not.

Sunday, a Human Institution

Liberal Protestants shared with their adversaries a commitment to Sunday as a special day in the weekly calendar. Shortly after the Civil War, the radical abolitionist Charles K. Whipple wrote that he did not want to eradicate the day, but he could not countenance its status as the Sabbath. He noted that religious education and propaganda (by way of the Sunday school) tended to strengthen the conviction that Sunday was the Sabbath. Sabbatarians, who directed and controlled "the religious instruction of the whole population," had "their doctrine in regard to Sunday" accepted "without demur, by a large and highly respectable portion of the community." It was high time for new Christian meanings for Sunday. Near the end of the 1870s, William Channing Gannett, one of the more famous Unitarians, formulated a "secular Sunday" as an alternative to the Sabbath, but most religious liberals found the idea unpalatable. They wanted to sanctify Sunday, but with the inclusion of uplifting activities and innocent diversions. To accomplish this reform, liberal theologians needed to reinterpret the biblical basis for the Christian Sabbath.[8]

So, clergy who had been trained in historical and literary methods of biblical exegesis in seminary began to spread their vision of Sunday as "man's day." They described the Sabbath as part of the covenant between God and the Jews, suggested that Sunday worship had pagan origins, and explained that Christ's actions and words abrogated the fourth commandment.[9] When Christ declared that the "Sabbath was made for man" he outlined "the principle that human welfare must take precedence" over "external observances." Men and women needed rest for their bodies and souls. Sunday, as a human institution, could meet both needs, but only if Americans would turn to the Gospels for guidance about how to rest.[10]

In addition to meanings for Sunday rooted in the New Testament, liberal Protestants promoted Enlightenment ideas concerning human nature and the potential of culture. Sunday was one of the few available avenues for overcoming peoples' base nature, a nature that led them to be ruthless competitors, to lose their sense of community, and to neglect both home and Nature. Accordingly, men and women needed "to attune" their souls "to the beauty and music of creation," and to come to love and be at peace with their neighbors. The person who thus spent Sundays would have *"the savage in him tamed."*[11] Pleading from a "higher ground than the physical" for a Sunday devoted to body and soul, liberal Protestants claimed: "We are animal, but we are more: we are *spiritual.*"[12] The universal basis for sanctifying Sunday would be in its physical and spiritual value for mankind, rather than in the fourth commandment. It would be as a day of leisure rather than of rest that Sunday would flourish.

The liberal theology concerning Sunday mandated different kinds of Sunday laws from the ones on the books.[13] Liberal Protestants exhumed the anti-Sabbatarian streak found in Colossians 2:16, where Paul exhorts Christians to restrain from judging each other's observance of Sabbaths, new moons, and holy days.[14] More important, they believed that Sunday laws created a false and stressful relationship between the individual and God. As one wrote, "We shall never win the Sunday that we need, by means of negations and prohibitions—'touch not, taste not, handle not.' "[15] But without any laws at all, the day would face ruin. Laws that prevented needless labor and willful dissipation were necessary.[16] Devoted to liberty though they were, religious liberals rarely defended Sunday saloons or other commercial recreational enterprises.[17]

In general, liberal Protestants appealed to individual consciences concerning Sunday observance. When prescribing methods of sanctifying the day, Sabbatarians quoted an array of biblical texts that urged Christians to do no work, "abstain from all worldly enjoyments," publicly worship God, participate in "private acts of secret and social worship," and perform works of "necessity and mercy." Religious liberals, on the other hand, believed that Christian men and women had the natural capacity to figure out how to spend Sunday without reliance on commandments, rules, or laws.[18] The perplexed should ask, "What would Jesus do?" when trying to decide how to behave on Sunday. "His example of morning instruction and afternoon recreation seems eminently reasonable and in the spirit of the meaning of the day, whether regarded from a sanitary or a religious point of view."[19]

The "practical theology" that characterized the liberal Protestant approach to Sunday emerged out of faith in the immanence of Christian time, the inherent goodness and rationality of human nature, and the redeeming power of God's love. It elevated every day of the week to the level of Sunday—all days were equally holy, all time was sacred. One liberal Protestant declared that "we cannot impart to it [Sunday] a sacred content by declaring it holy from sun to sun, by inference asserting that the other six days are unholy or secular . . . To the believer every day is the Lord's day."[20] Another claimed that "a good man, indeed, spends all his days and especially his Sabbaths, as in God's sights."[21] Still, they wanted Sunday "to go on being a 'Sunday,' " but they wanted it "for life's best uses."[22] Where Sabbatarians saw temptation to sin everywhere in the world, liberal Protestants saw manifestations of God's greatness, perhaps sullied by impure uses, but capable of great good. Seeking to reform, rather than reject, the world, they embraced what had been considered worldly, and therefore sinful, activities. Protestants of all inclinations had sought to transcend the world's cares, distractions, and pleasures each Sunday, but liberal Protestants sought to fuse themselves with the world and thereby remake it.

Much of the impulse behind religious liberalism came from the sense that conditions of American life were changing in ways that put democracy itself in danger. The state was expected to make every man a citizen, but to do so involved more than granting the franchise and showing the way to the polling booth. By the same token, democracy would not thrive if the understanding of politics was limited to elections, politicians, and policies. As the genteel cultural critic Thomas Wentworth Higginson pleaded, "the essential thing is, that we should recognize, as a nation, the value of all culture, and resolutely organize it into institutions."[23] Although Higginson was referring to universities in particular, he could have been speaking equally well for the religious liberals who aimed to make Sunday into an institution of culture.

The possibility that Sunday might become an institution of culture outraged Sabbatarians. They argued again and again that Christ had claimed the Sabbath for himself, not for man. When they interpreted Mark 2:27, "a saying" that they acknowledged was "at once orthodox and liberal," they concluded that it simply universalized the privilege of one day's rest in seven.[24] The Princeton theologian Benjamin Warfield explained that "not man but the Son of Man is Lord of the Sabbath." To Warfield and other Sabbatarians, the Sabbath was "not an invention of man's," but "a creation of God's."[25] And even though the day was made for man, it was different from "a weekly bank holiday."[26] Since God made the Sabbath, He was its ruler. Liberal Protestants, in the opinion of Sabbatarians, encouraged Americans to "treat the day as if it were a human convenience rather than a divine gift. We stress so much the fact that the 'Sabbath was made for *man*' that we slur the fact that the Maker of the Day is God, and that in a unique sense the Day is God's *gift to man*."[27] Under the direction of liberal Protestants Sunday would become

a gift [used] in such a way as to injure the giver. Our friend gives us a walking stick, and we employ it directly as a weapon wherewith to

maim *him!* . . . He gives us a jeweled knife, and we place its sharpness
against his throat in an effort to gash *him!* The illustrations are strong,
but they are suggestive too. God made the Sabbath for man; while man
in his turn often remakes the Sabbath against God! The gift is turned
against the Giver.[28]

More than routine desecration of the Sabbath was at stake. If the line
between rest and leisure were erased, Sabbatarians and conservative
Protestants feared that Christianity itself would suffer.

Opening the Boston Public Library

Between 1859 and 1872, the debates over opening the Boston Public
Library on Sundays illustrate the interplay between conceptions of culture and Sunday. The trustees of the library first considered Sunday
opening in 1859 but voted unanimously against the motion, claiming
that there was no demand for Sunday hours. Shortly before the end of
the Civil War, the Boston city council ordered the public library kept
open on Sundays from ten in the morning until ten at night. This order
applied to all the library's departments, including circulation. But the
city council's Committee on the Public Library, to which the order was
referred, did not support it, reasoning that the trustees would protest by
withdrawing endowments. To bolster their pecuniary rationale, they
cited the librarians' and the community's need for a day of rest. Nevertheless, the following year the city council handed the mayor an order
for Sunday evening hours, five until ten, for the reading room. The library's committee discussed the issue, but "as a unanimous report
could not be procured, owing to radical differences of opinion on the
part of the members, the subject was laid aside." Before the order could
be sent to the library's trustees, Mayor F. W. Lincoln vetoed it; in justification he invoked the language of Christian stewardship, affirming
that "as a Christian community, we are bound to the extent of our
power to conform to the proprieties, at least, of the Christian Sabbath."
Boston must "beware lest we do anything in an official capacity which
will apparently justify others in lowering the [city's] standard of character." In addition, the mayor reminded councilmen of the state law that
forbade unnecessary Sunday labor.[29]

In 1867 a coalition of workingmen and "liberals" petitioned the city
council to open the library on Sunday. In response, the city council recommended the opening of the reading room from two in the afternoon
to ten in the evening on Sundays. When the library committee made

public its report recommending Sunday opening, Boston's clergy re-
acted strongly in pulpits and city newspapers. Responding to minister-
ial pressure, the city council held a series of hearings in July 1867 to
allow remonstrance. At least forty people testified against Sunday opening, numbering among them most of Boston's more influential ministers, such as Jacob Manning of Old South Church, as well as political
leaders like W. W. Story, who had been president of the city council,
Harvey Jewell, a powerful member of the Massachusetts Whig and Republican parties, and William Greenough, a trustee of the library, as
well as two library assistants and the library janitor. A much smaller
group—two workingmen, a physician, and one of Boston's prominent
lawyers, Charles Mayo Ellis—favored Sunday opening.[30]

The first, and almost only, issue addressed in the 1867 hearings was
Sunday's religious meaning and value. Those against Sunday opening
described it as a plot to destroy religion and decency that would give
"the friends of liberal Christianity an opportunity to boast that Puritanism is rapidly weakening." When the doors of the library opened on
Sunday, declared one, "this old Puritanical City of Boston" would lose
its prestige. An avid opponent of Sunday opening, M. Field Fowler, devoted most of a pamphlet (published at his own expense) to the familiar
argument that the Old Testament's prescription for the Jewish Sabbath
mandated similar observance of the Christian Sabbath. As did many
others, he concluded that the city of Boston would be violating the explicit wishes of God found in the Old Testament and the Decalogue if it
opened the doors to its library on Sunday afternoons.[31] Those in favor
of Sunday opening, however, argued that whatever fed the intellect nurtured the soul, and vice versa. Charles Mayo Ellis suggested that "learning promotes morality," and that the library was "the best auxiliary and
test and stimulant of the pulpit."[32]

The debate drew, as well, on differing understandings of church and
state. The library committee held that opening the library on Sunday
would protect and uphold democratic rights, would avoid favoring one
set of beliefs over another, and would extend the privileges of culture to
the entire community. Opponents characterized uplift as sectarian,
contending that its advocates were trying to enforce their own version
of Sunday observance with the aid of the city treasury. One minister
claimed that if the library were to open on Sunday, the city government
would "become a propagandist" of a specific and sectarian "opinion on
Sunday observance." Under this scheme the city might turn the library
into "an instrument for working out certain ideas of the Sunday." He
urged those who wanted to provide an open reading room on Sunday to
"put their hands into their own pockets, as old fashioned people who

believe in another sort of Sunday are doing, and let us be taxed only for
that which shall afford equal protection to us all." His opponents, however, argued that keeping libraries *closed* was sectarian: "All pay. To
give to all the chance to use when they can and as they will, is free, fair,
and equal. To debar any on set days and seasons in obedience to the
faith or taste of others, is to force them to conform to the standard of
such taste and belief."[33] Was uplift in the form of Sunday opening a
civic, and therefore universal, ideal or a theological, and therefore sectarian, plan?

At stake in the debate was the nature of democratic culture. The library committee noted that other nonchurch organizations functioned
on Sundays, including a horse-car company, several private reading
rooms, and two social clubs. Patrons of these institutions were "among
the most substantial of our citizens." Furthermore, the city's elite did
not have to depend on the public library for reading matter; its members
could turn to their private clubs and reading rooms, or read their own
books at home. It did not seem fair, then, that the public library, which
aimed to give the entire community access to books and learning, was
closed on the one day when most of the population had the time to read.
Sunday opening would remove the grounds for calling the library a
"class institution," a characterization that had troubled the library's
trustees during its early years. In addition, the city council's mandate to
look after public welfare pushed it to consider its citizens' Sunday observances. It was found that even if all of Boston's 115 churches were
filled on Sundays, three-quarters of the city's population would still
have no place to go and nothing to do. The problem was most acute for
those who lived in boarding houses, who "seldom or never attend any
church, but seek the country or the streets for recreation." In the face of
such activity, considered the same as idleness, why not keep open
places of "attractive resort" on Sundays? Along these lines, then, closing the library on Sunday was both cruel and undemocratic. As lawyer
Ellis, Sunday opening's eloquent defender, asked in the final hearing:
"Who are the men here, and what is their sanction, and to what end is
it, that they ask the large mass of this community to surrender their
only time to those on whom time hangs heavy? Give up the sole time
left them for books because you have time enough to read on other
days?"[34] Ellis maintained that excessive concern for "preserving the
day" violated natural and democratic rights.

In response, Sunday-opening opponents claimed that the working
classes would only misuse and otherwise violate library privileges. One
minister suggested that it would not be long that "our library be an ornament and honor to our city if it be opened, as are beer and tobacco sa-

loons, for a similar or this very class of visitors." Like apprehensions characterize the comments of the Tremont Temple's minister: if the library opened on Sundays, then "no decent person could go there with propriety, as even now the place was used for assignations." (Later a witness "repudiated as an insult that the petitioners would use the library room for the purpose of making assignations with the other sex." He pointed out that the "Tremont Temple was known to be quite available for that purpose.") Insult and retort seethed with class tensions, exacerbated by nativism. In the off-chance that Sunday opening proved beneficial, opponents argued, it would still provide the "opening-wedge" for the Continental Sunday, and thus would irrevocably damage the city and its polity. They warned that it would "plant a lever which may eventually heave all our religious liberties from their sure foundation." Boston would head the way of infamous New Orleans, toward a Sabbathless state and a sinful existence. It seemed a few short steps from open reading rooms, to the Continental Sabbath, to despotism itself.[35] Americans, in their opinion, had to keep leisure, whether or not it was uplifting, separate from rest.

In response, Ellis characterized the library as a place that "tends to peace and quiet, to study and thought. It does not counteract, it supports the institutions of religion." Sunday opening would diminish demand for demoralizing Sunday amusements. In other countries, "rural excursions, botanical gardens, crystal palaces, and bands of music," explained the library committee of the Boston City Council, "are among the more decorous means, favored by philanthropic and religious men, for keeping the mass of the population from vice and dissipation on [Sunday]." It was subscribing to the conventions of polite culture in the attempt to lift the city's opinion makers' eyes away from prophecies of immoral and indecent behavior. Was it better to "allow these throngs to thus pass the day in comparative indifference and idleness, or offer an inducement for even a very small advantage to their minds by furnishing an open reading room?"[36]

In spite of weighty theological and sectarian arguments over Sunday opening, the sticking point turned out to be the state law against Sunday labor. The city council could not order Sunday opening without violating the state law against all Sunday labor except that done "of necessity and charity." After calling the Sunday law "a very ancient one," and noting that it "prohibits many of the transactions now permitted by general custom," the library committee recommended in 1867 that no further action be taken to open the library on Sunday.[37] Each session of the state legislature during the following years witnessed unsuccessful attempts to modify the Sunday statutes. Yet despite the intransigence of the legislature, the Committee on the Public Library held to its faith in the necessity of opening the library on Sunday. In 1872 the city council presented Mayor William Gaston with an order to open the public library from two in the afternoon to nine at night for the use of books and periodicals within the building. Gaston vetoed the order.[38]

Meanwhile, other cities opened their newly established public libraries on Sundays. The Milwaukee Public Library introduced Sunday hours in 1869; the Mercantile Library of Philadelphia, one of the largest libraries in the nation at that time, opened its doors on Sundays in 1870; the Cincinnati Public Library introduced longer Sunday hours than any other library in the nation in 1871; in 1872 and 1873 the New York Mercantile Library, the St. Louis Public School Library, the Worcester Public Library, and the Chicago Public Library likewise opened. Proponents of Sunday opening in Boston marshaled support from these so-called experimental openings of libraries on Sundays.[39] Finally, on Sunday, February 9, 1873, the doors of the Boston Public Library were opened at two o'clock in the afternoon. Since the Massachusetts legislature had not amended the blue laws to allow for Sunday opening, the city council and the library's trustees had decided to take their chances by violating the rarely enforced statute. In September they extended Sunday hours: "the large number of readers" had made it "desirable to delay the hour of closing."[40]

Sunday hours at the Boston Public Library and other libraries were popular. Visitors, according to library reports, included a large portion of "those who work early and late in their daily vocation," as well as the unemployed and "idle." Before the turn of the century the library was the preserve of men, young and old, who may have had nowhere else to go each Sunday. Although women were never explicitly barred from public libraries, they used them infrequently during the week and on Sundays until after the turn of the century.[41]

Library reports suggest, however, that Sunday opening did not immediately lead to uplift. Individual uses for libraries varied, often far from the intentions of Sunday-opening advocates. Urbanites seeking warmth found refuge in the library, especially during the winter months: January, February, and March were the months with the highest Sunday attendance in libraries across the nation. Data concerning the genres of books as well as the volume of newspapers issued on Sunday suggest that patrons sought a range of reading material: not much theology, considerable fiction, mostly newspapers and periodicals.[42] But these realities did little to tarnish the image and ideal of Sunday opening as progressive, benevolent, and civilized.

The Gilded Age's public library movement, based as it was in ideologies of republicanism, moral warfare, and uplift, coincided with the "opening up" of Sunday. Mary Salome Cutler, one of the newly emerging class of library professionals and an advocate of Sunday opening, emphasized the confluence of the public library and Sunday by contrasting blue laws with library discipline: "Strangely enough, something of this notion of Sunday reminds me of the library of the olden time. A Sabbath stillness at all times pervaded this temple of wisdom . . . Like the old-time Sabbath, its work has been limited, because, like the Sabbath, it has existed for its own sake and not first of all for man." Cutler expanded on the "Sabbath for man" theme, praising cities that attempted to adapt both libraries and Sundays to human needs: "The library aims to do for the community by the aid of books and personal contact that [which] the Sabbath supplies by a wider circle of influences, both taking the mass of people as they are, and working to build them up in all that tends to a life of higher aims."[43] The civic obligations of libraries and Sundays were strikingly similar, and could be expressed in one pithy word—"uplift."

Librarians' deep sense of public service, which they shared with other professionals working in the public sphere, intersected neatly with the program of uplift. Gilded Age issues of the primary organ of the American Library Association, the *Library Journal*, are thick with statistics proudly detailing ever-lengthening hours of service. So strong was the commitment of librarians to public service and uplift that they convinced trustees to appropriate money to establish branches throughout the nation's rapidly growing cities, suburbs, and slums. In the mid 1890s one librarian observed, "In these days, when every one reads, a library is almost as much as a necessity as schools or parks, or art galleries, or anything else which means a higher or broader life. It goes abreast with Progress. Its work goes on, without stopping, every day in the year. It has no narrow sphere of usefulness." By the mid 1890s, almost half of the nation's public libraries were open on Sunday. After the turn of the century the Library of Congress opened on Sundays, libraries in small New England towns opened during the hour after church, and a majority of the nation's public libraries at the very least experimented with Sunday hours. What is more, as many as a quarter of public libraries' weekly visitors came on Sunday alone.[44]

Visitors went to the Boston Public Library to read the large collection of foreign and American newspapers, use the reference section, or entertain themselves with biography, poetry, and fiction. When the magnificent Copley Square building opened in 1895, Sunday attendance

ballooned; during the following three years not a Sunday passed without 3,000 visitors passing through the open doors. Later, large crowds
came to the library each Sunday to look at "the new decorations,"
which included a ceiling painting by John Elliott called *The Triumph of
Time*. In 1912 the library introduced free Sunday afternoon lectures,
and by the end of the 1920s it was sponsoring Sunday evening concerts.[45] Boston's public library aimed to guide citizens to "the higher
life" through its collections, architecture, decoration, and sponsored
events, and a great many Bostonians sought such uplift. By the first
decade of the twentieth century, the Sabbatarian spokesman Wilbur F.
Crafts, who had adamantly opposed opening libraries on Sunday during
the nineteenth century, described it as "of great benefit in a city's revival of Sabbath observance."[46] By the time Crafts had changed his position on Sunday opening, Sunday itself had joined the pantheon of
American institutions devoted to uplift.

The theological position that the Bible mandated church worship,
private prayer, and scriptural study as the only routes to rest underwent
significant revision after mid century. Liberal Protestants, believing
that Sunday should be transformed into a day for culture, looked to the
New Testament for support. There they found passages that suggested
the necessity of adapting Sunday to solve contemporary society's problems. The American people and nation needed the day to lift them out
of materialism and greed into a higher sphere where culture would
transform individuals into citizens. Rest and leisure would become one.
Opening libraries on Sunday was one of the first efforts to put liberal
meanings for the day into practice. Later in the century, museums and
world's fairs would also open on Sunday.

5 Opening Up Sunday

> The presence of United States troops at Fort Sheridan holds the Chicago Anarchists in check. Cannot the administration notify the Directory [of the World's Fair] that those troops will be promptly used, if necessary, to maintain inviolate the Nation's authority and keep the Fair closed on the Lord's Day?
>
> —TELEGRAM FROM EVANGELICAL ALLIANCE TO UNITED STATES ATTORNEY GENERAL (May 1893)

A few days after the Evangelical Alliance sent a telegram to the attorney general, the First United Presbyterian Church in Boston telegraphed President Grover Cleveland: "Guard the gates next Sabbath with troops if necessary." With this missive it joined millions of other Americans in efforts both sane and desperate to keep the Chicago World's Fair of 1893 closed on Sunday.[1] The protest was the culmination of decades of tension over making "the Sabbath for man." The hysterical telegrams are but two of many artifacts from the long struggle concerning the imposition of culture onto Sunday, of which the movements to open New York's Metropolitan Museum of Art and the Chicago World's Fair on Sunday, the subjects of this chapter, are examples.

"The Vestibule of the Church": The Metropolitan Museum of Art

When residents of New York City began to challenge the Sunday closing of the Metropolitan Museum of Art (the Met) in 1881, they embraced a broad-based theology of uplift. Supporters claimed, "We are not [so] extravagantly sanguine as to suppose this opening of a museum" will "change the moral aspect of the city at once. It is only a step in the right direction, but it is a very important one; it is a recognition of the higher needs and higher possibilities of the people."[2] Some New Yorkers disagreed: in their view only the church's ministry was appropriate on Sunday. Among opponents of the museum's opening were those who desired to support "the traditional Sabbath" and believers in a cultural hierarchy that presumed only those with wealth and education had the capacity to appreciate art. When the Met did open on Sunday in 1891, a heterogeneous group—"an old Quaker and his wife, an East-side Russian and his wife, and smart looking colored women with marvelously decorated male companions," among others, according to the *New York Times*—visited the galleries, transforming culture from the province of the few with time on their hands to that of the many for whom time was scarce.[3]

Art museums were novelties in the United States until after the turn of the century. Trustees and benefactors, rather than the state, sustained the few that existed, including Boston's Museum of Fine Arts (MFA) and the Corcoran Gallery in Washington, D.C. In the mid 1870s, about a year after opening, the MFA freely admitted visitors Sunday afternoons, partly because Saturday attendance had reached capacity. Some of the art and natural history museums that sprang up in the 1880s and 1890s also had Sunday hours. Although the Met in many ways competed with the MFA for national prestige, it did not see fit to emulate its rival's admissions policies. It restricted admission to daytime hours, charged an entry fee, and did not open on Sundays. But not until the collections were moved to a city-owned building in Central Park in 1880 did the museum's Sunday-closing policies arouse comment.[4]

Sunday opening was not a new topic for New Yorkers, but in the 1880s it attracted the interest of a large and diverse group. An 1859 *New York Times* editorial prophesied that Sunday afternoon concerts in Central Park would "cause that worst of civil quarrels,—a dispute between the different classes of the community on a point of theological belief and religious ritual."[5] The subsequent conflict over opening the city museums on Sunday pitted different groups against each other just as the *New York Times* had predicted. Many of the city's conservative and evangelical ministers, churches, and organizations joined with the Met's board of trustees and wealthy patrons, who included John D. Rockefeller, J. P. Morgan, and John Cornell, in opposing Sunday opening.[6] Those in favor, however, were both plentiful and powerful. Some of the city's leading men signed petitions demanding Sunday hours. In addition to marquee names—such as former mayors Abram S. Hewitt and William R. Grace, Reverends Lyman Abbott and R. Heber Newton, businessmen Louis Tiffany and the Vanderbilt brothers, statesmen Charles F. Adams, Elihu Root, and Theodore Roosevelt, and intellectuals George William Curtis, Walter Damrosch, and Chauncey Depew—more than 50,000 "workingmen" signed petitions requesting the reform.[7]

VOL. XXIV.—No. 617. NEW YORK, JANUARY 2, 1889. PRICE, TEN CENTS.

"What fools these Mortals be."

PUCK

KEPPLER & SCHWARZMANN, Publishers. COPYRIGHT, 1889, BY KEPPLER & SCHWARZMANN. PUCK BUILDING, Cor. Houston & Mulberry Sts.

ENTERED AT THE POST OFFICE AT NEW YORK, AND ADMITTED FOR TRANSMISSION THROUGH THE MAILS AT SECOND CLASS RATES.

THE METROPOLITAN MUSEUM.
"It is intended as much for the humblest artisan as for the most refined lover of the fine arts."—*Henry G. Marquand.*
And this is how the workingman enjoys the Museum on his only day of liberty. —*PUCK.*

"The Metropolitan Museum." Cover, *Puck* (1889).

"It is intended as much for the humblest artisan as for the most refined Lover of the fine arts."—Henry G. Marquand

"And this is how the workingman enjoys the Museum on his only day of Liberty."—PUCK

The movement to open New York City's premiere museum on Sunday reached high pitch in the 1880s. Since the museum received city tax revenues, many citizens believed that it ought to open on Sunday, the only day when most taxpayers were free to visit the collections. Opponents hoped to prevent the desecration of Sunday and expressed concern about the imposition of "Culture" on what they considered sacred time.

Theological principles played a small but important part in the controversy. Leaders of the Sunday-opening movement claimed that they did not "want to start a religious controversy," declaring "the population of New-York too varied and cosmopolitan and its foreign and liberal element too large to admit of the strict application of the old-fashioned idea of the Sabbath." They simply hoped to put into practice a liberal exegesis of Christ's words "the Sabbath was made for man." Liberal Protestants claimed that the path to salvation was broad enough to include visits to art museums. Charles Eaton, one of the most outspoken Sunday-opening advocates, argued that "there are many and contrasted methods by which the mind and heart are prepared for the incoming of the spirit. Many agencies are required to make the soil ready for the seeds of truth." Not seeking to cast the church aside, Eaton and other religious liberals were convinced that "we may at one time magnify the offices of the church, and at the same time defend open museums and galleries of art, and music-halls as appropriate means of Sunday instruction and grace." Henry Clews, a member of the metropolitan gentry and a leading financier and philanthropist, agreed, stating that "the old notion that in order to secure salvation one should attend religious service thrice on Sunday no longer prevails. Contact with and study of anything that is ennobling and beneficial helps the masses." Some attributed their liberal views to "personally observing European museums open on Sundays."[8] Clerical opponents spoke out against such views strongly. Carlos Martyn—minister of the Bloomingdale Reformed Church, Presbyterian in lineage, and champion of the Puritan legacy—blamed the city's newspapers and journals for promoting a "secular Sunday." He feared that an open museum might "Coney Islandize the Sunday—fuddle it with beer, and desecrate it with the clatter of glasses clicking and accompaniment to the coarse melodies of the *Opera Bouffe*." Some of the museum's trustees also predicted that the Continental Sabbath was ascendant. William Cowper Prime, a Presbyterian, resigned from his position as vice president of the board due to just such a conviction when the museum opened its doors on Sundays.[9]

The Met's board of trustees thwarted Sunday opening for more than two decades. The museum's founders had unwaveringly opposed it in 1871, believing that they were protecting the museum from becoming a place of amusement and a drain on the community's morals. Unconcerned with attracting visitors, trustees accepted and solicited bequests made with the clause that the collection in question never be shown on Sunday. They secured two endowments in 1871 with the pledge never to open on Sundays.[10] Most of the trustees admitted that they were afraid "to give offense to a large and influential section of our citizens—

particularly potential donors." Their critics concluded that "it would be the wise plan for the Trustees in future to decline to receive objects which are not fit to be seen on Sunday."[11] Under the telling caption "The Growth of Provinciality," the *Times* advised the museum's trustees and patrons to try importing broad-minded attitudes in addition to European masterpieces.[12]

Some advocates suggested that if the museum opened on Sunday generous donors would materialize. Others hoped that once the trustees and patrons witnessed the success of Sunday opening, they would recant.[13] But even talk of opening the museum on Sunday led to the loss of an endowment of $50,000 from the estate of Robert Stuart, a businessman and the second president of the American Museum of Natural History. Stuart's widow had willed the Met and the natural history museum $50,000 each on the condition that they never open on Sunday. In 1887, when it appeared that eventually the museums would open on Sunday, she revoked these bequests and left everything to the Lenox Library, which a decade later itself opened on Sunday.[14] On the other side of the spectrum, however, were separate attempts to bequeathe funds for Sunday opening by William Vanderbilt and a wealthy philanthropist from Baltimore, each of which the Met's board of trustees turned down.[15]

Sunday observance, then, was central in the debate over access to and participation in "high culture" during the last third of the nineteenth century. Culture and politics are never far apart, however, and New York City's political dynamics affected this conflict. The Met's trustees conceived of high culture as the right of the few, a point of view that was becoming increasingly outdated near the end of the century. Some joked that if the trustees could not compromise concerning Sunday opening they might exhibit themselves "in a gallery apart as specimens of paleozoic patrons of art."[16] An observer noted that part of the resistance to Sunday opening was a result of the fact that "immigrants control municipal politics, which makes it difficult for educated Americans to assent, especially because local politics are so corrupt." Nevertheless, Sunday opening was sound politics: one petition argued that "if the people are to be taxed for the support of the museum," it must be open on the only day of the week when most of the people had liberty from work. City politicians and public servants vocally shared this opinion. At an opening ceremony for a new wing of the Met in 1888, the mayor and the president of the parks department each stated that until the museum had Sunday hours its goal of providing instruction for all classes would go unmet. The mayor expressed "sorrow for any man who chose to prohibit the people from reveling in the contemplation of the beautiful in art on Sunday."[17] Opening its doors on Sundays was one of the first things the Met's trustees could do to heal the rift between democracy and "culture."

Class tensions prolonged and embittered the movement for Sunday hours. "The restriction upon Sunday-opening," commented one New Yorker, "looks like an oppression of the poor by the rich."[18] Labor unions endorsed each Sunday-opening petition presented to the trustees, and made arguments that dovetailed with those of the metropolitan gentry. The preamble to a resolution in favor of Sunday opening prepared by the Central Labor Union noted the complaints of the elite and well educated that working people showed little interest in learning or culture. It argued that Sunday opening would provide the well off with the chance to provide the opportunity for uplift. By continuing the Sunday morning work of ministers, museums would become "vestibules of churches."[19]

Unwilling to respond to these arguments, the trustees claimed they could not afford Sunday hours: extra assistants would have to be hired, heating bills would be enormous, and the museum's treasures might suffer injury at the hands of the untrained and willful masses. Furthermore, opening the museum on Sunday would jeopardize the day of rest: it would require labor, and would sanction labor in other enterprises. As one trustee theorized, "Break down the popular reverence for the day as a holy day—destroy the distinction between it and the week days, and it will inevitably become a working day." In addition, visitors might spend their day of rest "copying the designs found in paintings, and therefore extend their working hours," which would further compromise the day of rest.[20] Working people needed more time in church, or if not in church, then at home—a contention to which the editors at the *New York Times* responded, "To those who know what are the allurements of New-York tenement houses, the advice to people who are doomed to inhabit them to spend their Sundays 'at home' seems a piece of ghastly satire."[21]

The Sunday-opening movement in New York City thus cast Sunday as time for the recognition and fulfillment of democratic ideals, arguing that those ideals could be sustained in the public sphere. Tensions rising out of the reorganization and reappropriation of culture, rather than the theological conflict that had kept the Boston Public Library closed, kept the museum shut on Sunday for several decades. In mid May 1891 a delegation from a city newspaper, the *New York World*, presented the Met with a check for $2,500 to cover the expenses of Sunday opening. The trustees rejected it. A few days later a Committee of Citizens that included a local magistrate and two ministers presented a petition in favor of Sunday opening with 30,000 signatures from prominent citizens along with a subscription of $4,000 to pay for keeping the museum open. Responding to the Committee of Citizens' pleas as well as internal pressures on the board, the trustees finally opened the Met on Sunday, May 31, 1891, even though Louis P. di Cesnola, the museum's secretary and de facto curator, complained that a mob would overrun the museum's corridors, mistreat the valuables, and behave obnoxiously.[22]

After the first open Sunday, the curator sneered that the crowds had gotten their idea of a museum of art "from the specimens to be seen in Dime Museums on the Bowery, and had come fully expecting to see freaks and monstrosities similar to those found there." He also reported that "some [visitors] went to the length of moving, scratching, and breaking articles unprotected by glass." In contrast to his observations, several newspaper reporters described the crowd of 11,000 as orderly and respectable: "Those who expected to see Essex Street Polish Jews and Thirty-ninth Street and Eleventh Avenue hod carriers in ragged clothing and dilapidated hats, were agreeably disappointed."[23] On a rainy and cool summer Sunday a week later "there was nothing of the holiday gathering in those who came [to the Met]. They were rather, apparently, imbued with a fitting sense of the day," even though a few boys were playing tag in the front hall and a young woman "apparently not of the working class" tried to smuggle in her small dog. Between June and December 1891, 200,000 Sunday visitors came to the museum, out of more than 900,000 total for the year. The flow of Sunday admissions was steady over the next few years, though the total number of visitors declined.[24]

"A Silent Exhibition": The 1893 World's Fair

When the struggle to open the 1893 World's Fair ensued, liberal Protestants and evangelicals arrayed themselves, respectively, for and against it; each side's arguments incorporated theories about the way to salvation, the nature of religion, and the ideal Sunday. The conflict returned to earlier sets of fears and hopes, but the attempt to reap profit— in the form of admission fees—from uplift posed new challenges. The hazy distinction between commercial culture and "culture" underwent revision, which opened up Sunday more widely than most of its advocates had anticipated.

The World's Fairs that characterized nearly a century of industrial and technological innovation began in 1858 in London. Until the 1920s, whenever the fair was held in the United States the question of whether or not it would open on Sunday loomed. Previous fairs had faced the question individually, with some opening and others remaining closed.

New Orleans' "wide-open" exposition of 1884, complete with bull-
fights and Mexican fiestas the whole Sunday through, showcased the
"Continental Sabbath" but incited little protest.[25] But the 1876 Centennial Exposition in Philadelphia was closed on Sundays because the
fair's commissioners suspected that unruly crowds would start fires,
damage "the walks and shrubberies," and require policing. Even though
more than 60,000 of Philadelphia's citizens protested, the gates remained locked except on several Sundays when the fair commission's
president opened them for personal friends and dignitaries such as the
Brazilian emperor Dom Pedro and a Swedish prince, leaving "the thousands of poor people from the work-shops of Philadelphia kicking their
toes against the fence and peering through the pickets," according to
newspaper accounts. The New York Unitarian minister Henry W. Bellows (president of the U.S. Sanitary Commission during the Civil War)
and others, speaking in favor of Sunday opening, concluded that the fair
could "be the means of promoting and diffusing the spirit of a pure religion." It would enable "thousands of industrious and excellent men and
women to pass their only day of leisure among scenes of mental and
moral instruction and culture."[26]

At the same time as tens of thousands of people paid fifty-cent admission fees to wander through the incomplete exposition grounds in
Chicago each Sunday during the summer and winter of 1892, Sabbatarians and sympathizers worked to keep the upcoming World's Fair closed
on Sundays.[27] Methodists were most active in their opposition, along
with Baptists, Congregationalists, Episcopalians, and Presbyterians, although there was dissent within each denomination over the issue.
Extradenominational groups were the primary locus of opposition: the
1892 Christian Endeavor Convention made Sunday closing its center-
piece, Sabbatarian organizations agitated locally and nationally, and a
National Committee on Sunday Closing of the World's Fair was formed
out of a coalition of the American Sabbath Union, the Women's Christian Temperance Union, Christian Endeavor societies, and five state
Sabbath Associations.[28] These groups had learned from the efforts to
prevent Sunday opening on the local level that political acumen, rather
than theological erudition, was effective. Thus when the suggestion
that the fair open on Sunday first arose, influential Sabbatarians went
straightway to the fair's directors and commissioners. After their personal appeals failed, they organized a grassroots effort that resulted in
miles of petitions (literally) sent to congressmen and senators demanding that the fair be closed on Sundays.[29] The petitions worked some influence; the House of Representatives voted to amend an appropriation
of five million dollars for the fair with the clause that the gates close on

Sundays and with another clause prohibiting the sale of liquor at the fair. The Senate rejected the latter, but left Sunday closing in effect.[30] The fair's directors had no choice but to accept this condition since they were in somewhat desperate financial straits.

Before and after the passage of the Sunday-closing amendment a coalition of religious liberals, workingmen, and metropolitan gentry argued that a closed fair symbolized mean-heartedness, hypocrisy, and selfishness, as well as disregard for republican and Christian values. In their view, an open fair would sanctify Sunday by expanding the opportunities for cultural and Christian uplift, improving the lives of those who labored six full days a week, and keeping promises fundamental to the American Constitution and the Bible. Advocates ranged from the president of the World's Fair Commission, to assemblies of the American Federation of Labor; from the World's Fair Board of Lady Managers to the Knights of Labor; from Professor Felix Adler of the Ethical Culture Society to Catholic Cardinal Gibbons and to clergy and members of Unitarian, Universalist, Catholic, Anglican, and Seventh-Day Adventist churches.[31] Even a powerful Episcopal bishop, Henry C. Potter, who had earlier been a part of the opposition, cited opening the World's Fair on Sunday as a worthy goal. As he argued, it allowed the day to be "put to the best uses of man," which included anything that would "rouse the soul to an appreciation of what is good and beautiful and true."[32]

Behind this movement lay the hopes that the exposition would uplift and enlighten the underprivileged. Education took on the broadest meaning when connected with an open Sunday. A Catholic bishop wrote that opening the fair would teach "that while Sunday is a day of worship, it is also a day on which the whole people should be invited to cultivate and improve themselves." In addition, it would bring "a great multitude of ill-conditioned and unfortunate souls nearer to God." An active Sabbatarian joined those in favor of Sunday opening when he suggested that "in place of closing the gates and inviting the crowds" to church, "it would be much nearer to the primitive order to close the churches and do personal work by seeking men at the Fair." A few adjustments to the fair would provide an appropriate Sunday ambiance. On Sundays it "should be a silent exhibition: no hum of machinery." Ministers would preach, bands would play, fountains would flow. The Midway Plaissance and many exhibitions would be open, but some exhibits of states and organizations with Sabbatarian sympathies would be allowed to remain closed. Great pains would be taken to give those working at the exposition on Sunday another day of rest during the week. The exposition itself would be a healthy alternative to Chicago's five thousand or so open saloons. Chicago, after all, was considered "a city in which the Sunday sentiment is not strict." Sunday closing might reap "a harvest for the saloon, the brothel, and the gambling hell."[33] Even when it was decided that the fair would close on Sundays, religious and cultural leaders continued to speak in favor of Sunday opening and newspapers still speculated that Congress would rescind the clause.

May's first Sunday in 1893 strengthened the impression that Sunday opening was desirable. Reports suggested that more than 60,000 people went to the fairgrounds to gain entrance; when they found the gates closed they turned to other entertainment. Buffalo Bill's Wild West Show amused 18,000 and turned away another 5,000, saloons were packed, "brawls were numerous," and "the police had their hands full." Meanwhile, another 5,000 laborers were admitted to the Jackson Park fairgrounds—to finish the buildings and exhibitions as well as deliver the mail. A week later crowds barred from the fair wandered around Chicago spending their money on "cheap amusements." That same evening, a Trade and Labor Assembly meeting in Chicago resolved to "march to the grounds and tear down the fence" if people were not admitted to the fair the following Sunday.[34]

After mid May, the fair's directors decided to return the portion of the five million dollar appropriation that they had received to Congress and open the fair on Sunday. The U.S. attorney general responded by declaring that if the fair was open on Sunday, its directors would be breaking the law, and his office would file an injunction. The commissioners decided to open anyway; so the attorney general instructed the U.S. district attorney to file a suit for federal injunction. Since there were delays in filing, the fair was open on Sunday, May 28, 1893, with crowds of over 200,000. On the following Monday, the only Jewish judge in the Chicago circuit at that time issued an injunction against closing the gates on Sundays because the contract between Congress and the directors was null. At this point the federal case was still pending. When hearings began on May 31, with three judges sitting to decide the case, ministers, male and female onlookers, and businessmen packed the courtroom. The court refused to restrain Sunday opening, keeping the fair open for a third Sunday. Finally in mid-June, the federal court of appeals decided in favor of the directors, allowing the fair to open on Sundays. The attorney general considered going to the Supreme Court, but since its next session would not be until October when the fair would be nearly over, he did not pursue litigation.[35] The legal aspects of closing or opening the fair filled pages of newspapers for days on end.

Evangelical protests disintegrated. Neither boycotts nor doomsday prophesies materialized. A newspaper editor wryly commented after the first open Sunday, "The United States are still in existence, no thunderbolt has rived the Union and no deluge of water or shower with burning sulpher has erased the American people from the face of the earth; yet the gates of the World's Fair were open on Sunday."[36] Newspapers in fact did their best to valorize the fair's first few open Sundays. Reports emphasized that the Continental Sunday was absent, that the supposed "entering wedge" was nonexistent, and that uplift through culture was in evidence. They made much of the absence of rowdyism, drunkenness, and disorderly conduct, and lingered over the fact that only five arrests were made on the first open Sunday. Reports indicated that most saloons and "cheap amusements" in Chicago were deserted and the police force idle. According to the papers, there was a lack of interest in the Midway Plaissance (where amusements could be found); it was only "thronged" because "so much had been written about it." Families packed the Art Building and other exhibitions: "As to the eyes of Columbus dawned an unknown continent, so to them was this an undiscovered country full of miracles preaching the gospel of sweetness and light." In sum, as the papers would have it, "the plaissance only piqued curiosity; the main exhibition satisfied the soul." Fair president Harlow Higinbotham concurred: "The Art Building proved most attractive," he reported. It was "often thronged on Sundays, when other parts of the grounds were comparatively deserted." A reporter transcribed (or fabricated) a conversation he overheard on the fairgrounds one Sunday:

> An old man, who had the face of Beecher and a head of snowy hair, took the arm of his daughter and, as he was passing over the lintel of the door, he was heard to say: "Daughter I came here against my will, but I had rather stay here than listen to any sermon I ever heard."

The waterways, landscape, and architecture all served to uplift the visitor's soul. Sunday remained: "It was plainly the people's holy day."[37] To many it seemed as if Sunday opening reconciled culture and democracy.

On the symbolically potent first open Sunday, Sousa's Marine Band played sacred and popular music into the evening, providing an emblematic narrative, one version or another of which turned up in many accounts, even the dry and precise report to the fair's directors. Whether it was fantasy or fiction, the described moment encapsulates the Sunday, as holy day and holiday, that many hoped would displace the Sabbatarian ideal. A reporter for the *New York Times* wrote:

> Sousa's Band was surrounded by a crowd of 20,000 or 30,000 people while the illumination was in progress. The programme included sacred

and popular music. Some of the airs were in waltz time. The young people enjoyed these immensely, and tapped their feet on the walks impatiently, as if wishing that they might dance.

None danced, however—a sign, it was said, of a respect for the Sabbath. When the band struck up the hymn "Nearer, My God, to Thee,"

> every head was uncovered, and in silence, in the peaceful moonlit night, surrounded by the marvelous beauty of the exposition buildings in their robes of electrics, the assemblage listened to the song hallowed by the tenderest memories. When the music died away there was deep silence for several minutes. Then the audience applauded with their hands, because everybody there wanted to emphasize the fact that the opening of the fair on Sunday had not made the hearts of those present callous, nor driven away all religious feeling.

Those present belonged to, and respected, a common Protestant culture that held Sunday sacred. It was a time to celebrate beauty, truth, and godliness. The *Chicago Tribune* was more explicit in its construction of this seminal moment: "it was at the Fair grounds that these people, with look and act, paid homage to the Creator . . . The evening prayer, involuntary, unexpected, had been said."[38] They paid homage to "culture": the fairgrounds became a sanctuary.

But though at first hundreds of thousands came to the fair on Sunday, attendance diminished, and soon almost all who had been committed to Sunday opening were embarrassed by their passion. Perhaps after making several trips to Jackson Park on Sundays when the fair was rumored open, potential visitors had given up. Perhaps the admission fee of fifty cents was too high during a time of financial panic and economic depression. Perhaps those who went to the exposition on the first open Sundays felt cheated because many displays and buildings were closed, including the exhibits of Pennsylvania, Missouri, Virginia, Delaware, and all the New England states except Vermont, the United States government's building, and Canada's and England's. Whatever the reason, the anticipated crowds did not descend on the fairgrounds. Six weeks after the first Sunday opening attendance was so disappointingly low that the directors voted to close the fair on remaining Sundays. The headlines ran, "White City's Gates Closed: Even Scrubwomen Were Barred." The defenders of Sunday opening had disappeared, their place taken by "a drink-flushed individual mounted on a box across from the Fifty-Seventh Street entrance in the forenoon, calling vociferously for 100 volunteers to aid him in tearing down a section of the fence in order to allow poor laboring men to see the Fair free." A policeman "stopped the harangue." People did not want to pay full admission to see a half-shut fair with machinery exhibits covered in black drapery and state exhibits locked.[39] (Those who had the spare fifty cents probably could go on a weekday when the machinery was running and all the exhibits were open.) The fair's directors were charged with contempt of court, since the injunction issued by a local judge restraining Sunday closing was still in effect and remained so throughout the exposition. Forced to keep the gates open, the fair's administration did little to make Sunday attractive—no music, no religious services, no running machinery, sparse concessions. The fair remained open in name, but not in spirit.

Opening the Chicago World's Fair on Sunday failed to meet expectations—not because the crowds were rowdy, not because the Continental Sunday made a grand entrée, but because gate receipts were small. Harlow Higinbotham, the fair's president, reported that "there was little profit in the Sunday business, for as a rule attendance was less on that day than on the preceding week days."[40] He marveled that the fair's directors had had different expectations, but the historical record suggests that there was every reason to anticipate crowds; after all, libraries and museums, with much less to show, bulged with visitors each and every Sunday. The difference was the price of admission.

Although museums and libraries continued to open on Sundays across the nation, the 1901 exposition held in Buffalo and the 1904 St. Louis fair were shut on Sundays. A letter urging the directors of the 1901 fair to open invoked the oppositions that had been at play in most debates over Sunday opening: it advised, "Do not give the opportunity or occasion to view us as a narrow, provincial, sectarian aggregation of superstitious peasants. Be cosmopolitan, be open-hearted." It warned that "a narrow and shrunken policy would ruin it [the exposition], reducing it to the level of a country fair, a pumpkin show for provincials." In 1915, when resistance to the opening of commercial attractions on Sunday had worn thin, the San Francisco World's Fair was "wide open." When Philadelphia sponsored the World's Fair in 1926, fifty years after the Centennial Exhibition, its Sunday opening policy elicited the protests of Baptists, Presbyterians, Methodists, and other religious groups.[41]

On Sunday, April 30, 1939, New York City's World's Fair (themed "The World of Tomorrow") opened at 11 o'clock in the morning, the same hour services commenced in most churches. For the occasion, seventy-five "special excursion trains," in addition to hundreds of regular Sunday trains, ran between points along the Atlantic Coast and New York City, including one from Washington, D.C., carrying members of the Supreme Court, Cabinet, Senate, and House of Representatives.

The first official action on the opening day of the fair was the dedication of the Temple of Religion by Protestant, Catholic, and Jewish leaders; followed by that of the Plaza of Four Freedoms (press, speech, assembly, and religion) later in the day. The opening ceremonies, which featured President Roosevelt, were broadcast locally and globally via radio; newly developed televising technology also carried images of the events to the 200 or so receivers in the area. On the first day, more than 600,000 people paid the fair's seventy-five cents admission fee (twenty-five cents for children), leaving the streets of Manhattan deserted, and Coney Island with only a quarter of a million visitors.[42]

6 The Sunday Drive

No other form of Sabbath pleasuring has ever assumed such magnitude; it is hardly possible that any other ever can. Railroad excursions, steamboat excursions, horse-back or carriage riding—none of these can ever attain to such proportions as the present use of the bicycle on the Sabbath.

—WILLIAM NAST BRODBECK, *The Sunday Bicycle* (1897)

Because of technological and economic developments—the boom in the building and running of railroads (1850s–1880s), the extensive investment in resorts and vacation spots (1870s), the vogue in cycling (1880s and 1890s), and the popularization of the automobile (after 1900)—many Americans began to take pleasure excursions on Sundays after the Civil War, following an example largely set by the German-American community. Before mid century, however, few Americans traveled on Sunday, except when it was unavoidable. They went to and from nearby churches, camp meetings, and neighbors' homes, perhaps by carriage or wagon, often walking the distance. At first new means of transport permitted travel to distant churches where famous preachers might have been in residence, to extraordinary sites, such as civic monuments and soldiers' homes, and to parks and other nature spots. In the 1830s and 1840s some of the nation's wealthier citizens took their carriages out on lovely Sundays, but it was with the advent of the bicycle, and later the automobile, that the excursion to nowhere in particular became a widespread phenomenon. Excursions, rides, and drives contributed to the collapse of the distinction between rest and leisure. While some Americans believed that such "Sabbath pleasuring" threatened the sanctity of the day, others looked forward each week to going on Sunday excursions, riding bicycles, and driving automobiles.[1]

Excursions

Until mid century, only individuals with private means of transportation or willing to go on foot could take Sunday excursions. These
unorganized and impromptu affairs were disruptive on occasion, which
aroused comment and sometimes action. One Sunday in the 1840s, a
resident of a town along the route to Coney Island (which at that time
was just a beach), counted 300 carriages passing through. Around the
same time, some Brooklyn churches stretched chains across the streets
near their sanctuaries, and in other towns chairs were placed in the
streets around the churches to prevent disturbance from passing vehicles.[2] Railroad companies experimented with "Sunday trains" in the
1840s, but found that there was little demand. There were usually one
or two passengers on the small trains leaving the countryside early in
the morning with milk for the urban market. The mail trains that ran
Sundays, by government order, customarily carried a few passengers as
well. Even commercial boats and ferries followed sporadic Sunday
schedules. By the 1850s small groups of unattached young men rode
mail and milk trains through the countryside around New York City,
and reportedly attacked pedestrians and pillaged fields on occasion.[3]

When a number of railroad and streetcar companies attempted to introduce Sunday service in the 1850s and 1860s, they faced several ob-
stacles. There was the possibility of being viewed as encouraging
Sabbath-breaking, or of losing the weekday business of those who ob-
jected to Sunday trains, or of failing to attract enough passengers to earn
a profit. Nevertheless, when streetcar companies began to offer limited
service in cities such as New York, Boston, Philadelphia, St. Louis,
Chicago, and San Francisco, as well as smaller cities such as Worcester,
Massachusetts, they found that in general, as one officer of a streetcar
company put it, passengers "dressed in their best clothes" and were "on
their best behavior." At first, patronage of the somewhat limited routes
and schedules was light, but business boomed once service was provided to excursion spots such as rural cemeteries, picnic groves, parks,
and beach resorts. Foremost among such places were camp meetings—
weekend and vacation religious gatherings in rural or semi-rural areas.[4]

One of the first sites to attract large numbers of urban residents on
Sundays was Cambridge's Mount Auburn Cemetery, which Bostonians
began visiting soon after it was founded. Between 1830 and 1860 the
cemetery served as a park, and was so popular that commercial transportation to its gates proliferated. Pleasure seekers, tourists, and
mourners mingled in the sprawling landscape filled with monuments,
winding paths, and fountains. Mount Auburn inspired the founding of

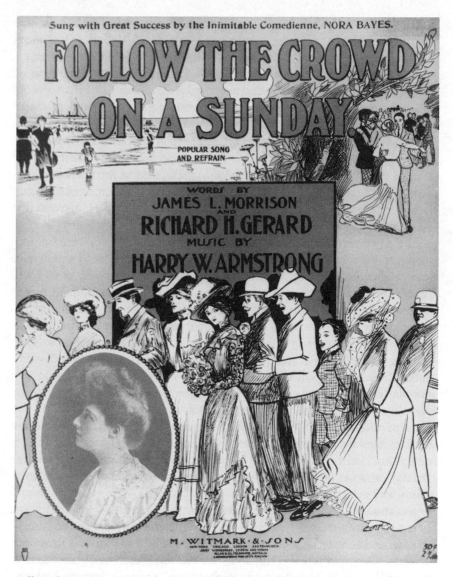

Follow the Crowd on a Sunday (1897). Sam DeVincent Collection of Illustrated Sheet Music Covers, Archives Center, National Museum of American History, Smithsonian Institution.

In the 1870s Americans began lining up Sunday afternoons for entry to rural and seaside resorts, dramatic spectacles and displays, instrumental and vocal concerts, and spectator sports. They followed one another out of the home and the church into commercialized spaces, such as the dance hall and the beach.

public parks, and later the "City Beautiful" movement, each of which aimed to improve cities and their residents. New York City's Central Park, which opened in 1859, was another popular Sunday destination. In the 1860s visitors in carriages trundled along the park's paths on all days except Sunday, when pedestrians, who tended to be of the working classes, crowded into the park, despite the prohibitive cost of transportation to what, at that time, was a somewhat remote area of Manhattan. The park board was none too sure that it wanted to accommodate the working classes; in the 1860s it prohibited music and boat rentals on Sundays, although it did allow the sale of refreshments (but not beer).[5] During the nineteenth century Sunday was almost the only time when crowds of diverse classes descended on Mount Auburn and Central Park.

Entrepreneurs began to build picnic groves on the outskirts of American cities around mid century. These were similar to rural cemeteries and public parks, except that visitors paid an entrance fee and could rent boats and buy beer. Patronized heavily on fair-weather Sundays, these prototypes of amusement parks offered visitors restaurants, saloons, game halls, concerts, and exhibitions of skill and daring. Diversions such as tightrope performances, shooting galleries, wooden horses, live donkeys, and pictorial shows made Jones's Woods—153 acres of New York City's Upper East Side—one of the East Coast's most popular resorts before the development of Coney Island. Here, as the *New York Times* noted, "beer reigned supreme, the favorite potable." In Harlem and near High Bridge, a bit further away from the city, pleasure seekers could find places to "sit over lager beer and hear Dutchmen sing." Still others could go on organized fishing excursions, spending the day on deck, and paying a fee that covered the transportation, equipment, and refreshments.[6]

At the same time that picnic groves and public parks were flourishing in cities, entrepreneurs were building seaside and lakeside resorts meant to cater to the various classes living in the cities. First among these was Atlantic City, known as "the lungs of Philadelphia" and connected to that city by a railroad built in the early 1850s. The railroad was designed specifically to take "artisans and the urban masses" out of Philadelphia to the seaside on their one day off from work, which usually was Sunday. In partnership with the railroad's owners, other entrepreneurs financed resorts along the Jersey coast to entertain Philadelphia's working people, such as the Seaview Excursion House, the Narrow Gauge Excursion House, and the West Jersey Excursion House. A few years after the first Sunday train ran (1854) one critic noted that in Atlantic City there is "no Sunday; that is, so that you would notice it." Bar rooms, billiard halls, shuffle boards, and bowling alleys did bustling business. Along the beach, groups gathered around barrels of beer.[7]

Other kinds of resorts developed during the 1860s and 1870s. Shortly after the Civil War, residents of Elmira, New York, began to take Sunday excursions to Eldridge Park, sixty acres of "tastefully laid-out" landscape next to a lake belonging to the town's wealthiest resident, Edwin Eldridge. Eldridge built a small chapel, hired a brass band to play church music, and invited Elmira's clergy to hold services in the park's chapel. When streetcars began running on Sunday to the park, some of the town's clergy complained that their pews were empty, in contrast to overflowing ones in Eldridge Park's chapel. Soon they claimed that between the Park's attractions and the streetcars' service, every Sunday in Elmira was "a circus day."[8]

"Except Sundays," a typical qualifying phrase found in the railway schedules of the 1840s and 1850s, nearly disappeared by the end of the century. This was due in part to the insistence of travelers and shippers on uninterrupted long-distance journeys, and to the multiplication of excursion trains and special Sunday schedules during the last quarter of the century. Sporadically labor and religious leaders protested the running of trains on Sunday as well as the work done on the rails and in railroad yards. Occasionally railroad managers and superintendents responded sympathetically. A Vermont railroad required its conductors to read Scripture to all those who took Sunday trains. At one time or another, railways of all sizes banned Sunday traffic during the Gilded Age. After the turn of the century, general passenger agents met to consider the abolition of Sunday excursion trains, with few results. Despite the fear that running trains on Sunday fostered work and vice, most railroads could not afford to ignore the passenger and freight demand, nor the extra profits from excursion travel connecting cities with outlying resorts.[9]

Sunday trains and boats running out of and into Boston, New York, Philadelphia, and other cities multiplied during the 1870s as more and more diversions were made available. Fraternal, social, and political organizations, steeped in the homosocial masculine culture that characterized much of nineteenth-century America's public life, sponsored most Sunday excursions during the Gilded Age. They rented steamships and picnic groves for the day and then offered members a ticket that covered transportation, food, entertainment, and usually beer. Excursions were not always occasions of good-natured sociability; for instance, one hosted by New York City's "Our Yacht Club Association" ended with a bookbinder stabbing a bricklayer in the throat. The police, conveniently cruising by on their boat *Florence*, came on board to arrest the assailant, causing another brawl that took some time to settle down.[10]

On the Beach. Photograph taken at Coney Island between 1900 and 1905. Library of
Congress, Prints and Photographs Division, Detroit Publishing Company.

It is likely that this photo was taken on a Sunday, since it was on that day alone
that most Americans would have had the time to go to the beach. A scene such as this
one would have been quite unusual before the 1880s, and unheard of before the 1840s.
It represents the development of recreation as a legitimate way to rest and to spend
Sunday.

Toward the end of the 1870s, women and children began to take more
Sunday excursions, transforming them into family-centered activities,
which spurred the development of extensive mass transit routes and
numerous resorts, large and small. Taking note of horse-car companies'
success with Sunday routes and the increasing number of excursion
destinations, local train and steamship companies entered the competition for Sunday pleasure-seekers, offering to take city residents to the
countryside and seashore. Milk and mail trains as well as "through-
trains" (completing trips begun on Saturday) became so crowded that
Sunday locals were introduced, quickly becoming well patronized.[11]

As a variety of resorts emerged to take advantage of the Sunday trade, public parks changed their behavior codes in the attempt to provide alternatives to commercial resorts. Boats, ponies, and goat carriages for children became available Sundays in Central Park in the 1870s and in other public parks a few years later. In 1877 the Central Park board allowed concerts in the park after 7 P.M. on Sundays. And in 1884 it sponsored Sunday afternoon concerts, the first of which attracted 60,000 New Yorkers. In the 1890s, when transportation was more affordable and Central Park was more central, twice as many New Yorkers went to Coney Island, primarily because the range of amusements was vast in comparison to those available in the public park.[12]

Many kinds of resorts ran solely for profit. During the 1880s, for example, the entrepreneur John H. Starin founded a seaside resort for New York City's middle classes on a beach called Glen Island. At first he hoped to appeal to the German trade by serving imported cheeses, breads, and beer in a three-sided building that opened onto a view of the ocean. Soon, however, Starin strove to appeal to those who embraced domestic and didactic plans for Sunday with additional dining facilities (including pits for "Rhode-Island style clam-bakes"), swings, merry-go-rounds, zoological gardens complete with sea lions, and stages for musical groups. The advertisements and newspaper reports about Starin's resort highlighted the abundance of children's diversions and the wholesomeness of the entertainment. Because steamboats ran between Starin's Glen Island and New York City from early in the morning until ten at night, families were not bound to a strict schedule: they could choose when to leave and when to return. Starin discovered a profitable formula; between 10,000 and 12,000 people went to Glen Island each summer's Sunday in the 1880s and 1890s.[13]

During the last two decades of the nineteenth century, entrepreneurs across the nation built and financed transportation systems and designed resorts meant to attract nearly all solvent urban residents on Sundays (as well as on the other days of the week). This was the same moment that some Americans focused on the "problems and possibilities of the recreational," in the words of one recent scholar, especially the relationship between play and commodified culture. In the creation of a "new politics of pleasure" the elasticity of the meaning of play made it endlessly commodifiable, and yet it somehow remained separate from the market.[14] The same could be said for Sunday. With electric lights, promenades, and countless attractions in the vanguard, resorts near cities such as Worcester, Boston, New York, Cincinnati, Chicago, Denver, and Philadelphia attracted visitors young and old each Sunday. Trains, steamships, and ferries ran more routes than on any other day of the week, with standard hourly and half-hourly schedules. Excursions drew hundreds of thousands of people every summer Sunday. It is debatable whether or not Sunday at the beach, framed by market transactions (buying train tickets, paying admissions, purchasing refreshments), transformed the day into a commodity, but it certainly contributed to the process of transforming rest into leisure.

Objections to Sunday excursions sought to maintain the distinction between rest and leisure. One Sabbatarian argued: "Valuable as the Locomotive may be—it is less valuable than the Decalogue; and if it cannot do its appointed work without running over 'the tables of stone,' it were better that it never run at all."[15] Others pointed out that excursions could take a variety of possible shapes. The Presbyterian minister David Mitchell, for instance, "strongly condemned Sunday junketing parties with dancing and music," but refused to "blame the laborer for taking his necessary airing in Central Park or the shaded heights of Staten Island."[16] Legal distinctions between travelers and pleasure seekers, which remained in effect through the end of the century, also posited a difference between rest and leisure. People injured on Sunday in accidents caused by poor roads, defective transportation machinery, or negligent workers could recover damages only if they could prove that they were traveling for charity or necessity. In 1881, for instance, a man drowned after being thrown overboard while on an excursion up the St. Croix River in Minnesota. The steamboat company met his estate's suit with the argument that when the deceased accepted passage on the steamer he engaged in an unlawful act, that of participating in the steamboat company's violation of Sunday laws. Others injured on streetcars, in private carriages, or while walking faced questions from the court about why they were traveling. If their answers even hinted at pleasure, then it was assumed that they were violating the religious and legal order to rest on Sunday. By the end of the century this changed; most cases were decided in favor of the plaintiff, whether or not, in the words of one court, "he was traveling for pleasure on the Sabbath day."[17]

The relationship among three resorts on the New Jersey coast— Atlantic City, Ocean Grove, and Asbury Park—exemplifies the typical resolution of the conflict between religion, rest, and leisure. Atlantic City, with a national reputation for immorality and insouciance, was close to Ocean Grove, where middle-class Protestants (mostly Methodists) strictly observed the Sabbath, even to the exclusion of seabathing. Perhaps emulating Ocean Grove, perhaps trying to lift itself out of the muck of Sunday amusements, Atlantic City passed an ordinance in August 1890 prohibiting all public amusements on Sundays, although it did not close saloons and other drinking establishments. After much agitation, the ordinance was repealed, and entrepreneurs sought to combine the holy with the profane in their Sunday amusements. Methodists rented out a skating rink on Sundays for services; the owner of a hotel built an open-air church on the boardwalk; Applegate's Pier became a site for concerts of sacred music on Sunday nights; and Young and Mc-Shea's Ocean Pier sponsored church services at their merry-go-round on Sunday afternoons and "sacred musicals" in the evenings. As one historian has noted, "the efforts of churches and citizens to make Sunday in the resort holy persisted for many years, despite the long odds against righteousness presented by the critical Sunday-excursion trade."[18]

At around the same time, Asbury Park, a seaside resort that began as a Methodist camp near Ocean Grove, also moved toward adapting Sunday to amusements. Its city council sanctioned trains, "high-class" vaudeville, and musical concerts on Sundays as well as all other days of the week. Furthermore, it sponsored the building of Ocean Boulevard, meant specifically for Sunday driving. Most dramatically, Asbury Park's city council approved of providing licenses to large hotels for Sunday amusements and liquor.[19] While Atlantic City tried to make its Sundays more closely approximate to a holy day, Asbury Park tried to make its Sundays into holidays. In the meantime, the Sabbatarianism of Ocean Grove became unfashionable, even for pious members of the middle classes. A cleaned-up set of diversions and an opened-up Sunday appealed to the majority, who no larger heeded the distinction between rest and leisure.

Thanks to the development of a culture of excursion taking, special events and sites drew throngs of sightseers out of the city on Sundays. Funerals were often held on Sunday, sometimes drawing thousands: near the turn of the century, a funeral, in a small town outside of New York, for three sisters who had drowned the previous week attracted 5,000 mourners. Military installations were also popular destinations. Near the end of the century, the Long Island Railroad sponsored Sunday excursions to Camp Black, where 5,000 encamped soldiers demonstrated maneuvers, infantry drills, and artillery drills. On a summer Sunday in 1898 the Staten Island Railroad Company's ferry boats carried more people to and from Staten Island than ever before to inspect the seven steel warships that would vanquish Spain later that year. Over 200,000 men and women arrived at the docks, many by seven in the morning. At ten the Navy opened a few gangways to the public. At the end of the day, spectators in hired rowboats surrounded the ships. Construction sites were also destinations: nearly all of St. Louis spent one Sunday or another out on the grounds of the 1904 World's Fair as the buildings were going up.[20] Going somewhere, anywhere, whether it be a beach, park, military camp, or construction site, was a part of the American Sunday by 1900.

The Driver's Seat

Cycling first became a rage in the late 1860s, although the equipment was dangerous and the roads treacherous. Some cyclists pedaled on Sundays, though the practice does not seem to have been widespread until the 1880s. Letters to *The Bicycling World* in the 1880s solicited opinions about Sunday spins, and received soothing advice:

> In Massachusetts many wheelmen ride on Sundays, some to church, more to call on relatives or friends, and many take short spins for exercise or recreation, or go on all day runs for discovery. They use the wheel as they would a horse, or would walk. Riding the bicycle quietly and decorously on Sunday is as appropriate as riding a horse or in a buggy, or as taking a pedestrian stroll.

Others advocated Sunday riding for a range of reasons, including the alternative it provided to less savory activity. Thus it was argued that "RIDING COMBATS TEMPTATION," keeping men from dawdling in the streets, loafing in saloons, and drifting into evil and bad habits. The founder of the Women's Christian Temperance Union, Frances E. Willard, echoed this sentiment in her memoir, *A Wheel within a Wheel: How I Learned to Ride the Bicycle.* Bicycles were her ally "in winning young men away from public-houses, because it afforded them a pleasure far more enduring, and an exhilaration as much more delightful as the natural is than the unnatural." Others, less approving, described the boulevards as being "black with bicyclists on the morning of the Sabbath."[21]

After the safety bicycle was developed in the late 1880s, the ensuing bicycle craze turned Sunday cycling into a mass activity. Preachers, saloon keepers, livery stablemen, and surprisingly, piano salesmen complained about the safety bicycle: it gave men and women something to do with their free time besides going to church or to the saloon, or staying at home (and playing the piano). Even though a depression wreaked havoc in the 1890s, the profits of bicycle manufacturers, such as Pope, Overman, and Spaulding, boomed. Furthermore, riding academies as well as rental places, which tended to be open on Sundays, flourished. The safety bicycle worked against the individualistic and male-oriented nature of early cycling. It enabled men and women to cycle together, ministers and their wives to ride to church (frequently on tricycles), and deacons to lead congregations on "church runs."

As with other kinds of excursion taking, cycling fit into a web of leisure activity. Cycling clubs sponsored "club runs" on Saturdays and

"Fifth Avenue after Church." Drawn by C. G. Bush. *Harper's Bazaar*, May 14, 1870. Museum of the City of New York, Print Archives (92.50.217).

"The Uptown churches all strive to get in, or as near as possible to, the Fifth avenue. One reason for this is doubtless, the desire that all well-to-do New Yorkers have to participate in the after-church promenade. . . . The congregations of distant churches all find their way to the avenue, and for about an hour after church the splendid street presents a very attractive spectacle" (*Lights and Shadows in New York Life*, 1872).

Sundays. A group riding from Gloucester to Boston one Sunday in the 1890s left at 7:30 in the morning. When they arrived at Beverly Farms they rested, then rode a bit further and "refreshed at Salem." Their dinner in Lynn was "with cider," which usually was alcoholic during the nineteenth century. Finally, in Malden they "assaulted a man who tried to arrest them for breaking the Sabbath."[22] This "spin," as cyclists usually called their rides, was typical. Cycling clubs proliferated; in Chicago alone there were more than 500 in the mid 1890s, some of which met on Sundays in front of the Michigan Avenue hotels.[23] Cycling, like Sunday, was fashioned as a safety valve—an escape from the mundane and worldly. On the bicycle, "the time for the duties of the day is over. You mount your silent steed, and there is motion and speed and change of scenery . . . Sunshine fills the soul. The cares of life, and its duties thereafter are cushioned with the pneumatic tires, and the fun of youth becomes projected through our maturer years."[24]

The distinction between rest and leisure animated objections to cycling on Sundays. Near the end of the century, one critic noted that Sunday riders interfered with church attendance, forced others to work, and sought nothing more than "exercise or recreation." Edward Everett Hale, a leading liberal Protestant reformer, agreed. In his opinion, cycling, regardless of the exhilaration and contact with nature that could result, ensured that "the next generation shall have no Sunday." Although an advocate for opening libraries, museums, and world's fairs on Sundays, Hale believed that recreation would detract from the opportunity to uplift Americans. As he said: "The institution of Sunday, if it is to be maintained at all, will be maintained for the nobler purposes of the higher life."[25] Recreation was suitable for other days of the week, but only uplifting—in other words, mental and spiritual—activity could make Sunday the day of rest.

The number of Sunday cyclists paled in comparison with the popularity of Sunday drives, first in carriages, then in the automobile. When automobiles were still a novelty and a luxury item, most owners drove them only on Sundays, preferring to use horse-drawn carriages on weekdays. With the increase in car ownership, more and more appeared on the road each Sunday. Many commentators hoped that drivers and passengers alike were on their way to the church of their choice, but clerical pessimism, legal restrictions, and superstition countered such optimism. In the 1920s some religious groups warned that even though the auto could be a "servant of man," it was not religious to drive on Sunday. Robert and Helen Lynd's study of a representative American town, *Middletown* (Muncie, Indiana), quotes a preacher decrying the epidemic of "automobilitis"—"the thing those people have who go off mo-

Fifth Avenue on a Sunday Morning. Photograph taken between 1900 and 1910 in New York City. Library of Congress, Prints and Photographs Division, Detroit Publishing Company Collection.

Although forty years may separate this photograph from the *Harper's Bazaar* drawing, little seems to have changed. Note the preponderance of horse-drawn carriages. The Sunday drive was a practice that came into vogue long before the mass production of automobiles extended the distances traveled.

toring on Sunday instead of going to church." A Baptist weekly advised those who used the car on Sundays to "display a placard or pennant to indicate that they are going to church."[26] Opponents of Sunday driving tried to close service stations and auto shops on Sundays; by the end of the 1920s it was clear that their efforts had failed. Frequent Sunday breakdowns and accidents gave rise to suggestions that God disapproved. But this did little to discourage Sunday drivers. Nor did clerical reprobations, such as this one from the mid 1920s: "When you spend

Sunday after Sunday on the road and neglect your church you are a slacker, and you disgrace decent standing."[27]

Criticism was in fact minor compared to the praise the automobile received. The Sunday drive facilitated the mixing of religious, domestic, didactic, and commercial meanings for Sunday. Families could drive to church *together* and then roll off into the countryside, or to the beach, or to a relative's home. Observers cited the automobile as the cause of an increase in church attendance; urban and rural residents were willing to drive "that extra mile" for the church service of their choice. At the same time, there was an acknowledged mixing of driving for pleasure and for religious reasons. The automobile made religious practice in rural areas more ambiguous: going to church no longer took the entire day for farmers and their families who lived far from town.[28] Even families that left for Sunday drives in the morning might attend church somewhere along the way.

Wherever they were going, hundreds of thousands took to the roads on Sundays. The automobile contained the potential to enhance or to undermine family togetherness and church attendance. Alone or in pairs, youth headed out on Sunday afternoons for drives. All roads did not lead to church; farmers drove by neighbors' fields to see how and what they planted; and no small number spent Sunday afternoons washing, waxing, and fiddling with their cars. Today, the enormous parking lots adjacent to nearly all American churches, sports arenas, and shopping malls attest to the incorporation of the automobile into all aspects of American life, including Sunday.

After 1850, excursions began to commercialize Sunday and to herald the collapse of the distinction between rest and leisure. Americans bought tickets for rides on milk, mail, and Sunday trains; they paid fares for trips on horse-cars, electric streetcars, and subways; they spent their wages on admission fees to picnic groves, resorts, and amusement parks; they purchased bicycles and automobiles. The rise of various networks of mass transportation and the numerous examples of spending Sunday in public places, rather than just in the church and the home, enabled the expansion of leisure, in the shape of amusements, spectacles, and commerce itself. In significantly reshaping Sunday, the commercialization of American life destroyed the distinction between rest and leisure, and turned Sunday into another work day for millions of Americans. The next chapter takes up this development.

7 Putting the Dollar Mark on It

> Organized forces are determined to destroy the sanctity of the Sabbath
> and put the dollar mark on it in an even bigger way than this trade
> mark of commercialism is registered on the other days of the week.
>
> —PRESBYTERIAN CHURCH OF THE U.S.A. (1923)

"The dollar mark" was gradually imprinted on Sunday. Between the
late nineteenth century and the 1960s, the near complete ban on entertainment, sport, and commerce on Sunday disintegrated.[1] In large part,
the inability to uphold the distinction between rest and leisure contributed to the demise of "blue laws." For the most part the few restrictions that remain in certain localities and states are considered oddities.

Two sets of objections impeded the tide of commercialization. One
was that commercial attractions kept Americans out of pews and par-
lors, both considered sites essential to the health of the community.
The other was that they threatened to turn the day of rest into "a day of
gain." Although neither objection prevented the imprimatur of the dollar mark on Sunday, each influenced the manner in which the day was
commercialized. This chapter covers several moments in the commercialization of Sunday. The development of vaudeville and motion-
picture theater circuits, professional sports, and a vast world of buying
and selling goods and services forced decisions about Sunday observance, and Americans made their choices within well-established religious, didactic, and domestic parameters.

Commercial Leisure in the United States

The relationship between Americans and commercialized leisure has
a long and uneasy history.[2] Thomas Morton's raising of the May Pole

and dancing around it one Sunday in the seventeenth century warranted his expulsion from Plymouth. Although some in the southern
colonies raced horses and gambled, by the nineteenth century such
practice was far from common on Sundays. Diversions that sought
solely to entertain, amuse, or distract had no place, since it was felt that
they might deprave the citizenry, and therefore jeopardize the republic.
Theaters, concert halls, and stadiums were unusual in the antebellum
period, and the few that existed rarely opened on Sundays. Men from all
occupations gathered in firehouses, brothels, and taverns during time
free from work. Picnic groves, minstrel shows, melodramatic theater,
and, of course, saloons catered to working-class men (native born and
immigrant), who in terms of population distribution dominated nearly
all American cities. Much commercialized leisure tapped into a hodge-
podge of urban activities, remaining decentralized and somewhat illicit
until the later decades of the century.

After mid century, liberal Protestants reevaluated amusements. Although theatrical productions, concerts, and spectator sports did not
morally elevate, scientifically instruct, or culturally refine (which had
been the criteria for legitimate leisure pursuits), they should have a
place in American life. If managers would censure overt bawdiness,
there would be little cause to ban these spectacles, even on Sundays.
And this is what they did in the 1870s and 1880s, reaping large
middle-class audiences. We have seen how the resistance to opening
libraries, museums, and world's fairs on Sundays drew on the deep
commitment to the distinction between rest and leisure. Liberal Protestants once again challenged that divide when they heralded the imposition onto Sunday of leisure activities that promised one thing
only—diversion

The connection between liquor and leisure, which had long provided
the rationale for keeping organized leisure separate from Sunday, complicated the process of opening up Sunday to amusements and recreation. As the temperance movement gained momentum in the 1870s,
some leisure activities severed their ties with the world of drink. At the
same time, saloon owners and politicians began to forge compromises
that maintained space for liquor consumption by containing it within
specific places and times. Popular resistance tended to overcome efforts
to quash Sunday liquor sales altogether. In 1895 New Yorkers refused to
comply with Police Commissioner Theodore Roosevelt's campaign to
prevent liquor from being served on Sunday in any venue. In 1908 the
governor of New Jersey threatened to send the state militia to Atlantic
City to shut down the saloons on Sundays if city officials would not.
Several years later, Chicago's Mayor "Big Bill" Thompson declared, in

THE FAMILY CIRCUS®　　By Bil Keane

12-13
©1997 Bil Keane, Inc
Dist. by Cowles Synd., Inc.

"Roughing the kicker! A fine way to keep holy the Sabbath!"

"Roughing the kicker! A fine way to keep holy the sabbath." Cartoon by Bil Keane (1997). Reprinted with permission of King Features Syndicate.

Football was primarily a college sport played on Thursdays and Saturdays during its first few decades, but a loose-knit league of professional teams began to schedule games on Sunday during the 1920s. The National Football League's games have been played on most Sundays between August and January since 1949. As Knute Rockne, American football icon, once said, "Outside of the Church, the best thing we've got is good, clean football!" (Quoted in A. M. Weyland, *American Football*, 1926).

the face of riots, that henceforth all saloons would lock their rear and front doors on Sundays and do no business. In reaction to these various efforts in some of the nation's hardest-drinking towns, "organized saloonkeepers" agreed among themselves to limit, but not end, their Sunday business.[3] To this day there are many states and cities that ban package liquor sales on Sundays, but most allow drinks to be served in commercial establishments after noon.

The processes of opening up Sunday and legitimizing amusement complemented each other. The nation's first great amusement park, Coney Island, "declared a moral holiday for all who entered its gates," as one historian put it, by offering a stark contrast "to conventional society, everyday routine, and dominant cultural authorities." Coney Island "located its festivity *not in time* as a special moment on the calendar but in space as a special place on the map."[4] The fact that until after World War II the "moral holiday" usually fell on Sunday complements the emphasis on special places in the American landscape—amusement parks, theaters, saloons, baseball parks—set aside for holidays, for fun, for turning the world upside down. Theater owners, baseball managers, and the like made concessions to Sunday's special needs because they could not afford to close every Sunday, which was, after all, the most likely day for vigorous business. When else did large groups of people have free time, except when they were unemployed (and therefore less likely or able to pay for entertainment)? Sunday was *the* time during which much of American leisure was experienced, just as baseball stadiums, amusement parks, vaudeville halls, and movie palaces were the places where commercialized leisure flourished. Neither space nor time can be studied separately, each needs to be understood in relation to the other.

"Sacred" Concerts, Shows, and Games

In the late nineteenth century, Sunday spectacles, such as theater and sports, posed a series of increasingly intense challenges to Sunday's status as holy and as a day of rest. In the 1850s and 1860s such spectacles took place sporadically and haphazardly. Ethnic societies sometimes sponsored Sunday evening concerts to raise money for widows and orphans or other causes; periodically an entrepreneur would sponsor a "Grand Sacred Concert" to commemorate a special occasion, such as Easter. Few in the entertainment business considered scheduling Sunday shows. In 1864 and 1870 two frontier states, Oregon and California, sanctioned Sunday theater, but elsewhere, with a few exceptions, Sunday theater did not become legal or popular until the 1890s.[5] Initially baseball games, foot, bicycle, and boat races, and even prizefights posed more of a threat to Sunday than did the theater. In the 1880s large-scale commercial culture was just beginning to emerge, breaking away from while at the same time reshaping middle-class codes of conduct, which usually included types of Sunday observance associated with church and home.

After mid century, new circumstances in theatrical production and marketing facilitated the performance of certain kinds of shows on Sunday. The spontaneous, rowdy, and often bawdy mixture of Shakespeare, melodrama, comical skits, animal tricks, and other such displays—

which characterized most theatrical shows in the United States until the 1850s—threatened Sunday's sanctified status. When theaters began to specialize in one type of performance and when managers gained more control over players, it became possible to guarantee a show's "cleanliness." Producers and managers could then stage innocuous melodrama, musical concerts, and the B. F. Keith brand of family variety on Sundays without blaspheming the day. By the same token, theaters began to cater to the different classes found in every American city, and so audiences that had once contained representatives from every social strata became homogenous. Theater became far more predictable than it had been, and therefore it was easier to sanction some kinds of shows and theater as appropriate for Sunday.

In the early 1890s commercial culture began to make itself increasingly felt on Sunday. Dissent over the meaning of Sunday within mainline Protestantism, the Sunday opening of public institutions of culture, and the popularity of Sunday excursions inspired theater managers and owners to sponsor Sunday spectacles. "Uplifting" cultural events, such as orchestral concerts, were relatively easy to introduce to Sunday, despite some objections. Theodore Thomas, one of the conductors responsible for bringing symphonic music to the United States, did not sanction Sunday performances. Yet others did. In the summer of 1890 Eduard Strauss conducted his Royal Vienna Ball Orchestra in a series of Sunday evening "Sacred Concerts" in Madison Square Garden ("The Largest, Coolest and Most Magnificent Place of Amusement in the World"). This series and others given in the early 1890s were liminal. Strauss and his orchestra played waltzes, polkas, and dance music, but it was reported that the audiences' "inherited respect for the Sabbath" kept those present from dancing. Still, on one evening (at least) those present could not resist swaying to the music. Feet beating "a tattoo to the measures of the merry polkas" could be heard, the *Times* reported. Meanwhile on stage, Strauss danced "an accompaniment to the conducting of his orchestra," rousing in his auditors "the impulse to join in his terpsichorean exploits." It was only when he played songs with titles like "Pestering the Devil" that the concerts were construed as improper for a Sunday. Despite (or because of?) his occasional lapses, Strauss's concerts drew larger and larger crowds each Sunday at 8 P.M. For some time other New York theaters remained closed on Sundays, although a few introduced Turkish Lady Orchestras, Hungarian bands, and waxworks exhibits to compete with Strauss.[6]

Efforts to exclude vulgar and "low" entertainment from Sunday persisted well into the twentieth century. Sunday performances were banned, theaters were closed, and plays were censored. Legal and religious authorities tried to prevent what was considered low culture from entering the domain of Sunday because they believed that demoralizing and degrading spectacles contravened the day's meaning and purpose. However, it was difficult to legislate in favor of some and against other types of commercialized amusements. By the middle of the 1890s variety shows and concerts had become a permanent part of Sunday afternoons and evenings. By no means were a majority of theaters and concert halls open on Sunday, but enough were to provide still another way to spend the day. Shows ranged from "FAT LADIES' RUNNING RACES: SIX FAT BEAUTIES, whose combined weight is 2,000 pounds" at Hunter's Museum on New York's Lower East Side to Walter Damrosch at Carnegie Hall conducting one of Haydn's oratorios, to the "Consolidated Minstrels" at St. Louis's Olympic Theatre, to the "picturesque melodrama" in five acts entitled "The James Boys" at Wallace's Comedy Theatre in Chicago. Uplifting concerts garnered the acclaim; for instance *The Chautauquan*, bastion of middle-class respectability, described Sunday evening concerts in New York City as tasteful and attractive to discriminating audiences. Meanwhile critics characterized vaudeville and moving pictures as demoralizing, especially on Sunday.[7]

The categorization of cultural products and activities consumed a great deal of energy, and so did the efforts to protect Sunday from low culture. The outcome of a controversy over Sunday performances of Verdi's Requiem at the Metropolitan Opera House reveals the intensity with which authorities worked to separate the uplifting from the debasing. The New York police attempted to shut all theaters on Sunday during 1906, which resulted in a cycle of openings and forced closings. Around the same time, the screening of motion pictures on Sundays was declared illegal. When such provisions were challenged, a local court found that the "singing of the mass" (Verdi's Requiem) on Sunday did not interrupt "the repose and religious liberty of the community." On the other hand, it concluded, the performance of "tragedy, comedy, opera, ballet, farce, Negro minstrelsy, Negro or other dancing, boxing with or without gloves," and a range of acts of skill and strength were violations of the Sunday codes. The court claimed that these activities disturbed the community's rest and religious freedom.[8] Texas witnessed similar scenes, with police arresting vaudevillians in the middle of shows and carting them to jail, only to have the performers post bail and return to the theater to finish their performance.[9] Similar events regularly occurred across the country. Serious or uplifting culture was deemed acceptable on Sundays, even when an admission fee was charged, but lawmakers cast low culture as inappropriate on Sunday and therefore a violation of the right to rest and worship. It was low culture alone that was accused of turning the day of rest into a day of gain. The persistance of the ideal of "uplift" fed efforts to attribute value only to certain kinds of cultural endeavor.

In the 1910s, when theaters of all sorts opened on Sundays, authorities were still attempting to censor what could be shown. In Massachusetts, for example, local police commissioners followed strict guidelines when licensing "Lord's day entertainments," prohibiting parodies, changes of scenery, the portrayal of any element of chance, and the use of firearms as props. Furthermore, theaters could screen only approved motion pictures, and could not sell "refreshments" (beer) or allow smoking. The Massachusetts state legislature published lists of approved movies for Sunday screenings: the lists from 1915 and 1916 include such titles as *The Birth of Our Saviour, The Baseball Pennant Chase, Alice in Wonderland, The Servant Question, Wrecks and Explosions, The Witches of Salem,* and *Carnivals and Celebrations.* Movie censorship called for removal of scenes of dancing, sleeping, abduction, and intoxication for Sunday screening. Connecticut's Sunday-opening provisions forbade both the screening of movies and the playing of jazz, on the premise that both were debasing.[10] Yet, the veneer of uplift was not difficult to maintain, since amusement proprietors had been modifying low culture for decades in their attempt to attract "the family trade." Witness the eradication of overtly sexual jokes. Furthermore, churches themselves had adopted motion pictures and other techniques of popular culture in their quest to reach more Americans. In the 1910s it became common for clergy to sponsor the screening of motion pictures on Sunday nights.[11]

In the 1920s movies and amusements characterized Sunday in rural and urban areas alike. Before American entry into war in 1917 only six states prohibited the opening of movie palaces on Sundays, but most communities exercised their option to refuse licenses for Sunday amusements.[12] After the war the National Association of the Motion Picture Industry sponsored a campaign to legalize the screening of movies on Sundays, but it stressed that it did not wish to compete with religion. Movie exhibitors tried to work with churches: they offered to announce Sunday's sermon topics before Saturday shows and donated free films to churches to screen on Sunday evenings. They also waited to begin shows until after morning church services let out. Some of their efforts were more aggressive; before the feature, theater owners showed slides that solicited signatures on petitions in favor of Sunday movies. One such slide read, "Do you want this theatre closed on Sunday? It provides you decent, clean amusement at a price within reach of your pocketbook. Signify your desire by signing the petition at the box office." After the war, states that had refused to grant local option, such as New York and Idaho, relented. Furthermore, these and other states began to grant licenses for Sunday operations to a range of commercialized amusements, such as dance halls, roller-skating rinks, and bowling alleys.[13] When all else failed, theater owners were willing to pay "Sabbath-breaking" fines out of the large Sunday box-office profits. In Providence, Rhode Island, for example, theaters regularly opened in violation of the law on Sundays in 1919, and continued to do so until 1926 when a bill was passed legalizing Sunday movies.[14] Furthermore, and most telling, residents in towns where movie theaters were closed on Sunday regularly went to neighboring towns for the matinee or evening show. The residents of a Nebraska town that did not have Sunday movies until 1929, for instance, drove to one of the thirteen neighboring towns whose theaters were open on Sunday.[15] Still, some towns, such as Knoxville, Tennessee, did not allow Sunday movies until after World War II.

Led by baseball, amateur and professional sports also worked to close the gap between "high" and "low" culture. Professional baseball's National League banned Sunday games (and all beer sales) in 1878—and in 1882 made good on its ban by expelling the Cincinnati club for playing on Sunday. These regulations helped transform the sport into the province of middle-class men, and increasingly women and families, since they could be assured that rowdy working-class spectators would be in short supply. The National League sanctioned Sunday games in 1892, although sometimes star players chose to observe Sunday as the Sabbath, and went to church rather than to bat. Managers of baseball teams made gestures that symbolically paid homage to Sunday as a holy day, as in 1892 when sacred concerts were held on the ball field before the first pitch on Sundays in Muncie, Indiana. In the 1890s nearly every city with a population that was two-thirds or more immigrants had Sunday baseball, and many cities in the Midwest and West with a majority of the native-born did also.

On Sundays in the 1890s, some families and groups of young men also played baseball in public areas inside and outside of cities. By the turn of the century, many newspapers were publishing a sports page each Monday to report the outcomes of the previous Sunday's many events: tennis, golf, rowing, athletic meets, cycling, horse races, cross-country foot races, amateur skating, sledding, but above all else, baseball. During World War I, owners of baseball teams in states that banned Sunday games, such as Massachusetts and Pennsylvania, scheduled Sunday exhibition games after military parades and concerts and slated

THE BULLETIN

of the

NEW YORK SABBATH COMMITTEE

31 Bible House, New York City

| Vol. II | AUGUST–SEPTEMBER, 1915 | No. 4 |

"The Break in the Levee." Cover, *New York Sabbath Committee Bulletin*. General Research Division, The New York Public Library, Astor, Lenox and Tilden Foundations.

Many Americans refused to equate baseball with manual labor, believing that baseball games and other amusements enhanced, rather than endangered, Sunday's position as a day of rest.

the proceeds for the families of servicemen. As well as making canny use of patriotism, baseball also deployed religion to conquer prejudice against sporting Sundays. In New York City ministers held "baseball services" on Sunday nights, which sometimes featured players from the Giants testifying about their religious faith.[16]

After World War I Sunday baseball was legal in most cities, with some exceptions. Long-standing prohibitions held in Boston, Philadelphia, and Pittsburgh until the 1920s and in all southern cities, except those in Texas, New Orleans, Mobile and Memphis. Legalization of Sunday baseball was positively correlated with higher proportions of foreign-born to native-born in each city, with some variations in this patterns.[17]

During the 1920s proto-professional football players began to stage games on Sunday, a practice that culminated in the creation of the Super Bowl in 1967. This event, which occurs in January or February, reflects the division of the football schedule—Fridays and Saturdays for high school and college games, Sundays for professional ones. Before the 1920s, football games had been limited to amateurs who mostly played for colleges on Thursdays, Fridays, or Saturdays. But the athletes who began to play football for pay during the 1920s tended to be available for games only on Sundays, since they were either working or attending (and playing for) a school on the other days of the week. This precipitated a crisis in some places, such as Pittsburgh, where professional sporting events were prohibited on Sundays. The titles of professional football players' memoirs—Ray Nitschke's *Mean on Sunday* for instance—speak to the centrality of Sunday to the sport, as does the title of Oliver Stone's film about pro football, *Any Given Sunday*.[18]

The commercial aspect of such diversions continued to discomfit many during the "Jazz Age." Within the Protestant establishment some complained that commercialized amusements and sports turned the day of rest into a "day of gain." Throughout the 1920s church organizations made efforts to highlight baseball and theater managers' thirst for profit: accusations that the "moving cause of this measure is the money back of it," that "organized forces are determined to destroy the sanctity of the Sabbath and put the dollar mark upon [it]," and that "the prime motive is the love of money" characterized state hearings about bills legalizing Sunday baseball.[19] The New York Sabbath Committee editorialized, "The real question is this: Is the financial prosperity of the baseball and movie fellows of such sacred and transcendent importance that the whole state must sacrifice its Sabbaths to bring it about?" Prominent clergymen agreed that Christians should "play on Sunday," as long as sports and games were not commercialized.[20] Antipathy toward commercialism replaced that toward popular culture in the protests against Sunday movies and baseball. This became clear when churches began to include topical movies in their Sunday evening services. After hearing that the pastor of the First Christian Church in Hastings, Nebraska, screened movies at the Sunday evening service, local theater owners petitioned for licenses for their Sunday movies. When the issue was put to vote, the town decided that movies in church were acceptable because they were not for profit. Even though some argued that they could "illustrate the gospel and spiritual truth," it was the noncommercial nature of the screening that was the legitimizing factor. As one Sabbatarian group declared: "It is true that some churches have movies, but they *do not commercialize Sunday;*—do not imprison employees, operators, in close quarters, who have been at the same business all week and need fresh air." Another minister simply argued that "people must be entertained," so if churches were going to close theaters, they were obliged to provide amusements.[21]

Complaints about commercialization, the last coherent set of arguments put forth against Sunday amusements, coalesced in the 1926 congressional hearings on Sunday observance, the stated purpose of which was to consider a set of proposed Sunday laws for the District of Columbia. Testimony at the hearings bespeaks the mixture of religion and amusement, church and commerce, rest and leisure. "I go to church and to movies on Sunday," testified one man. Another stated that it was "a fact" that religion is amusement. A third stated that "there is no institution so devoted to commercialism as the church."[22] Over five days, representatives of church associations, labor unions, and amusement and motion picture associations testified for and against the bill, which aimed to "secure Sunday as a day of rest" in the District of Columbia by prohibiting labor, excepting "whatever is needful during the day for good order, health, or [the] comfort of the community." The authors of the bill specified that needful Sunday labor included the sale of motor oil and gasoline, the maintenance and running of streetcars and railways, and the operation of private golf and tennis clubs. They hoped to prohibit the opening of "any place of public assembly that charges an admission fee" and make it unlawful "to engage in commercialized sports or amusements on the Lord's Day."[23]

In the course of the hearings distinctions were drawn between golf as private and baseball as public, between church services that ended with collection plates being passed around and movies that charged entrance fees, between the rich man's access to private recreations and the workingman's dependence on public, and therefore commercial, provision of amusements, between paying an organist to play hymns in church on

They Can't Stop You

*from breathing on the Sabbath.
Neither can they interfere with
your eating. Exercise and recreation are just as vital in the
proper care of our physical
well beings. Shall we permit
a few narrowminded people to
bring about the distrucion of
our health, upon which all
else depends?*

THE REAL SIN

GOD made our bodies after His own
image and commanded us to keep
them as such. Moses laid down the rules
of health as they were known in those
days, and all God-fearing men observed
them. In the New Testament, our Savior
said to keep our bodies as the Temple of
the living God. Not six days in the week,
but every day. It is a real sin to disobey
this command.

THE PERFECT SABBATH

DON'T neglect your Christian duties!
But don't forget that God gave you
a body to care for and preserve. You
cannot do this without outdoor exercise
and recreation any day and every day
possible.
You should also have some concrete form
of home exercise to follow up daily and
keep yourself in perfect shape at all times. Call at my office if possible. Otherwise write me at once. Mention this magazine and ask for

EARLE E. LIEDERMAN,

"They Can't Stop You From Breathing on the Sabbath." Advertisement in *Anti-Blue
Law Magazine* (1921). General Research Division, The New York Public Library, Astor,
Lenox and Tilden Foundations.

As more and more Americans worked in offices rather than in fields and factories,
fitness experts and social scientists introduced physical exercise and recreation to Sunday. During the 1920s some of the few remaining Sabbatarians attempted to prevent
such activity.

Sunday morning and paying her to play waltzes in a dance hall on Sunday afternoon. It was said several times in several ways that "seeking pleasure may be just as religious as worshipping Almighty God in a church." The hearings took on a national scope when witnesses referred to commercial amusements on Sunday in cities other than Washington, exposing a national, particularly urban, landscape well stocked with amusement parks, theaters, baseball fields, and golf courses open every Sunday in the year, regardless of regulations to the contrary. Commercialized amusements and recreations collided with the ideal of Sunday as a day set apart from the world. But the mingling of religious and domestic observances with excursions, amusements, and recreation reveals patterns of accommodation to commercialized leisure that continue to this day.[24]

After the 1926 hearings closed, little was heard again in Congress concerning Sunday observance. The bill went through several drafts, and was approved by a subcommittee, but neither legislative house voted on it in 1926. It was reintroduced in 1927, only to be tabled and never heard of again. Around the same time that the Sunday debates died down in the nation's capital, it was proposed that a "Sports Bay" be built in New York's Episcopal Cathedral of St. John the Divine; later the bay was christened as "a witness against the mistaken view of religion which was expressed in the Puritan Sabbath and in the old Blue Laws."[25] The "modern Sunday" had assumed primacy even in church.

"Work of Necessity?" Shopping on Sunday

During the 1950s and 1960s commercialism and materialism intensified their pressure on all aspects of American life, including Sunday. Blue laws were amended to provide more space for commercial activity. They persisted—some new ones were written—but their stated aim was to "preserve an atmosphere," as opposed to earlier commitments to preserve the Christian day of worship or provide a common day of rest. At the center of debates was the problem of the commercialization of Sunday, rather than the older problem of Sunday labor. Religious edicts that had guided state and federal courts during the previous century ceased to wield much power. The American political and social obsessions with work and rest, which had augmented anxieties about industrialization, had been eclipsed. Cold War–era debates over what could and could not be sold on Sunday and who could and could not sell such items or services rarely ventured into discussions about the value of rest. Americans had let go of the ideological commitments necessary for keeping Sunday isolated from leisure.

Postwar attitudes toward the problems of commercially regulating Sunday had their roots in several larger economic transformations concerning work. Since the end of the nineteenth century the American economy had been moving toward efficient, capital-intensive, labor-saving production, and mass provision of services ranging from telephone assistance to televised entertainment. This reorientation from a producer to a service calculus can be chronologically grounded by pointing out that in 1956, for the first time, more workers wore (at least symbolically) white and pink than blue collars. The imbalance continues to favor the service workers. To close (at least in name) factories and plants on Sunday, to minimize the amount of plowing, tending, and harvesting each Sunday, and to cease digging, hauling, and building every Sunday were all reasonable. But what of closing restaurants, padlocking amusement parks, clearing the airwaves, closing down the switchboards? Services could reap large profits on a day when so many people were free from the constraints of the workplace. Furthermore, much that the service sector does is central to American leisure practices. As the economy became service oriented, few enterprises could afford to lie fallow for an hour, let alone a full day.

Although the two were not causally related, the rise of the service sector accompanied the demise of the six-day workweek. Since the late nineteenth century American productivity (measured in output per person per hour) has continually risen. Workers have been able to put in fewer hours and produce more units; in many cases, machinery has eliminated the need for labor altogether. Increases in productivity enabled the truncation of both the workweek and the workday. This process came to a standstill in the 1930s, when, as one historian points out, political deals with industry artificially created a standard of living that forced Americans to work somewhere between forty and fifty hours a week.[26] Still, by the 1950s, nearly all Americans had at least one and usually two days off from work a week. Such mass leisure was a novel phenomenon.

Resulting in part from the maturation of the service economy and increases in productivity, and in part from the proliferation of technological aids such as the airplane and telephone, new concepts and orientations concerning time began to pervade Americans' awareness. Technological developments allowed people to transcend what had seemed like natural and everlasting weekly, daily, even hourly, constraints. Distances such as that between Boston and San Francisco, which had required a week to traverse via railroad (itself a great improvement compared to seven months at sea or two seasons rolling through prairie grasses and dust), now took less than a day. Relationships that had withered over the distance of little more than a mile flourished owing to "telephony." Shut-ins could hear and eventually watch church services in their living rooms. It no longer mattered so much which day of the week it was—with an electric washing machine one could do laundry on any day, at any time of the day. Washing on Monday became as obsolete as the Saturday paycheck. The specificity of Sunday further blurred and receded. With more free time, larger incomes, and increasing appetites for and access to services and goods, many Americans ceased to recognize in Sunday the gift of time for spiritually grounded and noncommercialized forms of rest.

As is usually the case, laws lagged far behind custom. Several states in the late 1950s revised their Sunday codes, prohibiting activities, such as stock-car races and telephone solicitation, which were unknown at the turn of the twentieth century. In 1960 all but one state had laws characterizing some form of conduct on Sunday as illegal.[27] Because police erratically enforced the new and old Sunday laws, several cases concerning the constitutionality of such laws went to the Supreme Court. Along the Atlantic seaboard, orthodox Jews, who had for years opened their groceries, department stores, and other enterprises on Sunday with the tacit approval of the local powers, began to face arrest warrants and fines in the mid 1950s. This new vigor resulted in a set of Supreme Court decisions in 1961, whose terse dissenting and lengthy supporting opinions are found in *McGowan et al. v. Maryland*. McGowan et al. were seven employees of a Jewish-owned department store in Anne Arundel County, Maryland, who had been arrested for selling "a loose-leaf binder, a can of floor wax, a stapler, and a toy submarine" one balmy Sunday afternoon. Other accused "Sabbath-breakers" whose cases reached the Supreme Court included kosher butchers from Worcester, Massachusetts, and retail clothiers in Pennsylvania. That these defendants kept a Sabbath—from sundown Friday until sundown Saturday—was irrelevant in the opinion of the Court, in spite of the Constitution's establishment and free exercise clauses. The Court found that states could pass and enforce Sunday laws in the quest to protect the health and general welfare of their residents. Its final finding (in response to the claim that the usual exemptions mentioned in Sunday laws for "works of necessity and charity" were vague and subject to competing constructions) was that the laws in question were sufficiently lucid.[28]

In the face of this decision, retailers looked for loopholes in the largely symbolic bans on Sunday sales. Lawyers and judges considered whether the items or services being sold were necessary, rather than focusing on the labor being performed on Sunday, as earlier courts had done. Before automation, objections to commercial activity on Sunday had focused on the requirement that some people had to sacrifice their day of rest. Over time it was agreed that certain services were for the public good (such as the continual operation of public utilities) and therefore worth the loss of Sunday rest for some (preferably small) portion of the population. Nearly all states exempted manufacturing labor from Sunday statutes, under the assumption that most industrial plants needed to run continuously. It could have been argued that fewer and fewer hands were needed to run factories, and therefore that continuous manufacturing did not imperil (in any real fashion) the day of rest. (However, the symbolic power of factories remained potent through the 1970s: steam puffing out of chimney stacks, machinery grinding, and cars in vast plant parking lots surely detracted from Sunday's appearance as a day of rest.) But working hours were no longer a central social, political, or cultural preoccupation. Since laundromats and car washes did not require the presence of an attendant on Sunday, cases about their opening illuminate how Sunday adjudication and legislation after World War II had very little to do with the goal of securing a rest day. Courts ruled instead that neither car washing nor clothes washing was *necessary.*[29]

Nineteenth-century Sunday laws sought to contain the meanings and styles of rest; Sunday laws in the mid twentieth century attempted to halt the commercialization of everyday life. The endeavor failed. Courts could not contain commerce. Consider, for instance, the Missouri Court of Appeals 1973 decision that a retail furniture store could open its doors each Sunday, with the invitation to "browse today, buy tomorrow." The court found that this procedure constituted neither Sunday sales nor Sunday solicitation, and therefore did not violate Missouri's Sunday Sales Act.[30] Such sales tactics had been multiplying throughout the 1960s even though most courts tended to find them in violation of Sunday-closing laws. By the end of the decade, courts had assented to telephone and door-to-door solicitation on Sundays. Contrast this with the voluntary closing of most commercial establishments on Sunday during the first half of the twentieth century. The Chicago retailer Marshall Field and Company, for instance, not only closed each Sunday, but also pulled "down store window curtains Saturday night until Monday morning," as did other department stores, including Lord and Taylor and those in John Wanamaker's empire. A 1920s advertisement in the *Chicago Tribune* for Marshall Field and Company described the owners' "old-fashioned background." It continued that they were "taught in childhood that six days are enough for the things that are seen. The first day of the week" Marshall Field's owners averred, "is for the things unseen—rest, and worship, and family life, and freedom from thoughts of business."[31]

The application of the exception for "works of necessity and charity," which has muddled many debates since the middle decades of the nineteenth century, undercut most efforts to protect Sunday from commercialization. Legislatures declined to define necessity, leaving it up to police and courts to untangle the mess, which they rarely did to anybody's satisfaction.[32] Previously used to contain labor, by the 1950s the meaning of necessity had traveled a tortuous route, arriving at the prevention of profit. Whereas reformers during the nineteenth century worried about the transformation of the week into a never-ending grind, with Sunday as yet another working day, those in the mid twentieth century worried about the ubiquity of materialism, which was turning Sunday into another day of gain.

As American culture moved toward an individualistic orientation, the meaning of necessity became increasingly unclear. One sign of this enervation was confusion over whether necessity pertained to people generally or to the individual—and how to make the distinction. "The emergency room is the true domain of necessity," observes a contemporary essayist as she laments American decadence, "the place where there is no drawing back before the bleeding wound, the broken bone, the last minute contractions." But Americans do not see the difference between necessity and convenience; they equate the services of the emergency room staff with a cashier willing to sell "a Poptart or a six-pack of Coke in the middle of the night."[33] In the early 1960s, many state supreme courts defined "necessity" in social rather than individual terms, as they had been doing for many decades. But some states were in the vanguard of validating personal definitions of necessity. For example, Texans in the early 1960s were required to sign "certificates of necessity" when purchasing on Sunday items ranging from uncooked meats to writing paper to screwdrivers. These binding certificates guaranteed that the item or service purchased was *for an emergency*. Most states skipped the certificate stage, and during the 1970s allowed stores to open Sundays. Practically anything could be, and was, defined as a necessity.[34]

Today the term necessity is nearly meaningless. Americans are no longer willing to differentiate between necessity and luxury. And yet, courts have continued to affirm Sunday's unique place in the calendar. Into the 1970s lawyers and judges defended Sunday legislation because, to paraphrase a decision issued in Bismarck, North Dakota, it aimed to preserve an atmosphere.[35]

In the long run commercialization has simultaneously depleted and shored up the various meanings of Sunday. This was obvious even in the early 1960s, when a marketer predicted that "Sunday will involve family shopping," that "fun" would return with "carnivals, the circus, miniature golf, bowling, and entertainment."[36] Today Sunday is one of the busiest days at the grocery store, the outlet mall, and the super-store. Since the mid nineteenth century, excursions, bicycle rides, the Sunday drive, concerts, vaudeville, theater, movies, baseball—all the stuff of American culture—have converged in such a manner that the "dollar mark" has permanently tattooed Sunday. This does not mean that the day is any less valuable or meaningful than it had been, and it does not prevent religious, domestic, or didactic ideals from shaping in-dividual meanings and practices. But in significantly, and radically, al-tering what it means to rest, the dollar mark has transformed rest into leisure.

Thus far I have outlined religious, didactic, and commercial contests over Sunday. I have lingered over nineteenth-century disputes about Sunday mails, about the biblical Sabbath, about Sunday in the city, on the frontier and during war, about opening noncommerical and com-mercial venues for culture on Sunday, about Sunday excursions, rides, and drives, and about selling goods and services on Sunday. The per-ceived difference between holy day and holidays, between sacred and secular, between rest and work framed these struggles. By and large they concerned policies, and so my discussion has relied on the stuff of institutional history—reports, documents, sermons, speeches, news-paper reports and editorials, pamphlets, tracts, laws, and court deci-sions. One important sphere remains for me to explore, Sunday at home and among family. The next chapter takes us back to the 1830s, when controversy about the religious mandate for Sunday raged, and brings us to the end of the twentieth century. It uses personal papers, as well as homemaker's manuals and other prescriptive kinds of sources. The ma-terial allows for an interpretaion of Sunday in relation to dominant cat-egories shaping contemporary inquiry into America's social history—race, class, and especially gender. It also illustrates how institutional practices and policies shaped the Sundays of individuals and families.

8 Daddy's Day with Baby

Another use of Sunday is as a family day. It is the day on which the father is at home, the day for playing a new piece on the piano, singing hymns and songs.

—JOSEPH LEE, "Sunday Play" (1910)

In the course of the nineteenth century, yet another layer of meanings for Sunday, ones that we can term "domestic," proliferated. Joseph Lee, leader of the progressive movement to build playgrounds and develop recreation programs in the United States, affirmed what mothers, social reformers, and clergy had been saying since the mid nineteenth century, that is, that Sunday should be "the father's opportunity."[1] The family of kin, rather than the family of believers, became central to the American Sunday. With such a shift in emphasis, both Sunday and rest settled into long-lasting forms based on domesticity.

The church's diminishing monopoly over Sunday, new understandings about how to be religious, and the growing legitimacy of leisure pursuits all supported the development of "the domestic Sabbath." Some felt that church Sundays fatigued rather than rested congregants, drove potential converts away from religion altogether with their rigidity and dogmatism, and "left nothing to the home." Although it was clear that Americans had religious yearnings and impulses—after all, the proportion of the population who claimed church membership increased between 1850 and 1930—the church building may have not been at the center of their faith. A minister for an African Methodist Episcopal Church in Oakland, California, after mid century, for instance, described his inattentive congregation: "Some sit and sleep—others present, look around at each other—the clock—occasionally pulling out watches." Dues-paying members were absent, exacerbating his difficulties. "Have to wait for my brethren—where are they? Elsewhere went in good season, no doubt—

Sunday is Daddy's Day with Baby [1930s]. Sam DeVincent Collection of Illustrated Sheet Music Covers, Archives Center, National Museum of American History, Smithsonian Institution.

   Ethnicity, generation, class, and above all gender determined one's quantity and style of rest. It seemed that men, busy getting a living and running the world, had little time other than Sunday to spend with their children. Mothers were encouraged to prevent children from exhausting their fathers, who, after all, needed the kind of Sunday rest represented here by the smoking pipe. Little was ever said about a mother's rest, although some acknowledged that "her work was never done."

Remember the Sabbath-Day, To Keep It Holy. Published by Currier & Ives [1870]. Museum of the City of New York, The Harry T. Peters Collection (56.300.523).

Reading the Bible, praying as a family, and other like devotions in the home constituted some of the many ways Americans were instructed to spend Sunday. The refined and orderly home, as represented in the composition of the figures and the fine china on the mantle, was an image of what heaven would be like. Sunday thus spent did not neglect the day's religious duties—reading was religious, meals were simple and required no work, and social intercourse was limited to the spiritual. The publication of the Sunday newspaper after the 1880s altered domestic scenes such as this one, as did the domestication of radio in the 1920s and television in the 1950s.

cold tired of house—love variety."[2] After mid century churches began to offer fewer and shorter services, and by 1900 most Americans attended just one service per Sunday. Changing understandings about how to behave as a Christian further contributed to the dissolution of boundaries around Sunday, religion, and the church. Liberal Protestants, for instance, posited a transcendent and omnipresent God who could be found anywhere and everywhere.

In Our Parlor on a Sunday Night, (1922). Sam DeVincent Collection of Illustrated Sheet Music Covers, Archives Center, National Museum of American History, Smithsonian Institution.

This song gave new meaning to the saying "There's No Place Like Home" with its lyrical tale of "girls dolled up right", a mother handing out lemonade ("No one knows from what it's made"), and youngsters singing duets from *Tosca*. Sunday in this parlor has little in common with the scene depicted by Currier & Ives in *Remember the Sabbath-Day, To Keep It Holy* reprinted on page 113.

Both liberal and orthodox Protestants frequently represented the home and the Sabbath as institutions that God made for Adam and Eve: the two were essential to each other, to Christian living, and to "the restoration of man's lost innocence." Sunday, with its connection to eternal rather than mundane time, was similar to the afterlife: "earthly Sabbaths were foretastes" of heaven. Heaven was pictured as a domestic paradise, an idealization that emerged out of the emphasis on the home as a sphere devoted to purification and uplift.[3] It was widely believed that for Christianity to thrive, it had to enlist the home in the effort to civilize, uplift, and ultimately save souls.

Protestants were wont to depict the home as a sanctuary, which became easier to do after the 1830s, because of improvements in home construction and the mass distribution of home furnishings. "The home was supposed to be a haven apart from the industrial and commercial world," writes a historian of domestic architecture in the United States. "Home was idealized as a retreat for men and a refuge for women." The growth of suburbs in the late nineteenth century, enabled by the development of rapid municipal transportation and new building techniques, allowed the "rhetoric proclaiming 'the home' and 'the world' as separate realms" in some ways to mirror a physical reality. Although home ownership was confined to a minority until after World War II, more and more Americans did come to own single-family homes over the course of the nineteenth century. Thanks to significant developments in print and electronic media, the home did not entirely constitute "a haven apart from the industrial and commercial world."[4] It did, however, provide space for the resolution of tensions between competing ideals for Sunday, for rest, and for leisure.

Children and Sunday

In the late 1880s and early 1890s the Bancroft family split its time between Helix Farms, their family farm near San Diego, and a home in San Francisco where Hubert Howe Bancroft, the father, ran a lucrative book and stationary business and wrote histories of the West and Mexico. The family's extensive extant diaries, their mix of rural and urban Sundays, and their internal disagreements about Sunday render them a good case for investigating the "domestic Sabbath." When at the farm on Sundays, the family's three preadolescent boys, Paul, Griffing, and Phil, would chase horny toads, engage in egg fights, capture owls, hunt and fish, pick grapes, sail on the pond, and torment their younger sister Lucy. Griffing's Sunday entries in his journals, which he began keeping at age eight, exemplify the tensions attendant on the accumulation of meanings for Sunday. One Sunday he went to German Sunday school in the morning and English Sunday school in the afternoon, another Sunday he saddled the pony and rode around the yard, on yet another Sunday he went hunting in the morning, and on still another one, as he noted, "We did not go to church to-day because we didn't want to." In Griffing's journals, as in many other nineteenth-century American sources, sacred and profane seem oddly mixed. Hubert Bancroft, a man without any obvious regard for Christian formalities, conducted business, tended to his farm, and drank on Sundays. For a short time after the revivals of 1858 he had been a trustee in a Presbyterian Church, but when his first wife died he became a self-proclaimed agnostic. Bancroft's second wife, Matilda Coley Griffing Bancroft, who moved to California from her home in Connecticut, harbored faith in a Christian God. While in San Francisco she ushered her four children and occasionally her step-daughter to church, Sunday school, and Golden Gate Park. Sometimes the family took Sunday excursions to Chinatown, climbed Telegraph Hill, or went to the public library. These activities were interspersed with singing hymns and reading the Bible at home.[5]

But on the farm Matilda Bancroft's family Sundays were a continuing problem. After three years of diary entries describing Sundays spent "shooting before supper," or returning "some bottles which we borrowed from a saloon man," or fertilizing orange trees with manure, Griffing mentioned what must have been the outcome of a great deal of familial conflict: "On Sunday mama wants us to take a good deal of time for reading." A week later he noted, "it being Sunday we did not burn the weeds." After a September Sunday of learning Bible verses (a day when Hubert Bancroft never got out of bed), the family reverted to old habits: October's Sundays were devoted to hunting quail, gathering tomatoes, "playing in the mud," and shooting down card houses. In the early part of that winter, Sundays on the farm were as usual—trapping squirrels, hunting lark, and doing chores. But again Matilda Bancroft's resolve returned. Griffing tersely recorded that one Sunday "Mamma would not let us shoot any today." A few weeks later he described a Sunday spent "quietly reading" and listening to "Mamma read to us from *Foster's Story of the Bible.*" The winter diary entries record a litany of church and Sunday school, with occasional asides such as "we have to learn four verses out of the Bible every Sunday."[6] The Bancroft family's Sundays tended to quiet, uplift, and rest.

Thereafter Griffing's Sunday entries were laced with resentment, as in an entry from his twelfth year: "We went to church as usual today.

After that we went to Sunday School. This all lasts from eleven until two." He clearly hated the Sunday his mother was trying to fashion. The remainder of his teenage Sundays were passed in frustration: he could not go rowing, he was not allowed to fish, and while visiting relatives in Connecticut he and his brother "started to shoot some early in the morning," but were ordered to stop. While visiting back East his mother tightened the rules even further, making it clear to her sons that their Sundays would be different than they had been in California— "Mamma makes us all go to church every Sunday and it makes Sunday more rotten than ever." Mother Bancroft told Griffing and his brother that once they returned to San Diego, they would no longer be allowed to "carry a pistol" or "shoot on Sunday." Once he returned to Helix Farms, however, his mother's dictates were either rescinded or ignored, since Griffing mentions hunting rabbit, deer, and quail, horseback riding, and playing football, all on Sunday, and sometimes in the morning. But then he left for a prep school in New Hampshire, Exeter, with the irate expectation that he would have to go to church each Sunday, since it was one of the headmaster's "blooming rules." Required church attendance only ceased when Griffing enrolled in Harvard College. There his Sundays were devoted to tennis games, horseback rides to Fresh Pond, and, occasionally, study.[7]

The Bancroft family's Sundays provide a template for understanding both ideal and lived Sundays in (and around) the home. For instance, sending children to Sunday school was not enough; parents were expected to conduct religious instruction in the home as well. Family prayer and Bible study constituted the standard syllabus. One guide book enumerated games that taught children about foreign missions, Christian Endeavor societies, and temperance groups. It also described Bible picture-puzzles (explicitly for boys), inexpensive Bible books (*Half Hours with Bible Heroes*), and cards inscribed with biblical texts. Publishing houses marketed literature, other than the Bible, for Sunday reading, such as the *Sabbath at Home*, a "monthly visitor" filled with religious and sentimental poems, stories, and essays, all designed "to help the followers of Christ employ the Sabbath at home to the highest advantage."[8]

The home Sunday's development was rooted in long-term changes in family life and child rearing. Child-rearing practices became more permissive after mid century, as some educators argued that play, if properly directed, could contribute to the task of awakening and shaping children's religious sensibilities. In the antebellum period parents had been instructed to treat their children as miniature adults, advice which profoundly shaped Sunday observance. Mrs. Child's *Mother's*

Book (1831) states that on Sundays children should remain quiet and not disturb their parents' rest, and that in turn adults should set an example for children by remaining sober and quiet.[9] But this view was revised only a few decades later. Newer theories about child development suggested that children required different stimulus and activity from adults (who benefited from a Sunday of quiet sobriety). Harriet Beecher Stowe, for instance, explained that "what was so very invigorating to the disciplined Christian"—quiet study, trancelike stillness— "was a weariness to young flesh and bones."[10] Mothers were urged to allow their children to play on Sunday, but to make this play "religious" by providing "special Sunday playthings" and activities built around Bible study. Advisers suggested games with religious purpose, books and toys, such as Noah's Arks, which were known as "Sabbath toys," and activities that would carry as much religious value as possible. The increased emphasis on the virtues of play for children deeply affected the home Sunday, to such a degree that as the century neared its end Sunday became, in the words of one historian, "child-oriented and mother-directed."[11]

The compartmentalization of American space and time, in many ways, accounts for Sunday's transformation into "Daddy's Day with Baby." Industrial and commercial development accelerated during the antebellum period, mandating the division of time and space. Employers began to insist that employees work for hourly wages, perform specialized tasks, and cease drinking on the job. Each demand furthered the effort to compartmentalize and closely control time. By the same token, remunerative work was moved from the home into the office, factory, and store, and in the process helped create the ideal of separate spheres. The emergence of residential, commercial, financial, and industrial districts as differentiated urban spaces further reinforced the notion of separate spheres. The home was reconfigured as an adjunct to the church and as antithetical to the market. Fathers and children spent more and more of their time outside the home getting a living or an education. "The less time families had together," notes a social historian, "the more certain times came to matter to them—that is, as real time grew scarce, symbolic time loomed ever larger." Sunday, then, became the time for family.[12] Families relied on Sunday to renew their bonds of affection and kinship.

After mid century women's responsibility for Sunday in the home increased. *Aunt Louisa's Picture Book* (1867), which was filled with biblical stories and admonitions, concluded, "We hope that Aunt Louisa will thus help Mamma in making Sunday the happiest day of the week." By the 1880s a mother's manual titled *Twenty-Six Hours a Day* sympathized that "it is true that if the mother spends all her spare time reading and

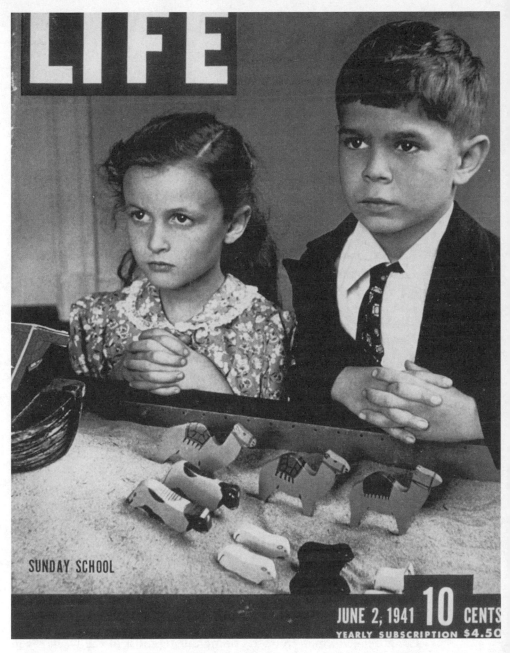

Sunday School. Photograph by Alfred Eisenstaedt, *Life Magazine* (1941). Copyright ©
Time Inc.

   The Noah's Ark toys in the foreground were popular among families that allowed
their children to play on Sunday, but wanted the play to be directed toward religious
learning and uplift. These toys, some of which are part of permanent displays at the
Metropolitan Museum of Art and the Museum of the City of New York, were often reserved solely for Sunday, thus making them special and contributing to the day's dis-
tinctiveness.

talking to them [her children], Sunday is anything but a day of rest to her."[13] In the first few decades of the twentieth century, Protestant churches, advertisers, confectioners, card companies, and florists invented Mother's Day, situating it on a Sunday. By the mid twentieth century, influential preachers heralded mothers as "keepers of the door," a phrase that encapsulated the ideal role of the Christian mother in relation to Sunday, which had begun developing a hundred years earlier: "The doorkeeper must shut out of her home those worldly intrusions which would destroy its integrity as a place apart."[14] If Griffing Bancroft's journals are at all representative, it seems clear that mothers often could barely direct their children's play, let alone keep the door shut.

Sabbatarians and orthodox Protestants received the home Sunday and especially women's growing authority over the day with ambivalence. Sunday observance had been the province of men: clergymen and interested laymen, with the emphasis on men, belonged to Sabbatarian organizations and debated the right uses of Sunday. Women had taken part in efforts to "save Sunday," but their mission was largely limited to keeping men out of saloons or from working. As women gained more responsibility, some Sabbatarians depicted them as unable to enforce proper Sunday observance. A children's book published in 1854, for instance, is replete with examples of weak mothers who, unwilling to prevent their children from playing on Sunday, end up with dead or injured progeny. One story blamed a "very indulgent" mother whose son died in a horrifying fall on a Sunday horseback ride.[15] During the 1880s and 1890s, however, religious authorities focused on women's role as preservers and shapers of the nation's Sundays. In 1884 the Women's Christian Temperance Union formed a "Sabbath-observance department," signaling a transfer to wives and mothers of public responsibility for Sunday.[16] The formation of the Women's National Sabbath Alliance in 1895 and Matilda Bancroft's efforts to shape her family's Sundays made manifest what could be labeled the "feminization" of Sunday, but what is better understood as its domestication. In addition to fashioning uplifting and religious home Sundays for their children, and to organizing reform associations to protect the day, women were expected to make Sunday "the father's opportunity."

The absence of men from the home during most of the week made Sunday even more a day apart for the family than it was otherwise. A boy's description in the 1880s of his father as "the man who spends Sunday here" neatly sums up the distance between fathers and children in modernizing America.[17] The transformation of Sunday into the father's opportunity suggests yet another way that Sunday bore the weight of multiple demands, which no single time or space could possibly fulfill.

THE BULLETIN

of the

NEW YORK SABBATH COMMITTEE

31 Bible House, New York City

| Vol. II | APRIL–MAY, 1915 | No. 2 |

A SABBATH QUESTION IN THE HOME

"A Sabbath Question in the Home." Cover, *New York Sabbath Committee Bulletin* (1915). General Research Division, The New York Public Library, Astor, Lenox and Tilden Foundations.

"The keeper of the door" tries to prevent her husband from leaving the home—site of rest—for the world of work. The illustration starkly opposes the home and the world and emphasizes how the responsibility for protecting Sunday came to fall more heavily on women than on men or even the clergy after the turn of the twentieth century.

"The Sunday Best": Socializing

Although every day was meant to be a day of preparation, Saturday was central in the Christian preparation for the Sabbath; it was then that baths would be taken, clothes mended and laid out, shoes polished, work finished, playthings put away, and thoughts turned toward God. Such preparations were also directed at more worldly ends: visiting and courting.

Part of the American fondness for Sunday no doubt had to do with clothes and appearances. Diaries record many observations about how both men's and women's grooming and clothing distinguished Sunday from the other days of the week. One mid-century Sunday, for example, Anne W. Booth, a migrant to California of New England origins, remarked in her journal that she "loved Sundays at sea," because she was "struck with the improved appearance of all": on Saturday nights the sailors would scrub the decks, press their white shirts and pants, bathe their bodies. On land on Sunday the very poorest might wear their only shoes, don a clean shirt, or pin an ornament to a rag of a dress. The wealthiest wore lavish hats, demure yet dazzling dresses, and the most delicate of shoes. Sunday clothes were the repository of a great deal of meaning; often they were the only thing of value an adult possessed. "When a man—and I mean by that, any male person over 16 or thereabouts—was able to accumulate the required number of dollars, one of his most important investments would be in a Sunday-go-to-meeting outfit," remembered an Oregon settler. The outfit, made by "eastern tailors," would include "a swallow-tail coat, a fancy, light-colored vest, and a striped pair of pants," topped off with "a high beaver hat." Even the indigent often managed to have a Sunday suit of clothes. James Agee described an African American tenant farmer who preached in a Baptist church on Sundays as being penniless and on the verge of ruin, but in possession of a Sunday outfit "that fits him as well as it did the deceased husband of the woman who gave it to him." Agee continues in his 1939 masterpiece, "He wears this only when he preaches. During the remainder of Sunday and all through the rest of the week he slips into the ill fitting garments he wears as a day laborer."[18] The change in personal appearance, like the closed doors of commerce and industry, like the long intervals between streetcars, trains, and ferries, visibly marked Sunday as different from the other days of the week.

"The Sunday best" has a long history of sanctifying the day and of rousing memories of family and home. As one historian has observed, "shoes, stockings, removed hats" were ways that colonial "Americans

His Sunday Best (1902). Library of Congress, Prints and Photographs Division, Detroit Publishing Company Collection.

    Americans both young and old, rich and poor, male and female, black and white—in sum, of all backgrounds and positions—have long donned their "Sunday best." This man is no exception.

might attest to the sacredness of the day." Some observers argued that dressing up for Sunday made the day different from the remainder of the week, and in the 1930s one even suggested "that it would be better for the race [to wear formal clothing] than the bathrobes and negligees which nowadays can be seen sprawled around almost any American home any Sunday morning." A few Sundays after she described the enlivening effect of the sailors' white shirts and linen coats, Anne Booth observed that the change in appearance of all on board took her thoughts to home and friends, enabling her to "enjoy an imaginary commune with those dear ones far away" and indulge "in the too pleasing anticipation of living again amid the scenes of my Home." Such reminiscences of homes left behind in the dust of time or space were potent. To help conjure memories, some would reread old letters from home each Sunday, others would write letters to the place or places where their families were, calling these places home, and still others would lapse into reverie. One woman on the Texas frontier at mid century asked her mother who was living in the East "to post a note every Sunday with the words 'All is well.' "[19] Sunday at home, then, was a resonant symbol and experience for Americans, meant to convey family, piety, and separation from the worldly, which the Sunday best enhanced.

Yet at the same time, suitably attired visitors and suitors traipsed through American homes both rural and urban, and unlike the other days of the week, men and women spent most of Sunday together, flirting, conversing, parenting, even quarreling. Charles Parson Bigelow, born in 1835 in upstate New York, kept a diary between 1859 and his death in 1917, which details his migration from New York to California, time spent in the gold mines, travels around the Northwest, his marriage, the birth (and death) of his children, the purchase of a farm, and his church attendance. Whenever there was a wedding on Sunday he made a note of it in his journal; about his own wedding he tersely noted on Sunday, April 13, 1870, "went to church in the forenoon got married in the evening had a jolly time." Ten months later he noted on another Sunday, "Did not go to Church. Mary [his wife] was sick. Mary Hester Born 10 past 2 P.M."[20] Different lives beget different Sundays, but certain aspects of the life cycle often converged with Sunday, either by choice (marriage) or chance (birth). Another example of the primacy of Sunday for socializing comes from the journals of someone who never married, a Californian named James Beith, an adventurer, miner, and farmer who also spent Sunday in a round of church, visits, courtship, work, and books. An 1862 entry records, "Took a bouquet to Miss Laphronia, who by the way was in the midst of her cooking & her beaus both ancient and modern." A few months later he proudly penned an entry about his amorous success with a lass other than Miss Laphronia: "Saw Mary and took *un beso bueno.*" A month after he enjoyed a kiss from Mary, he coyly wrote about yet a different woman, "Today the drag was put upon a certain pleasure, a hint for me to go slow." As much as Beith played the field, he was not immune to the strong sentiments surrounding the home, marriage, and Sunday in American culture. In another entry, written while he was in San Francisco, he described a sermon he heard one Sunday about the value of the home: "Spoke in feeling terms of what a home should be, the temple and the sanctuary of our holiest hopes. Saw a young couple married in Church." The next year he jotted one Sunday "Delightful morning. Rob [a friend] went to Eureka, to prosecute his new flirtation."[21] The record does not indicate the outcome of this flirtation, but marriage was the end result of much Sunday courtship. It was often said that "Sabbath bells and marriage bells ring together."[22]

Courtship flowed from the church into the parlor, and back again. As detailed in diaries, memoirs, and songs, it may well have been the prime motivation for Sunday visiting. Sunday as a day for courtship, whether in or out of the home, was as important to young men and women in the nineteenth and early twentieth centuries as Saturday night is to contemporary lovers. Some courted on the porch, others on bike rides, long walks, or at Coney Island, and still others at church. Margaret Scholl, living in rural Maryland at mid century, described in her diary a Sunday spent in church and courtship: "We were ready for church by ten o'clock and the beaux [were] there, so off we strung in church and up to our pew, Mr. P. Kunkel with me, Mr. P. with Mary, and Harry with Melia. We created quite an excitement." Her diaries are full of courting. One suitor came for years every Sunday: on May 15, 1853, Scholl went on a long walk with him after church; seven years later they went on such a long walk that he suggested taking a railroad home, but she refused, feeling it would desecrate the day.[23] Each Sunday in 1893 New Jersey matron Georgiana L. Vail recorded, "Russell here to see Belle."[24] Near the end of the nineteenth century, a southern man remembered, on "Sundays I'd go around to see girls," and he saw so many that he ventured, "twenty girls thought I was going to marry 'em." Born in 1854, he recalled that he "bought horses and fine buggies and went a-courtin'" every Saturday and Sunday. When he finally got married, he and his wife "always had a heap of company, ten or twelve extra for dinner every Sunday."[25]

The volume of visits between households was remarkable. Margaret Scholl made between two and five visits every Sunday during the 1850s,

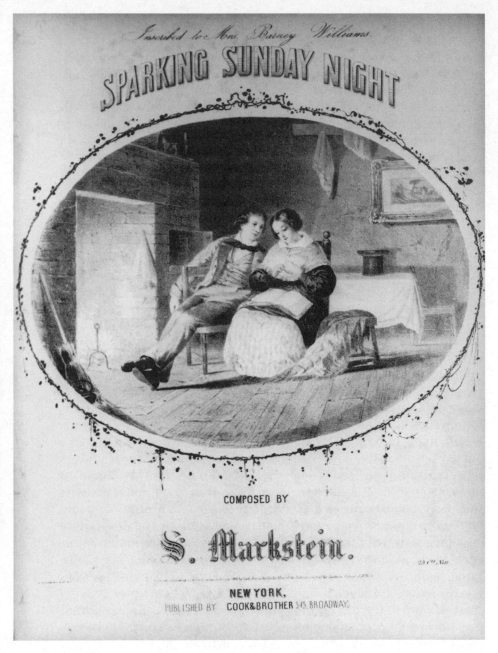

Sparking Sunday Night (1855). Sam DeVincent Collection of Illustrated Sheet Music Covers, Archives Center, National Museum of American History, Smithsonian Institution.

One version of this popular song, which was reprinted several times during the nineteenth century, was dedicated to "all who feel guilty." The lyrics suggest the origins of such guilt: "How your heart is thumping 'gainst your Sunday vest, How wickedly 'tis working on this day of rest! Hours seem but minutes as they take their flight, Bless me, this is pleasant, Sparking Sunday night!"

not to mention the visitors she received and the visiting that took place in and around church. Most Sundays she recorded visitors who left as late as midnight and never earlier than seven in the evening.[26] A young woman living in San Francisco in the mid 1870s spent her Sundays visiting before and after church; she often noted that visitors called while she was out, either at church or teaching Sunday school. Sunday night in particular seemed to be set aside for visiting; she made a point of mentioning when she did not go out or have visitors in the evening.[27] The diaries and journals of young men also reveal a preponderance of visiting and socializing:

> Al and I went to Stebbins church at noon to meet the people coming out.—I walked home with Miss Shew & afterwards went up Sutter St. where I met with Mrs. Wm. Macondary & Miss Fisher. Invited to dine with former, & went at 4 o'clock,—Newhall there.—To Davis' in eve, where I saw all the ladies, & was intro. to Horace D.'s brother Andrew.—Singing.[28]

This entry, from an engineer's 1871 diary, exemplifies the variety and intricacy of Sunday visiting: he did not go to church but went with a friend to meet the people leaving services. He escorted a young lady home, then ran into another single woman (Miss Fisher). At dinner he not only saw associates and friends, but also courted the few available women. As if he had not had enough visiting and courting, our young engineer then went to another home in the evening, where there were still more ladies, where he met a friend's brother, and where they all joined together in singing who knows what. His schedule was far from unusual; few diaries reveal Sundays spent alone.

The decline of the Sunday afternoon church service during the second half of the century contributed to the development of Sunday dinner as a central ritual in the life of a family. During the 1820s and 1830s Sunday evening supper parties were common, but few had a mid-day Sunday dinner. This was partly due to the proscription against working on Sunday (which included preparing a meal), the distances that families traveled to church (which required them to stay in the vicinity of the church rather than go home between services), and the sense that extravagance of any kind desecrated the Sabbath. Furthermore, family meals and dining (as contrasted with eating) began to be scheduled and ritualized only after mid century.[29] Then, although visitors and suitors often sat down with the host family, the Sunday dinner came to be understood as family time.

Starting in the second half of the nineteenth century, wives and mothers from the middle classes were urged to make Sunday dinner

Sunday after Dinner. Painting by Russell Vernon Hunter (1943). Dallas Museum of Art, Dallas Arts Association Purchase.

 After the Civil War, American families began to gather around a large midday meal each Sunday. Especially in rural areas Sunday dinner was the marrow of social life. Apart from holiday and Sunday dinners, when do American meals extend through several hours? When, other than Sunday, do Americans sit together on the porch, or anywhere else, in various states of conversation and contemplation?

"one of the principal delights of the day." As with most other aspects of everyday life, the family's socioeconomic status determined in large part the nature of its Sunday dinner; some families sat down to a formal feast that moved "from olives and celery through a heavy soup, a huge roast, ice cream (delivered in a wooden bucket every Sunday morning), to nuts and raisins;" others ate roasted chicken and potatoes. After the turn of the century homemakers began to advise simpler Sunday fare. One woman lamented that "Sunday is only too often apt to be one of the hardest days in the week for the active wife and mother" and recalled tearful breakdowns many a Sunday when she was a young wife. She suggested simplifying the day's meals and detailed how this could be done without sacrificing quality. Women's magazines, manuals, and cookbooks included menus and tips for preparing the Sunday dinner with the least amount of effort possible. Menus tended to include roasts, fish, eggs, and "something extra in the shape of a treat after dinner, either of candy or of something sweet, to mark the day."[30] Here was one of the many ways that rest was inflected with various meanings; a mother needed rest from food preparation, a family needed the kind of rest that a good meal could induce.

Around the turn of the century those working in the steel-producing town of Homestead, Pennsylvania, claimed that Sunday dinner was the only festive time of the week, an opinion that many families across the nation shared. Even if it was not enjoyable, it was family time, which bred its own kind of intimacy. Anatole Broyard described the streets of mid-twentieth century Brooklyn as being deserted Sunday afternoon, "since everyone ate dinner at the same time." After the meal of roast beef and mashed potatoes was over, Broyard noted, "At last I felt that I had eaten enough, an exemplary amount. With all my blood and nerves busy in my stomach, I relaxed, I became flatulent with affection. My mother saw my face go blank and she beamed. Belly to belly, that was the only true way to talk." The Sunday dinner, coming at the middle of the day, made time "flow backward and forward in a manner different from weekdays," one historian noted. The custom lingers. Today, almost half of all Americans report that they prepare a special meal for their families or friends on Sundays. Not long ago a second-generation Chinese American poignantly commented that "the only time we get together as a family is on Sunday. Sunday is the only time at night we have our dinner meal together," and then he added ruefully, "it is about the only time we have."[31]

Newspaper, Radio, and Television

Sunday in the home during the nineteenth century was a very social time. Even so we can discern seeds of an antisocial home Sunday, focused on the consumption of books, newspapers, radio programs, and in the post–World War II years, television shows. In the 1920s, the Lutheran Church, among many institutions, expressed concern about family life on Sundays. In its view, families forsook the home for public attractions. Or, if they stayed at home, they read the newspaper or listened to the radio, which prevented the "family as a family" from enjoying "the home as a home on the Lord's Day."[32] The Sunday newspaper, the radio, and the television each brought the world, in its commercial and noncommercial aspects, into the home. Each had the potential to enhance or to undermine religion and rest, and to contemporary observers it seemed that each did both.

"Let no Sunday newspaper invade the sanctity of a home," thundered many ministers during the last part of the nineteenth century. One critic contrasted the efforts of editors across the nation to perfect the Sunday edition with the experiments of scientists: "They have at last invented and launched upon the world this Frankenstein of the century, the fifty-page Sunday issue, to bewilder, to fascinate, to at last overpower and enslave, the ninety-nine out of every hundred."[33] The Sunday paper thrust "itself in the face of Sabbath-loving people as no other business is allowed to thrust itself." Although it was an "insidious and subtle evil" reaching into "religious homes" and upright hearts, Christians and non-Christians alike "hungered and thirsted" for it, reading the newspaper before and after morning services and neglecting domestic duties to savor it just a bit longer. One minister warned subscribers that they were allowing their homes "to be flooded with influences which are, when all is said, away from spiritual and helpful ones."[34]

This flood was barely at a trickle in the antebellum period, during which time Americans bought weeklies on Saturday night that they may have read on Sunday. In 1835 the publishing whiz James Gordon Bennett introduced the *Sunday Herald* in New York City, which quickly folded. It returned in 1841, however, and by 1860, 10,000 copies of the *Herald* circulated each Sunday, competing with Sunday editions of newspapers printed in French and German. During the Civil War dailies published seven days a week, and afterward a Sunday newspaper, which resembled daily papers with news, notices of arrivals and departures, and advertisements of all sorts, could be found in some cities. During the 1880s, Joseph Pulitzer and other publishers remade the Sunday edition. They divided it into sections appropriate for each family member and published special stories, features, and advertisements. Still, only about 15 percent (approximately 250) of the nation's daily newspaper companies published Sunday editions in the 1890s, though that was a considerable increase over the nation's four Sunday papers in the 1860s. After the Spanish-American War (1898), newspapers throughout the country developed Sunday editions, complete with comic supplements. By the 1930s, nearly 505 Sunday newspapers were published throughout the country, with a combined circulation of nearly 27 million, which would have placed a Sunday paper in nearly all American households. As they do today, New York papers circulated nationally, competing with, or supplementing, local Sunday editions.[35]

Sunday papers began to cater to the entire family and various classes of Americans in the 1890s. *The Springfield Sunday News* advertised it-

self as "the only Sunday paper in a city of 40,000 population and surrounding territory of 200,000 population. Society, Literature, News and
Criticism are leading features." Another paper promised that it was
"the best family Sunday newspaper published in Philadelphia." The
Sunday Globe of Pittsburgh claimed to be "the most widely read Sunday paper among the industrial classes." The Providence, Rhode Island,
Sunday Telegram was "welcome alike to the home circle, counting-
room, manufactory and lyceum."[36]

As critics had warned, Sunday papers were powerful agents of commerce. Near the close of the century, an advertising agency noted that
"the power of 'the Sunday paper,' or the 'Paper for Sunday reading,' "
could be harnessed. Was it not "designed expressly for perusal during
the public's rest from labor" and therefore would not advertisements
capture the attention of the entire family? Most publicists and publishers shared this realization of the paper's advertising potential. Feature
articles, photo essays, "the colored supplement," and the comics all
made the Sunday paper popular. Editors saved their best items—
interviews with celebrities, scoops concerning titillating scandals, syndicated cartoon strips, reports from special correspondents, stories by
the nation's leading writers—for the Sunday edition. The papers ranged
in size, but in the 1890s the *New York World* boasted that it had nearly
50,000 *more* words in each Sunday edition than there were in the Bible.
By the 1930s, according to one study, the typical Sunday issue ran to at
least 150 pages. The Sunday newspaper "takes time—millions of people
spend hours," noted one critic, "which ought to be devoted to higher
things."[37]

At the same time, it became apparent that Sunday papers could also
provide "incentive to religious duty and philanthropy." They could
evangelize. In their pages were lists "of the preachers who are to fill the
pulpits, together with the topics they will discuss," advertisements for
charities and their works, feature articles that supported "the cause of
the weak against the strong," and reports apprising Christians about politics, news, and "Progress." It was even claimed that "what a preacher is
powerless to do is easily accomplished by the press." By reaching into
"tens of thousands of homes, ranging from those of palatial splendor to
those of pinching penury," the Sunday paper could evangelize those "beyond the reach of any pulpit." Near the turn of the century, the Newspaper Sermon Association, whose membership included George Hodges
(dean of the Cambridge School of Theology) and Edward Everett Hale (a
leading Boston minister), furnished "the Sunday papers with readable,
non-sectarian religious matter addressed to and intended for their
20,000,000 readers in the United States." Such sermons and articles

were intended to encourage formal worship and to bring "the churchless Sunday reader into a purer and higher plane of thought" than the typical Sunday newspaper. Most of the nation's largest papers agreed to run the sermons and essays in the Sunday edition, which the association believed would encourage "a greater willingness to use the newspapers as a power for Christianity."[38]

In 1922 the cover of the Radio Corporation of America's catalog announced, "Radio Enters the Home." Sunday broadcasting blurred the line between the home and the world even more dramatically than had the Sunday newspaper. At first it hewed closely to a vision of Sunday as a day reserved for religion and cultural uplift, and such Sunday programming as there was centered around religious themes or "symphonies, choirs, and organ recitals." Devotees of radio in the 1920s hoped that it would become a "medium of Uplift," and Sunday was central to that project. In early radio days many stations went off the air on Sunday mornings, although some New York stations carried late-morning church services and Sunday school lessons. Several start-up stations broadcast only on Sunday mornings, such as WIBG in Elkins Park, Pennsylvania, which in 1925 began broadcasting morning services from St. Paul's Episcopal Church, and Chicago's WIBO, which broadcast Swedish church services every Sunday beginning in 1926. In the afternoons other stations went on the air with programming devoted to classical music and sermons. Soon each of the national broadcasting corporations, not content simply to broadcast sermons from the nation's more famous pulpits, was developing special religious programs. A typical program showcased guest speakers from different Christian denominations for thirty minutes twice each Sunday. More and more programs aired in the early 1930s, with some lasting until the 1950s. NBC dominated Sunday religious broadcasting. A few of its more important programs were *Young People's Conference* (1926–1933), *The Jewish Hour* (1928–1932), *Sabbath Reveries* (1929), and *The Catholic Hour* (1929–1956). But CBS and ABC also provided religious programming, such as *CBS Church of the Air* (1931–1956) and ABC's *National Church of the Air* (1927–1956).[39] All the broadcasting companies created programs for specific markets, with religious themes germane to particular religious traditions.

When the evangelical minister Charles E. Fuller formed the Gospel Broadcasting Association in 1933, he hoped to build a corporation that would equal, if not surpass, CBS, NBC, and ABC. (Around the same time, consumers could buy radios that looked like cathedrals, and once they were installed, families could worship at home.) By 1940, 150 stations nationwide carried Fuller's *Old Fashioned Revival Hour*. An extremely popular show built around religious music, testimony, and a sermon, it aired for a quarter of a century. Letters sent to Fuller over the decades suggest that the radio may have converted some homes into religious sanctuaries. One man wrote: "As you closed your meeting Sunday night, I got down on my knees by the radio and prayed that I would be forgiven. I once knew what it was to have peace with God and it seemed so hard to come back." The radio became an altar and a preacher—a means of conversion and forgiveness. Those known as "shut-ins" benefited particularly from being able to hear sermons and religious music while confined to their homes by age, illness, or inclement weather.[40]

Despite the success of religious programming, however, broadcasters also experimented with other kinds of formats, some of which would come to dominate the air waves. During the 1920s, several stations broadcast baseball scores, a practice which soon developed into play-by-play accounts of baseball games, boxing matches, and the like. In the 1920s and 1930s local stations featured "kiddie programs" on Sunday mornings during which the comics sections from the local newspaper would be read; children not yet able, or just learning, to read, would follow along. By the early 1930s, broadcasting companies were producing variety shows to be aired Sunday afternoons and evenings, such as *Sunday Bright Spots*, *The Buick Concert*, and *The Buddy Rogers Orchestra*, the last show devoted sixty minutes to "the latest thing in swing." Soon novelty shows and dramatic skits, such as *The Cheerio Canaries*, *Dog Dramas*, and *Club Romance*, joined these musical variety programs. Producers of name-brand goods sponsored most shows; for instance, Hoover Vacuum Cleaners sponsored the live broadcasts of the Metropolitan Opera during the 1934–1935 season, Iodent toothpaste provided the funding for a Sunday variety program that featured music, comedy, and oratory, and Gulf Oil sponsored a Sunday evening variety show with Will Rogers as the host. Variety show formats further diversified to include symphonic music, dramatic skits, news shows, and even an afternoon talk hosted by the astrologist Belle Barte. World War II introduced Sunday news programs such as *Close-Ups of the News*, comedy shows that would become famous, such as the ones featuring Jack Benny, and serialized dramas about the war such as *Chaplain Jim, U.S.A.*[41]

By the 1950s a steady rhythm of Sunday morning church services, afternoon symphonic music, and evening variety shows characterized radio. Although most radio programming today is devoted seven days a week to an assortment of musical formats or to "talk radio," many stations still have special Sunday programs, such as livecasts or replays of rock'n' roll concerts or symphonic performances, music programs devoted to specific kinds of music, such as "old-time jazz," or in-depth news coverage, such as National Public Radio's various Sunday shows. College radio stations may broadcast morning church services, local stations may cover baseball and football games, and in one way or another most radio stations recognize that Sunday is a different day for their listeners and try to accommodate that difference.

Listening to the radio was itself an experience that carried a variety of meanings. From its invention until after World War II, according to one of its recent historians, "radio pulled together blood-related families and created ad hoc extended families." In the 1920s most people listened to the radio in informal groups at the local dry goods store, on the porch of a neighbor who had a short-wave radio (and knew how to use it), or even in local schools where an amplifier would be set up. Broadcasters responded in innovative ways to radio's separation of audiences from performers. An interesting experiment in this vein was CBS's 1936–1937 *Community Sing*, aired each Sunday and originating from two different locations at once. Milton Berle and Wendell Hall would host a studio audience in New York while Billy Jones and Ernie Hare would lead another in Philadelphia; each audience as well as the program's listeners was encouraged to sing along as religious and popular tunes were played. A short-lived experiment, it speaks to the various meanings of Sunday, and of radio. By the 1930s, many American families had a radio in their home or in their automobile, and although they might have sung along with the radio, it was a private matter. People born in the 1920s and 1930s recall listening to the radio while on Sunday afternoon drives, hearing a variety of religious, educational, musical, and dramatic programs as the day passed. With the bombing of Pearl Harbor, which many heard about one Sunday on the radio, Sunday drives all but ceased owing to gas rationing, but they resumed after the war, and with them special radio programs.[42]

It is difficult to take television on the road, although it has been done, and so the next in the line of media innovations rooted people more firmly in their homes than ever before. Television programming on Sunday took much the same course as that of radio programming: most stations devoted the mornings to church services, afternoons to either symphonic music, educational documentaries, or sporting events, and evenings to variety shows, news programs, or special movies. *The Ed Sullivan Show* surely stands out as the premiere variety show on early television; it aired for the first time on Sunday evenings at 8 P.M. in 1948 under a different name, eventually became *The Ed Sullivan Show* in 1955, and remained on the air until 1971. In the late 1960s talk and news shows became popular on Sundays. With the development of Charles Kurault's *Sunday Morning*, which was designed to have an "uplifting nature," the still-running in-depth news program 60 *Minutes*, and the kiddie variety show *The Wonderful World of Disney*, Sunday television, until the advent of cable in the 1980s, was simply a visual version of radio.[43] Each made the home the site of participation in religious activity, spectator sports, and cultural uplift.

So the spread of print and electronic media altered the initial partnership between the home and the church, in which each offered Americans a sanctuary from the corrupting world. Each medium eroded the boundaries between public and private, market and nonmarket, home and the world. Nevertheless, it is necessary to realize that these developments do not point to a diminution in Sunday's status and importance, since each of the visitors to the home on Sunday enhanced the unique nature of the day.

With more than half the American population living near or in poverty around 1900, it is hard to imagine the majority of Americans celebrating Sunday at home. Such home Sundays as this chapter has described were almost impossible for many African Americans, working people, and newly arrived immigrants. It is well known that a great majority of African American families, who lived for the most part in severely restricted economic and social conditions, turned to their churches on Sundays (and at other times during the week) for spiritual and social sustenance. But in doing so they too devoted Sunday to family. Evidence from three generations of ethnically diverse Americans in San Francisco, born around 1900, 1925, and 1950, also documents the widespread and long-lasting commitment to the family Sunday. In the first decades of the century Sundays were filled with Sunday school, church, excursions, picnics, movies, and trolley rides, and memories of the day are fond and cheerful. Listening to the radio, making trips to the seaside in automobiles, and attending church services, often without their parents, characterize the recollections of Americans who grew up in between the two world wars. Sundays remained placid for the baby boom generation.[44] Sunday continues to be "Daddy's Day with Baby": there is many a divorced father with his children out among us on this day to which the family still has claim.

In the 1820s and 1830s, Americans were beginning to separate the private from the public sphere. The home began to appear to be sanctified space, and family health as needful of Sunday. So it was that church and home, by the end of the nineteenth century, were cast as the only appropriate places for observing Sunday. But, as Chapters 3–7 have shown, spaces, meanings, and uses for Sunday that were rooted in the public sphere of commerce and culture were also developing. The devotion of Sunday to cultural uplift, commercialized amusements, and domesticity together reoriented American rhythms of being from work and rest to work and leisure. Through the many decades that it took for this significant transformation to occur, religion did not diminish in importance; it simply shifted places. The closing chapter cursorily explores the rise of new times for rest other than Sunday and new meanings for rest other than those connected to the biblical term "Sabbath."

9 What Is Rest?

Sunday is a psychological institution which modern hygiene of the
soul and body would have to invent if religion had not provided it.
—G. Stanley Hall (1901)

The previous chapters have suggested that the maturation of the nation's manufacturing and service industries, along with a culture based
on consumption, contributed to the collapse of the divide between
work and rest. During the 1800s, Americans, especially those living in
cities, began to seek their rest in places besides church; at first in par-
lors, dining rooms, beer gardens, picnic groves, and parks; soon in libraries, museums, fairgrounds, stadiums, theaters, movie palaces; eventually in front of television sets or at the mall. With the proliferation of
new sites for rest, moreover, increasing numbers of men and women
had to work on Sunday. Concurrently, the number of hours and days
worked per week contracted, making times to rest other than Sunday
available. When the prominent psychologist and educator G. Stanley
Hall described Sunday as a modern psychological institution, he acknowledged its status as the day of rest.[1] But he, along with other social
scientists, physiologists, progressive reformers, labor leaders, and Sabbatarians, could not keep the nation's attention on Sunday or on rest
after the 1920s. With the threat of unending labor vanquished by the
Great Depression and subsequent New Deal legislation which capped
the number of hours worked per week, Sunday lost its contested place
in American life and culture. Many other factors contributed to this.
Most important was the increased availability of blocks of time other
than Sunday free from the obligation to work and the extensive development of leisure as a sphere separate from work.

Yet despite the attenuation of debate over Sunday, Americans continue to set the day aside. They attend church and Sunday school, have family gatherings and outings, go to baseball games and shows, and visit museums and other cultural sites. Few argue about the use of Sunday, either privately or publicly. The little-noticed repeal of blue laws across the nation since the 1970s, except in a handful of places, is but one sign of this. Americans continue to discuss rest, but they do so using "leisure" as their keyword or "the overworked American" as the object of their concern.[2] They no longer separate rest from leisure, and few seek to segregate holy day from holiday. But many continue to resist Sunday's transformation into a workday: Extra wages for Sunday work, shorter Sunday shifts, and Sunday's exemption from "workdays" on court, banking, and governmental calendars all make this evident. A recent poll shows that Sunday is the favorite day of the week for a large majority of Americans.[3]

The "Art of Resting"

It was widely agreed near the end of the nineteenth century that Americans were "not adepts in the art of resting."[4] P. T. Barnum, leisure impresario of the nineteenth century, himself was unable to define rest except as being the opposite of work. The chapter of his autobiography titled "Rest, but Not Rust," sketches a depressing summer spent mooning around Long Island after he went bankrupt because of overinvestment in a clock company. Barnum concludes his account with a chapter proclaiming "Rest Found Only in Action," where readers might note that rather than experience rest when not working, Barnum was restless.[5] Repose was fashioned as one avenue toward a rested state. Annie Payson Call's manual *Power through Repose,* published in the midst of America's frenzied industrialization, does not mention Sunday; instead it focuses on how to rest the body through sleep, exercise, even posture. In stressing the difference between repose and idleness, the manual continued to affirm the work ethic.[6] Although few could explain what it was, social scientists, physicians, and religious leaders prescribed rest as both an antidote and a cure for overwork, nervous exhaustion, and the panoply of ills that accompanied the acceleration of American life.

Sunday was also fashioned as a cure for modernity's side effects. It was widely believed that only Sunday could provide "true rest." Shortly before the turn of the century, John P. Hylan, one of G. Stanley Hall's doctoral candidates, prepared a study that argued that worship was necessary for human health. When asked if they experienced "a Sunday feeling," 95 percent of the polled students from New England colleges and universities assented. The feeling was "of quiet exultation, and had for its associations religious devotion, emancipation from annoyances, aesthetic enjoyment, pleasant anticipation." On Sunday, people felt free "from care and no need of hurrying to do ordinary things." Hylan claimed that the conditions of worship—cessation of ordinary pursuits and duties, quiet on the street, later hours for rising, distinctive food for breakfast, Sunday clothes, reading the Bible, special devotions—gave rise to the Sunday feeling. Much of his thesis was devoted to a comparison of the "Roman type" of rest—recreation—with the Christian type—cultivation. Recreation was enervating, and was a primary cause of the ruin of Rome. Cultivation, on the other hand, fostered Christian character and therefore guaranteed the survival of the nation.[7]

During Hylan's time the meanings and connotations of terms like "cultivation," "recreation," and "amusement" were undergoing as much revision as were those of the word "rest." Activities that catered to the senses tended to be considered recreation or amusement, whereas those working on the spirit belonged in the sphere of cultivation. The widening gulf between manual and mental labor, however, forced a reassessment of rest. For those who toiled with their hands, rest could be found in mental activity, whether reading books, gazing at great works of art, or contemplating nature. People engaged in brain work, on the other hand, needed physical activity.[8] In addition, liberal Protestants, European immigrants with a range of religious commitments, and progressive reformers had been reconsidering the relationship between the body and the soul since the 1880s, and in some cases even earlier. They argued for the full development of each, and refused to differentiate between recreation and cultivation. Thus, at the time that Hylan was setting one term against the other, more influential Americans were promoting "muscular Christianity," "rational recreation," and "Sunday play." A theology that celebrated play as the conduit for releasing "God present in every human soul" gained currency. At the same time, Protestant eschatology shifted emphasis from salvation through work to salvation through play.[9]

As the opposition between rest and play collapsed, the shape of the ideal Sunday changed. Social scientists, psychologists, and ministers cast play as a site of socialization, expression, and discovery. Politicians and citizens joined the celebration: the establishment of the National Park Service in 1916 and the passage of numerous local bond issues during the 1920s enabled the development of a string of national parks that catered to tourists and the construction and staffing of urban playgrounds and recreation centers that served adults and children. At the same time, hundreds of amusement parks, movie palaces, and baseball parks opened across the country.[10] Most communities did not close these various sites on Sundays; rather, they incorporated play and recreation into the day of rest.

In the decades between 1880 and 1930, then, the meaning of rest expanded dramatically. It came to include reading, exercising, playing, competing (in a friendly manner), and repose, as well as an ever-expanding range of mental and physical diversion found in the public and private spheres. These new meanings for rest were so powerful, so alluring, so desirable that Americans sought rest not only on Sunday but on other days of the week as well. In this way, Sunday ceased to be *the* day of rest, and rest ceased to have meanings that were unique to Sunday. A diverse group of people, however, resisted these changes.

Natural Law and the Scientific Sabbath

After the Civil War Sabbatarians increasingly turned to natural law and experimental science to affirm that "true rest" could be had only on Sundays. They feared that the gradual separation of ideas about rest from religion, along with the pervasive presence of leisure, threatened the unique nature of the day. Their efforts, however, served only to establish that periodic rest from work was necessary, not that Sunday should remain the day of rest, or that it was the only time to rest, or that rest was different from leisure.

One tack that Sabbatarians took was demonstrating that the material world adhered to the principles embedded in the term *Sabbath.* Since the eighteenth century theologians had argued that the Sabbath's spiritual meaning, use, and obligation "all grow up from the root of the original physical law that man requires one day's rest in seven." The biblical command to observe the Sabbath, then, was "based in nature, in natural laws." Violating it would corrupt body and soul. Citing biological and geological descriptions of the "vegetable and mineral kingdoms," theologians of all persuasions during the 1870s and 1880s claimed that the natural world affirmed the fourth commandment's division of the week between six days of work and one of rest.[11] They characterized God as a scientist who "measured out" the weekly Sabbath in accordance with how much rest humans required. The 6–1 ratio of work and rest had the same "scientific basis" as "the constitution of the atmosphere, or the law of gravity, or the succession of day and night."[12] Tests identified as "scientific" supported the banning of activities—such as reading the Sunday newspaper, riding trains, participating in commercialized amusements, playing or watching sports, and so on—on the grounds that they were not restful.[13] Such attempts to harness science to Sabbatarian meanings for Sunday produced a narrow set of meanings for rest.

Meanwhile, physiologists became interested in locating both the sources of and the solutions for fatigue and nervous exhaustion. In the 1870s Adolf Haegler, a Swiss physician, performed experiments that provided evidence that nightly rest only partially restored the body from fatigue. He summarized his conclusion, that a full day's rest was needed to overcome fatigue induced by either mental or manual work, in a chart depicting *The Natural Law of the Weekly Rest-Day*. In 1879, when presented in the United States for the first time, Haegler's chart was overlaid with the assumption that Sunday was the only possible day of rest. From that point forward it provided a visual representation of the thesis that Sunday was necessary for people's physical well-being, although the chart itself only aimed to prove the necessity of a day of rest.[14]

Consensus about the validity of the natural law of the weekly rest day was widespread. When a group of Progressive reformers, liberal and orthodox Protestants, and Catholic luminaries gathered in Chicago in 1893, references to it suffused their discussion of the Sunday problem. A lawyer proclaimed that "rest is a natural law"; a Lutheran theologian explained that seasons of rest are "an inherent right and demand of human nature"; and an evangelical Protestant stated that the need for the Sabbath was "written on the pages of man's nature and environment."[15] Over the next few decades, professionals committed to social welfare also cited natural law when arguing for the necessity of a rest day. Progressive reformers incorporated Sunday observance into their "scientific" project of adapting society to urbanization and industrialization. They chose Sunday as the day of rest, rather than simply advocating one day of rest a week, because they believed that "true rest" needed a spiritual component.

The theory of the weekly rest day as natural law suggested that in spite of efforts otherwise, people would do well to continue rationing the amount of time they worked and rested. It held that rocks, plants, and animals all followed rhythms of work and rest, and that it would be foolhardy to ignore the human need for such alternation. The theory posited that one day of rest in seven provided the correct amount of rest. It did little, however, to set a clear standard about what constituted rest, nor did it bind the day of rest to Sunday.

During the second decade of the twentieth century, scientists at Harvard and Columbia returned to Adolf Haegler's research of nearly half a century earlier concerning fatigue and rest. Ernest G. Martin, a professor in the department of physiology at the Harvard Medical School,

The Natural Law of the Weekly Rest-Day

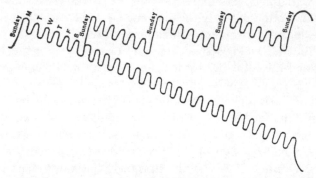

"Beginning on Monday morning, each downward stroke to E (Evening) marks the daily expenditure of energy, and the upward stroke the nightly recovery, which does not rise quite to the height of the previous morning; so that there is a gradual decline during the week, which only the prolonged rest of Sunday repairs.

The Natural Law of the Weekly Rest-Day [1870s]. Diagram from *Sabbath Essays* (1880). General Research Division, The New York Public Library, Astor, Lenox and Tilden Foundations.

Adolf Haegler's diagram suggests that nightly rest could not restore the body after a day's work; once a week a full day's rest was necessary. It was widely believed that Sunday provided the ideal conditions for recuperation, and therefore natural law confirmed the biblical mandate to cease working every seventh day.

conducted experiments on nine medical students over the course of the winter of 1912–1913 to discover whether or not recovery from fatigue could be attained through nightly rest. The nine subjects received electric shocks on a daily basis for eight weeks; their response to these shocks indicated their nervous systems' level of alertness. Martin found that sensitivity to the shocks was at its height on Mondays, and surmised that this was because the medical students took Sunday off from study. He concluded that fatigue accumulates despite nightly rest, and that therefore a day of rest was necessary for full recovery. Sabbatarians heralded his conclusions as scientific proof of the necessity of a Sunday free from work. But there was nothing in either Martin's or Haegler's research to prove that Sunday rest was essential, only that a day of rest was.[16]

In 1914, William J. Gies, chair in biological chemistry at Columbia University, promised the New York Sabbath Committee (NYSC) that he would conduct research concerning the influence of the Sabbath on "the physical well-being of the race." The same year, the NYSC inaugurated a fund-raising drive to support more research along these lines. Arguing that modern science could present more conclusive evidence than Haegler's *Natural Law of the Weekly Rest-Day*, the NYSC hoped that scientific research would present to the public, via the press and public schools, constructive ideas concerning Sunday, and thus mold Sunday observance in accordance with their ideals. The organization assured donors that "when we have secured a well-sifted body of scientific facts showing the influence of the Sabbath upon human welfare," Sabbatarians would have the necessary "arms and ammunition" to protect Sunday from further abuse.[17] They turned to the physical and social sciences in an effort to establish that there was such a thing as the "scientific Sabbath," and that it served the best interests of the American people and nation by providing the elusive, but necessary, cure for the ills of modern living—rest.

Little more than a year later, William Gies and collaborators made public a preliminary study concerning Sunday observance's effects on nutrition. But limited funds marred the experiments, and therefore the results. Scientists, under Gies's instruction, performed tests on two male lab workers. Since the volunteers were hard to monitor and supervise once the workday was over, the researchers also tested two dogs, whom they forced to work (by running on a treadmill) seven days a week and whose diet they controlled. The studies were meant to provide information concerning the relationship between nutrition, fatigue, and rest. It was hoped that the conclusions would speak to the necessity of Sunday as a day of rest. Results were inconclusive and the laboratory research program was abandoned.[18]

Isolating Rest from Leisure

During the Gilded Age states and territories passed, rewrote, and amended Sunday laws in the effort to regulate work, rest, and morality. In most places, the momentum in favor of Sunday laws was strong. Almost all the states, including the only two—Louisiana and California— that had never before regulated Sunday observance, passed acts that broadly prohibited all labor on Sunday. The new and revised statutes were generally similar in wording and intent.

> Every person who shall, on the Sabbath or Sunday, be found laboring, or shall compel his apprentice or servant to labor or to perform other services than customary household duties, of daily necessity, comfort, or charity, on conviction shall be fined one dollar for each separate offense.

These new Sunday codes mandated that breaking the law was a misde-
meanor, set parameters for fines, and made it clear that compelling another to work was as much a violation of the law as working oneself. In
states that had a long history of conflict over Sunday observance, such
as New Jersey, the statutes were lengthy and detailed, attempting to
clarify what was meant by "the Sabbath" ("between twelve o'clock Saturday night and sunset on the following Sunday") and "labor" ("traveling, worldly employment or business" or exposing "to sale any wares,
merchandise, fruits, herbs, meat, fish, goods, chattels").[19]

Many Sunday laws of the period, however, allowed labor for certain
kinds of transportation services, the running of industries that required
continuous operation, and the repair of machinery. They also exempted
the labor of people who observed another holy day, in some instances introduced local option concerning Sunday amusements, and began to
specify legitimate Sunday trade, such as "the sale of milk, bread and
other necessaries of life, or drugs and medicines."[20] Amended laws exempted news-crying, utility services (telephone, water, and electricity),
and ice delivery, which reflected the widespread opinion that "if all
work were to cease on Sunday, the day would be unendurable and too
full of discomfort to afford any benefit." Most Americans sanctioned
labor that gave Sunday the "highest possible value to society as a
whole." So legislatures began to explain what was meant by "works of
necessity and mercy," the phrase that had previously served to establish
exceptions to Sunday prohibitions. Most explanations remained pur-
posefully vague: in New York a "work of necessity" was defined as being
"anything needful to the comfort of the community."[21] The limitless
meanings of comfort became a loophole for Americans who sought to
hire or perform labor on Sunday. Soon the number of exceptions made in
the name of necessity and charity corroded both legal and religious in-
junctions protecting the day of rest. The longer and longer the lists of
"necessities and mercies" grew, the greater the inability (and unwilling-
ness in many cases) to enforce jumbled and contradictory laws, and,
more important, the vaguer the meaning of rest itself became.

Almost as soon as the ink dried on Sunday laws, Americans challenged them. Some religious leaders held to the view that persuasion
was the best means of assuring proper Sunday observance, and were
horrified that so many new laws were being written. They argued that
restrictive laws would only create antipathy for the day, rather than
love and respect. Even they, however, recognized that only legislation
could protect working people from employers' insistence that they
work seven days a week. Other dissenters queried whether or not Sunday laws were constitutional, often taking cases to higher courts and

usually losing.[22] Still more ran for office on platforms that proclaimed their intent to repeal noxious Sunday laws. In 1883, for instance, the Democratic Party in California won the governor's seat and a majority in the legislature after campaigning on a platform that promised to repeal the state's Sunday laws.[23] Sometimes the questioning transformed itself into direct action—banning the sale of liquor on Sunday sparked numerous riots in urban areas. The most effective challenge to the avalanche of Sunday laws, however, was their persistent violation, which provoked the passage of more laws, the repeal of some, and a variety of campaigns to "save" Sunday through other means altogether.

Sabbatarians, lawmakers, and courts argued that Sunday laws ensured the health of the state and therefore were an appropriate exercise of police power. When they faced objections that the laws were religious in origin and intent, they responded that the similarity between some civil and biblical laws did not mean that the church and state were colluding. Crimes and sins often resembled one another—for example, murder or adultery—but this did not necessitate the removal of state penalties. Blue laws enforced "man's duties to man," not to God. In their view it was incidental that biblical law also enjoined Sabbath observance.[24] Respecting the universal need for a day of rest was one of civil society's many obligations. Sabbatarians were fond of saying, "The law of rest for all is necessary to the liberty of rest for each."[25] Sentiment was widespread that continuous work would be the ruin of democracy. On the other side of the Atlantic, European social reformers were organizing Sunday rest-day societies in Germany, France, Italy, and Switzerland and convened international conferences on Sunday rest fourteen times between 1876 and 1915.[26] American Sabbatarians and labor organizers attended these meetings, returning home with a renewed sense of mission and a deeper conviction that Sunday ought to remain the day of rest.

By expressing their conviction that a day of rest was a citizen's right, Sabbatarians were able to enlist the support of various labor organizations across the country. Together they entered campaigns against Sunday labor in steel and chemical manufacture, gas companies, breweries, bakeries and barber shops, gaining the trust of working people. One of the most active leaders in the campaign to convert labor to Sabbatarianism was Wilbur F. Crafts, who, as will become clear, had an agenda that included defining what rest was as well as guaranteeing universal access to it. Crafts urged the Knights of Labor, the nation's largest labor union in the 1870s and 1880s, to "make a new Declaration of Independence" by insisting on Sunday rest: "Labor's right to the weekly rest is part of the right to life, liberty and the pursuit of happiness." He and other Sabbatarians asked workingmen to organize, to sign petitions, and to take pledges against working on Sunday. A typical pledge card read:

> With a firm reliance upon God, I hereby make my DECLARATION OF IN-
> DEPENDENCE against KING GREED, whose Sunday work I pledge my sa-
> cred honor never to do.

These appeals had some effect. Countless labor unions and working-men's groups endorsed the American Sabbath Union and other Sabbatarian organizations. Together they petitioned state houses, city halls, and corporate headquarters against Sunday labor. Sympathy and support for these efforts were abundant; numerous editorials, didactic stories, and forums decried Sunday labor in workshops and on the railroads.[27]

The joint and separate efforts to prevent Sunday labor had mixed results. In 1889 the Pennsylvania, Vanderbilt, Erie, Iron Mountain, and New York Central Railroads all curtailed the running of trains on Sunday.[28] This was one of the few outright successes in the campaign against Sunday work. Due to their close ties with large-scale industrialists, Sabbatarians were not as effective as they might have been. Steel manufacturers, for instance, financed the Pittsburgh Reform Association, which led a campaign in the 1890s to close drugstores and small shops on Sundays in the name of "Sunday rest," but turned a blind eye to the churning steel mills.[29] By the same token, services that small businessmen provided were largely prohibited on Sunday, while those sold by larger companies, such as public transportation or electricity, were exempted.

Despite widespread support, Sabbatarians failed to abolish Sunday labor because they had much broader goals than simply protecting working people's right to a day of rest. They wanted to define rest itself. The Sabbatarian effort to circumscribe the sphere of rest became clear in 1889, when a petition campaign for a national Sunday Rest Law swept across the country, producing more than fourteen million supportive signatures. As early as 1863, petitions in favor of "better Sunday observance" began to arrive in the offices of senators and congressmen. Several quiet decades passed, but in 1887 petitions against government work, interstate trains, and military parades on Sunday regularly began to arrive on the Hill.[30] After the Senate Committee on Education and Labor held a hearing concerning the issue in the spring of 1888, New Hampshire Senator Henry S. Blair wrote a Sunday Rest-Day Bill, which came to be known as the Blair Bill when he proposed it the following fall. Blair's Sunday Rest Law aimed to prohibit most of the recreations and activities that characterized working people's Sundays, a fact that some labor unions took note of when they refused to join the crusade. Still, handwritten and pre-printed petitions flooded the 50th and 51st Congresses, representing the will of millions of Americans. Enthusiasm for the legislation was the rule: an unlikely alliance formed between rural communities stretching from Maine to "Indian Country," Knights of Labor local assemblies, Brotherhoods of Locomotive Engineers, Sunday-school unions, national and local Sabbatarian organizations, denominations usually at odds with one another, and various other groups. Opposition was weak. One senator presented a remonstrance against the Sunday Rest-Day Bill with 230,000 signatures of judges, lawyers, doctors, and ministers living in every state; and small streams of petitions against the bill trickled in from Turnverein groups in Wisconsin, Minnesota, and Illinois, and Seventh-Day Baptists and Adventists across the nation. It seemed as if a national Sunday law would materialize.[31]

In 1891, however, before the Blair Bill came to a vote, Massachusetts Senator Henry L. Dawes introduced a bill to prohibit "the opening of any exhibition or exposition on Sunday where appropriations of the United States are expended," aimed at the 1893 World's Fair. His action destroyed whatever momentum the Sunday rest-day law might have had. The volume of supportive petitions for the Sunday rest law dramatically fell, while petitions poured in concerning Sunday at the World's Fair.[32] The subsequent controversy made it clear that defining rest would lead to the disintegration of the consensus in favor of Sunday as the day of rest. During congressional hearings about whether the fair should be allowed to open its gates on Sundays, Sabbatarians claimed to represent the interests of all Americans, above all the working classes. After all, in their view, they only sought to protect the right to rest. But it had become clear that Sabbatarian interest was not just in securing a day of rest but in dictating exactly how that rest would be procured. When Thomas Morgan, a self-proclaimed workingman and representative of 375 labor organizations from thirty-three states, held up his hands for the gathered congressmen, senators, and others to see, his testimony in favor of Sunday opening repudiated the Sabbatarians' mandate:

> You see I am a workman; there are the calluses and corns that are a necessary incident to manual labor. I come unprepared by education to meet the arguments presented here, or to present my case with the force and fluency that gentlemen in the opposition have, having been forced by my condition to labor all my life-time since nine years of age, without a single vacation; absolutely denied the opportunities of education except that which was wrested from my sleeping hours.[33]

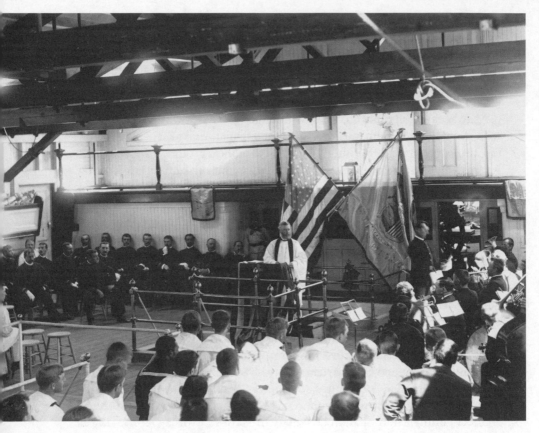

New York Naval Reserves at Church Service on U.S.S. New Hampshire. Photograph
taken between 1890 and 1901. Library of Congress, Prints and Photographs Division,
Detroit Publishing Company Collection.

    Although the National Sunday Rest-Day Law was never enacted, many branches of
the federal government have long paid heed to Sunday's unique status. Most government offices are closed, mail is not delivered (except at significant extra charge to the
customer), and all branches of the armed services provide religious services, which in
the United States Navy were mandatory. This photograph makes clear how deeply held
was the faith in the relationship between the state's health and a Christian Sunday:
both minister and flag were meant to inspire patriotism.

Morgan demanded that rest include diversion, amusement, and cultivation. In no time at all, the short-lived alliance between Sabbatarians and
those committed to the rights of working people fell apart, in large part
because of the multivalence of the term "rest."

    Although the battle over opening the Columbian Exposition on Sun-
day eclipsed the Sunday Rest-Day Bill, congressional representatives

from New Hampshire, North Dakota, South Dakota, Tennessee, and Mississippi reintroduced the bill in 1894 and 1896. Few Americans expressed interest or sent petitions.[36] The moment for a national law decreeing Sunday as a day of rest and worship had passed. For such a measure to become law, a majority of Americans would have to agree about what constituted rest.

As it became obvious that the demand for industrial and service labor would overpower Sabbatarian meanings for rest, groups began to fashion times other than Sunday when rest could be attained. In 1912 the American Association for Labor Legislation, an organization of social scientists and businessmen devoted to researching social policy, led a coalition of labor unions, progressive reformers, and Sabbatarian organizations in a movement in favor of one-day-of-rest-in-seven laws. Flagship organizations joined the movement, including the American Federation of Labor, the Federal Council of Churches of Christ in America, and the Progressive and Socialist Parties. One-day-of-rest-in-seven laws would "forbid an employer to work his employees seven days a week," but would "permit an industry necessarily or desirably continuous to operate seven days a week." The movement's participants recognized "that we must and can have continuous industries." They were, however, reluctant to create a class of "continuous men and women."[37] The one-day-of-rest-in-seven movement tried to accommodate the conditions of life in modern America. Instead of insisting that all activity cease on Sunday, demanding adherence to a Sabbatarian style of rest, reformers simply asked that working people be assured of a weekly day of rest. They realized that Sunday laws were not achieving their ends; signs of work were etched across the American Sunday. The industrial world ran continuously, and styles of rest that required labor were popular. Emphasis on *Sunday* rest shifted to *a weekly day* of rest, and eventually to leisure.

Sunday Is Eclipsed

Several years later the movement for one-day-of-rest-in-seven ceased, in part because supporters had been unable to prove its necessity, but mostly because the workweek was shrinking, and therefore the problem of rest did not loom as large as it once had. By the 1920s the per capita amount of time spent working each week had decreased, the result of a combination of successes in the Saturday half-holiday and the shorter-hours movements during the previous half century.[38]

Through the nineteenth century, the number of hours worked per day varied, but the figure tended toward double digits, and workers were enthusiastic about the campaign seeking "Eight Hours for Work, Eight Hours for Rest, and Eight Hours for What We Will." In addition, the Saturday half-holiday movement, initiated in the 1870s, gained momentum during the early decades of the twentieth century. Although some skilled workers had Saturday afternoons off, most of the employed, whether manual or nonmanual, worked through Saturday each week—when there was work—during the nineteenth century.

The first few decades of the twentieth century witnessed the freeing of more and more Saturday afternoons from the obligation to labor. In some instances the workweek ended on Friday. The first five-day work week in the United States was granted in 1908 in a New England spinning mill that employed many Jewish workers who wanted to observe Saturday as their Sabbath. The Bureau of Labor Statistics found in 1914 that the five-day week was "common" in three industries—clothing, printing and publishing, and the building trades. That same year Henry Ford introduced the five-day week at high wages in his automobile manufacturing plants. As it evolved, the five-day week provided workers with the time, and the higher wages with the money, to consume at a rate that would keep the rapidly expanding consumer economy afloat. After World War I the movements for shorter hours, most often in the shape of an eight-hour working day and a Saturday half-holiday, accelerated, as did employers' introduction of the five-day week.[39] Still, into the 1920s hundreds of thousands followed seven-day-a-week work schedules in industries ranging from canning to municipal transportation.[40]

These trends—shorter working hours, the Saturday half-holiday, the five-day week, and the seven-day week—all destabilized Sunday's status as the day of rest. As Sunday ceased to be *the* day of rest, convictions about what it should be unraveled. In large part this is a result of the multiple rhythms and routines that make up American life. The consensus that Sunday was the day of rest was strong enough during the nineteenth century to accommodate the rise of various practices that promised rest. What rest itself was went undefined.

At the root of conflict over Sunday were competing understandings and valuations of rest. Rest has persisted as an ideal among various groups interested in the health of the nation. The expansion of the meaning of necessity accelerated the slippage between rest and leisure, as proposed Sunday legislation for the District of Columbia in 1926 illustrates: it included exceptions for Sunday labor and business in connection with newspapers, automobiles, restaurants, drug stores, public transportation, and public utilities.[41] The list is even longer and more elaborate today. During the late 1970s, an ecumenical group took the position that "the rest from labor, the relief from the clamor of perpetual motion, is such a fundamental human need as to be a sacred duty." It argued that branding Sunday laws "as archaic" assumes "that these needs are outmoded."[42] Over the course of the century it seemed that Americans would have more and more leisure, and many assumed that leisure would provide rest. So disputes about Sunday's importance abated, in part because its multivalent meanings ceased to be in conflict with one another.

Religion has not lost its importance in the United States, secularization has not altered the calendar, and Sunday has not disappeared, as some critics in the nineteenth century feared would happen. It may be that conflict over places, rather than spaces of time, characterizes the late twentieth century. The Taos Indians' struggle to regain possession and control of Blue Lake—which figures as sacred in their religion—is but one example of such dissent.[43]

Americans loyal to many different Christian and non-Christian religions herald the coming of Sunday; they have learned to accommodate or ignore the diverse ways of keeping the day. They distinguish between work and rest as carefully as did the Revolutionary War generation; however, they no longer differentiate between rest and leisure.

Epilogue: Crazy Sunday

It was Sunday—not a day, but rather a gap between two other days.
—F. SCOTT FITZGERALD, "Crazy Sunday" (1932)

Sunday is nothing but empty air.
—REGINA MARLER, "Sunday" (1989)

In October 1955, about 1,800 technicians with access to more than 70 television cameras and 41,000 miles of telephone lines sought to capture a Sunday afternoon in the United States. The live show cut between Manhattan's Radio City Music Hall, the corner of San Francisco's Washington and Powell Streets where a cable car stopped, an Air Force base in Missouri, the community pier and the Church of the Lady of Good Voyages in Gloucester, Massachusetts, Princeton University's campus in New Jersey, and countless other places. The host, Dave Garroway, introduced the NBC show from a studio in New York City: "Today and for a lot of other Sundays, a 90-minute slice of this beautiful world of ours is yours." A poorly transmitted, by today's standards, live-cast took viewers close enough to witness Hopi Indian dances, to the deck of a speed boat, and to the middle of the Texas State Fair. The cameras also captured work—that of commercial fishermen in Gloucester, mechanical pickers in Nebraska corn fields, and steel workers in Ohio's Cayahoga Valley. From Florida, girls were televised dancing and eating bananas while submerged in the world's only underwater theater; and from the Associated Press newsroom in New York City came images of reporters hunched over teletype machines.[1] These snippets from across the nation highlight the multitudes of ways that Americans spent Sunday during the past century. Although some were at work, in common was the emphasis on relaxation, diversion, enjoyment. Contrast this with a Protestant minister's admonition more than a hundred years earlier to "spend no part of the Lord's day in seeking your own ease or pleasure."[2]

Waiting for the Sunday Boat. Photograph by William Henry Jackson (1902). Library of Congress, Prints and Photographs Division, Detroit Publishing Company Collection.

A great many fictional sketches have been written about Sunday during the twentieth century; to close *Holy Day, Holiday* I have selected two quotations from writers who find themselves ill at ease and at loose cnds on Sunday. Fitzgerald, one of the more poignant ethnographers of American leisure practices, depicts Sunday as a time out of time, a gap between two other days. Does this make it—a day without mail, work, the stock exchange—"empty air"? Or is it a time, as Fitzgerald suggests, when "individual life starts up again"? I want to agree with the latter conclusion, and commend what one essayist describing Sunday called "perfect relaxation." He fancied that it was something "that today is probably only known during a long voyage on a slow steamer. It was a state of mind in which even children found it quite pleasant to do nothing more than walk up and down the garden paths or sit under apple trees. It was the state of perfect relaxation—without even a book, a tool, or a pack of cards."[3]

We have the same amount of time today as did our ancestors one hundred, two hundred, and even two thousand years ago. How we think about time has changed, but the length of the day and night and of the week and of the seasons is the same. When we lament time starvation, we are conflating time itself (duration) with states of being and kinds of activity—working, resting, worshiping, playing—that we do not feel we have adequate control over. I have sought to tell the history of Sunday in terms of the tremendous struggles for control over time—between parents and children, employers and employees, clerics and co-religionists, politicians and citizens, and many others. That Sunday could be little more than "empty air" for some Americans suggests that several significant battles were lost along the way: not about the nation's religious vitality, but about the commercialization of everyday life.

Abbreviations

AHR	*American Historical Review*
ALLR	*American Labor Legislative Review*
AQ	*American Quarterly*
ASTS	American Sabbath Tract Society
AtMo	*Atlantic Monthly*
ATS	American Tract Society
CR	*Congressional Record*
CSP	Congregational Sunday-School and Publishing Society
GPO	Government Printing Office
JAH	*Journal of American History*
JER	*Journal of the Early Republic*
JSH	*Journal of Social History*
MBSL	Massachusetts Bureau of Statistics of Labor
NAR	*North American Review*
NRA	National Reform Association
NYSC	New York Sabbath Committee
NYT	*New York Times*
PBP	Presbyterian Board of Publications
WNSA	Women's National Sabbath Alliance

Notes

INTRODUCTION: A METHOD OF RECKONING TIME

1. Edward Bellamy, *Looking Backward* (1888; Boston: Bedford Books, 1995), 162, 173.

2. There are no published studies of Sunday in America apart from Winton Solberg's history of the Puritan Sabbath, *Redeem the Time: The Puritan Sabbath in Early America* (Cambridge: Harvard University Press, 1977). Witold Rybczynski devotes several chapters of *Waiting for the Weekend* (New York: Viking Penguin, 1991, chaps. 3–5) to the history of Sunday. Numerous dissertations and articles on various aspects of the history of the day are cited elsewhere in the notes. Primary sources available for the study of Sunday in the United States can be found almost anywhere, which made preparing this book endlessly exciting and frustrating. Almost any archive or repository of papers has pertinent materials. There is no single archive, hidden set of papers, or basic text where American Sundays are waiting for their historian. Clusters of small details support most generalizations, arguments, and summations that I make. Rather than give a source for each fragment the notes cite only direct references and quotations.

For a study such as this one, personal papers, especially journals and diaries, are invaluable. Institutional records, including the papers of Sabbatarian organizations and churches, are also useful and could be mined for much more information than this book evaluates. Newspapers, periodicals, and local histories form yet another set of indispensable resources. My archaeological approach to reconstructing Sunday is apparent in the notes, which suggest avenues for further research and provide a bibliographic guide for the great variety of topics the book takes up. In the bibliography I have arranged selected primary sources chronologically.

3. Anne W. Booth, Diary (Bancroft Library), entries dated July 4 and September 16, 1849.

4. Walter Van Loan, Diary (Bancroft Library), entry dated Sunday, February 5, 1854; James Beith, Diaries and Journals (Bancroft Library). My research for this book was facilitated by the fact that most diarists and letter writers noted not only the date but also the day in their headings. For mention of the bombing of Pearl Harbor, see Boxes 2 and 3, Frederick Wirt, interviewer, "Growing Up in the Cities: Oral History Interviews, 1977–1979" (Donated Oral History Collection, Bancroft Library). For more details about

the announcement of the bombing of Pearl Harbor on the radio on Sunday afternoon, see Ray Barfield, *Listening to Radio, 1920–1950* (Westport, Conn.: Praeger, 1996), 70–73.

5. Jane Addams, "Address on the Social Relations of Sunday Rest," in *The Sunday Problem*, ed. Alexander Jackson (New York: Baker and Taylor, 1894), 157; Mary Salome Cutler, "Sunday Opening of Libraries," *Library Journal* 14 (1889), 179.

6. W. R. Huntington, *Shall We Slur Sunday?* (New York: NYSC, 1901).

CHAPTER 1. WHAT IS A DAY OF REST?

1. Carroll D. Wright, *Sunday Labor* (Boston: Wright and Potter, 1885).

2. The early history of Sunday and the Sabbath has a vital and rich bibliography; some of the most helpful sources include: Roger T. Beckwith, *Calendar and Chronology, Jewish and Christian* (New York: E. J. Brill, 1996), 10–50; Tamara Eskenazi, ed., *The Sabbath in Jewish and Christian Tradition* (New York: Crossroads, 1991); Willy Rosdorf, *Sunday: The History of the Day of Rest and Worship in the Earliest Centuries of the Christian Church*, trans. A. A. K. Graham (Philadelphia: Westminster Press, 1968); and H. B. Porter, *The Day of Light* (Washington, D.C.: Pastoral Press, 1987, 1960), 1–13.

3. Lucy Larcom, *A New-England Girlhood* (1889; Gloucester, Mass.: Peter Smith, 1973), 51; E. A. Upton, Diary (Bancroft Library), entry dated September 22, 1849; Anne W. Booth, Diary (Bancroft Library) entries dated May 27, June 3, and June 10, 1849. My thanks to Richard R. John for pointing out an early draft's inconsistency in its usage of the terms Sunday, Sabbath, and Sunday-Sabbath.

4. Quotation from Francis White, the Anglican bishop of Ely (1635), cited in Nancy Struna, *People of Prowess* (Urbana: University of Illinois Press, 1996), 30.

5. Struna, *People of Prowess*, 29–30.

6. Studies concerning Sunday, the Sabbath, and Sabbatarianism in England include: Pallas Athene Reiss, "The Sunday Christ: Sabbatarianism in English Medieval Wall Painting" (Diss., University of Chicago, 1995); Frances Knight, *The Nineteenth-Century Church and English Society* (Cambridge: Cambridge University Press, 1995), 75–105; Kenneth L. Parker, *The English Sabbath* (Cambridge: Cambridge University Press, 1988); David S. Katz, *Sabbath and Sabbatarianism in Seventeenth-Century England* (New York: E. J. Brill, 1988); James T. Dennison, *The Market Day of the Soul* (Lanham, Md.: University Press of America, 1983), 18–44, 140; John Wigley, *The Rise and Fall of the Victorian Sunday* (Manchester: Manchester University Press, 1980); Douglas Reid, "The Decline of Saint Monday 1776–1876," *Past and Present* 71 (1976): 76–101; Christopher Hill, *Society and Puritanism in Pre-Revolutionary England* (New York: Schocken Books, 1964); George Ellis, "The Evangelical and the Sunday Question, 1830–1860" (Diss., Harvard University, 1952); W. B. Whitaker, *Sunday in Tudor and Stuart Times* (London: Houghton, 1933); and Struna, *People of Prowess*, chap. 1. Leisure and recreation in post-Reformation Europe and England can best be explored through the works of Peter Burke, *Popular Culture in Early Modern Europe* (New York: Harper and Row, 1978), and Robert W. Malcolmson, *Popular Recreations in English Society, 1700–1850* (Cambridge: Cambridge University Press, 1973).

7. Examples are from: T. H. Breen, "Horses and Gentlemen: The Cultural Significance of Gambling among the Gentry of Virginia," *William and Mary Quarterly* 34 (1977): 239–257; D. Wiggins, "Good Times on the Old Plantation: Popular Recreations of the Black Slave in the Antebellum South, 1810–1860," *Journal of Sport History* 4 (1977): 260–284; Russell Knight, "Tom Bowen's Church," *Essex Institute Historical Collections* 99 (1963): 58–63. See also Winton Solberg, *Redeem the Time: The Puritan Sabbath in Early America* (Cambridge: Harvard University Press, 1977), 301, 89–263, 292.

The literature on Puritans and the Puritan Sabbath in New England is diffuse. The most helpful sources are: Solberg, *Redeem the Time;* Charles E. Hambrick-Stowe, *The Practice of Piety* (Chapel Hill: University of North Carolina Press, 1982); Diana McCain, "Keeping Sabbath in Early Connecticut," *Early American Life* 19 (1988): 14–15, 64–66; David D. Hall, *Worlds of Wonder, Days of Judgment* (Cambridge: Harvard University Press, 1990); Bruce C. Daniels, *Puritans at Play* (New York: St. Martin's Press, 1995), especially chap. 3; and Struna, *People of Prowess,* 29–30, 59–63.

8. All quotations from Struna, *People of Prowess,* 91, 110, 168; Robert E. Cray, "Heating the Meeting: Pro-Stove and Anti-Stove Dynamic in Church Polity, 1783–1830," *Mid-America* 76 (1994): 93–107.

9. Wiggins, "Good Times on the Old Plantation"; Jerah Johnson, "New Orleans's Congo Square: An Urban Setting for Early Afro-American Culture Formation," *Louisiana History* 32 (1991): 117–157; Michael P. Smith, "New Orleans Carnival Culture from the Underside," *Plantation Society of the Americas* 3 (1990): 11–32.

10. E. A. Upton, Diary (Bancroft Library), entry dated November 11, 1849; James Beith, Journal (Bancroft Library), entry dated January 18, 1863; Hubert Howe Bancroft, Letter to wife, Matilda Bancroft, November 12, 1888, in H. H. Bancroft collection, "Letters to His Family," Box 1 (Bancroft Library).

11. Quote from Lucy Salmon, *Domestic Service* (New York: Macmillan, 1897, 1901), 146.

12. Daniel Rodgers, *The Work Ethic in Industrial America, 1850–1920* (Chicago: University of Chicago Press, 1974), chap. 7.

Studies of domestic labor are central to understanding Sunday. See especially: Harvey Green, *The Light of the Home* (New York: Pantheon, 1983), 86–91; Faye Dudden, *Serving Women* (Middletown, Conn.: Wesleyan University Press, 1983); David M. Katzman, *Seven Days a Week* (New York: Oxford University Press, 1987), 115; and Inez A. Godman, "Ten Weeks in a Kitchen," *Independent* 53 (1901): 2459–2464.

13. Report of the Bureau of Statistics of Labor (Boston: Wright and Potter, 1871), 65, 477, 598.

14. Charles L. Chalfant, "The Farmer's Sunday," in *Sunday. The World's Rest Day,* Duncan J. Miller ed. (NY: Doubleday, 1916) 403; Presbyterian Church in U.S.A., Presbytery of Utica, N.Y., *Sunday Cheese-Making* (Utica: Roberts, 1865), 6, 7, 12; Charles R. Osburn, "Sabbath Observance in the Irrigated Region," in *Sunday. The World's Rest Day,* 412; and David E. Schob, *Hired Hands and Plowboys* (Urbana University of Illinois Press, 1975), 94, 212.

15. It was almost impossible for me to estimate how many people worked on Sunday, let alone their hours, wages, conditions, and so on. Most industries and regulatory agencies did not keep track of Sunday workers, and even today the Department of Labor does not prepare indexes concerning Sunday labor. Helpful secondary works include: Betty Wood, " 'Never on Sunday?' Slavery and the Sabbath in Lowcountry Georgia, 1750–1830," in *From Chattel Slaves to Wage Slaves,* ed. Mary Turner (Bloomington: Indiana University Press, 1995); Ken Fones-Wolf, *Trade Union Gospel* (Philadelphia: Temple University Press, 1989); Ken Fones-Wolf, "Religion and Trade Union Politics in the United States, 1880–1920," *International Labor and Working Class History* 34 (1988): 39–55; James Price and Bruce Yandle, "Labor Markets and Sunday Closing Laws," *Journal of Labor Research* 8 (1987): 407–414; and David Brody, *Steelworkers in America* (Cambridge: Harvard University Press, 1960), 37–38, 94, 117.

For data and discussion about Sunday labor in primary sources, see: Wright, *Sunday Labor;* MBSL, *Annual Report for 1885* 16 (Boston, 1885), 99–101; MBSL, *Annual Report for 1899* 29 (Boston, 1899), 6–37; "Sunday Work," *American Machinist* 12 (May 30, 1889); Jesse H. Jones, "Sunday Labor," *The Chautauquan* 9 (1889): 398; *Twelfth Bi-*

ennial *Report of the Minnesota Bureau of Labor* (1909–1910); Margaret F. Byington, *Homestead* (New York: Russell Sage, 1910), 173, 176, 236; New York State Department of Labor, *Bulletins 45–49* (September 1910–December 1911); John J. Burke, "The Sunday Problem of the Toiler—'The Right to a Day of Rest'," in *Sunday. The World's Rest Day*, 440–441; NYSC, *History of the Struggle against Sunday Work in the Postal Service* (New York: NYSC, 1916); Richard T. Dana, *The Human Machine in Industry* (New York: Codex Books, 1927), 187–191; State of New York, *Second Report of the Joint Legislative Committee on Sabbath Law*, Legislative Document no. 48 (1953); *Report Submitted by the Legislative Research Council Relative to Legal Holidays and Their Observance*, Mass. Leg. Docs. No. 525 (1960); and U.S. Department of Labor Library, "Sunday Rest," Clippings File.

16. Quoted in "The Perfect Summer Sunday," *NYT*, July 7, 1996.

17. Sociologists, who introduced the term "secularization," have explored the theory extensively, the process less so. The most helpful secondary sources include: Mark Chaves, "Secularization as Declining Religious Authority," *Social Forces* 72 (1994): 749–774; José Casanova, *Public Religions in the Modern World* (Chicago: University of Chicago Press, 1994); C. Kirk Hadaway, Penny Marler, and Mark Chaves, "What the Polls Don't Show: A Close Look at U.S. Church Attendance," *American Sociological Review* 58 (1993): 741–752; Judith R. Blau, Kenneth C. Land, and Kent Redding, "The Expansion of Religious Affiliation: An Explanation of the Growth of Church Participation in the United States, 1850–1930," *Social Science Research* 21 (1992): 329–352; Oliver Tschannen, "The Secularization Paradigm: A Systematization," *Journal for the Scientific Study of Religion* 30 (1991): 395–415; Jeffrey C. Alexander and Paul Colomy, eds., *Differentiation Theory and Social Change* (New York: Columbia University Press, 1991); Daniel Bell, "The Return of the Sacred?" in Bell, *The Winding Passage* (New York: Basic Books, 1980), 324–354; and Andrew Greeley, *Unsecular Man* (New York: Schocken Books, 1972).

Other disciplines, namely history and literature, have begun to address and challenge secularization theories; James Hudnut-Beumler, *Looking for God in the Suburbs* (New Brunswick, N.J.: Rutgers University Press, 1994); Nicholas Birns, "Spirits Lingering: Christianity and Modernity in Twentieth Century American Literature" (Diss., New York University, 1992); and Mark Schantz, *Piety in Providence* Ithaca: Cornell University Press, 2000.

It is difficult to assess secularization by looking at rates of church attendance over time, partly because so much remains incomplete concerning the history of church attendance in the United States. Although numerous activities came to compete with church on Sunday, it would be almost impossible to argue that these have supplanted church. Although I did not follow through, I did find, in an essay by Jon Butler, bibliographic and methodological guidance concerning how to estimate church attendance historically: Jon Butler, "Protestant Success in the New American City, 1870–1920: The Anxious Secrets of Rev. Walter Laidlaw, Ph.D.," in *New Directions in American Religious History*, ed. Harry S. Stout and D. G. Hart (New York: Oxford University Press, 1997): 296–333.

18. George Barrell Cheever, *God's Timepiece for Man's Eternity* (New York: A. C. Armstrong and Son, 1888, 1883); H. A. Boardman, *A Plea for Sunday Afternoon* (Philadelphia: n.p., 1850), 17–18; Roger Lane, *Policing the City* (Cambridge: Harvard University Press, 1967), 127.

Recent works that seek to detail a history of shifting consciousness of time include: Mark Smith, *Mastered by the Clock* (Chapel Hill: University of North Carolina Press, 1997); Martin Bruegel, " 'Time That Can Be Relied Upon.' The Evolution of Time Consciousness in the Mid-Hudson Valley, 1760–1860," *JSH* 28 (1995): 547–564; Dennis Brailsford, *Sport, Time, and Society* (London: Routledge, 1991); Michael O'Malley,

Keeping Watch (New York: Viking, 1990); Stephen Kern, *The Culture of Time and Space, 1880–1918* (Cambridge: Harvard University Press, 1983); and David Brody, "Time and Work during Early American Industrialism," *Labor History* 30 (1989): 5–46.

19. Henry Ward Beecher, *Norwood* (1867; New York: Fords, Howard and Hulbert, 1887), 121–122.

20. On the history of the week, see: Anthony Aveni, *Empires of Time* (New York: Basic Books, 1989); Eviatar Zerubavel, *The Seven Day Circle* (Chicago: University of Chicago Press, 1985); F. H. Colson, *An Essay on the Origin and Development of the Seven-Day Cycle* (Westport, Conn.: Greenwood Press, 1974, 1926); and Hutton Webster, *Rest Days* (New York: Macmillan, 1916).

About the Protestant reformation of the religious calendar see: Ronald Hutton, *The Stations of the Sun* (New York: Oxford University Press, 1996); Maureen Perkins, *Visions of the Future* (Oxford: Clarendon Press, 1996); Ronald Hutton, *The Rise and Fall of Merry England* (New York: Oxford University Press, 1994); David Cressy, *Bonfires and Bells* (London: Weidenfeld and Nicolson, 1989); and Peter Burke, *Popular Culture in Early Modern Europe* (New York: Harper and Row, 1978), 207–243.

21. Eli N. Evans, *The Lonely Days Were Sundays* (Jackson: University Press of Mississippi, 1993).

22. About Jews and Sunday in the United States, see: Jenna Weissman Joselit, *The Wonders of America* (New York: Hill and Wang, 1994), 255–256; Naomi Cohen, *Jews in America* (New York: Oxford University Press, 1992); Susan Glenn, *Daughters of the Shtetl* (Ithaca: Cornell University Press, 1990), 139–143; Lance Sussman, "Isaac Leeser and the Protestantization of American Judaism," *American Jewish Archives* 38 (1986): 1–21; Kerry M. Olitzky, "Sundays at Chicago's Sinai Congregation: Paradigm for a Movement," *American Jewish History* 74 (1985): 356–368; Olitzky, "The Sunday-Sabbath Movement in Reform Judaism: Strategy or Evolution?" *American Jewish Archives* 34 (1982): 75–88; Ellen Sue Levi Elwell, "The Founding and Early Programs of the National Council of Jewish Women" (Diss., Indiana University, 1982); Benjamin Kline Hunnicutt, "The Jewish Sabbath Movement in the Early Twentieth Century," *American Jewish History* 69 (1979): 196–225; and Henry Gersoni, "How the Orthodox Jew Observes the Sabbath," *Independent* 47 (1895): 7.

23. About the Seventh-Day Adventist and Baptist positions on Sunday and the Sabbath, see: Paul L. Conkin, *American Originals* (Chapel Hill: University of North Carolina Press, 1997), 124–134; Siegfried Roeske, "A Comparative Study of the Sabbath Theologies of A. H. Lewis and J. N. Andrews" (Diss., Andrews University, 1997); George R. Knight, *Anticipating the Advent* (Boise, Idaho: Pacific Press, 1993); Yoshio Murakami, "Ellen G. White's Views of the Sabbath in the Historical, Religious, and Social Context of Nineteenth-Century America" (Diss., Drew University, 1994); and David M. Young, "When Adventists Became Sabbath-Keepers," *Adventist Heritage* 2 (1975): 5–10.

24. John K. Walton, "Leisure," in *Encyclopedia of Social History*, ed. Peter Stearns (New York: Garland, 1994), 413.

Recently scholars in various fields have begun to study American leisure, especially the economic, ideological, and physical choices and constraints that constitute its history. Labor historians have turned to workers' worlds outside the shop floor to better understand class formation and consciousness; social historians have followed the same route of inquiry to answer long-standing questions about race relations, gender roles, and social mobility. See: Priscilla Murolo, *The Common Ground of Womanhood* (Urbana: University of Illinois Press, 1997); Nina Mjagkij and Margaret Spratt, eds., *Men and Women Adrift* (New York: New York University Press, 1997); Struna, *People of Prowess*; Scott C. Martin, *Killing Time* (Pittsburgh: University of Pittsburgh Press, 1995); Lizabeth Cohen, *Making a New Deal* (Cambridge: Cambridge University Press, 1990); Ted

Ownby, *Subduing Satan* (Chapel Hill: University of North Carolina Press, 1990); Richard Butsch, ed., *For Fun and Profit* (Philadelphia: Temple University Press, 1990); Donna Braden, *Leisure and Entertainment in America* (Dearborn, Mich.: Henry Ford Museum and Greenfield Village, 1988); Benjamin Kline Hunnicutt, *Work without End* (Philadelphia: Temple University Press, 1988); Alex Keyssar, "Class, Ethnicity, and Leisure Time," *Radical History Review* 35 (1986): 112–117; Kathy Peiss, *Cheap Amusements* (Philadelphia: Temple University Press, 1986); Roy Rosenzweig, *Eight Hours for What We Will* (Cambridge: Cambridge University Press, 1983); Gunther Barth, *City People* (New York: Oxford University Press, 1980); and John T. Cumbler, *Working-Class Community in Industrial America* (Westport, Conn.: Greenwood Press, 1979).

25. William F. Russell, *Leisure and National Security* (Washington, D.C.: National Commission on the Enrichment of Adult Life of the National Education Association, 1933).

26. Joellen Kwiatek, "Brown Sunday," in Kwiatak, *Eleven Days before Spring* (New York: Harper and Row, 1994).

CHAPTER 2. A SERMON, THREE HUNDRED MILES LONG

1. Lewis Tappan, *Letter to Eleazer Lord, Esq.* (New York: John P. Haven, 1831), 22.
The literature on the Sunday mail controversy and antebellum Sabbatarianism is extensive. Most useful is Richard R. John, *Spreading the News* (Cambridge: Harvard University Press, 1995), 169–205, and Richard R. John, "Taking Sabbatarianism Seriously," *JER* 10 (1990): 517–567. See also: Isaac Kramnick and R. Laurence Moore, *The Godless Constitution* (New York: Knopf, 1996), 131–143; John G. West, Jr., *The Politics of Revelation and Reason* (Lawrence: University of Kansas Press, 1996), 138–170; Paul Conkin, *The Uneasy Center* (Chapel Hill: University of North Carolina Press, 1995), 116–117, 142–146; Michael J. McTighe, *A Measure of Success* (Albany: State University of New York Press, 1994), 62–65, 139–140; Robert Abzug, *Cosmos Crumbling* (New York: Oxford University Press, 1994), 105–124; Forrest L. Marion, "East Tennessee and the Sabbath Question, 1828–1832," *Journal of East Tennessee History* 66 (1994): 9–31; James Rohrer, "Sunday Mails and the Church-State Theme in Jacksonian America," *JER* 7 (1987): 54–74; Morton Borden, *Jews, Turks, and Infidels* (Chapel Hill: University of North Carolina Press, 1984), 103–129; Robert T. Handy, *A Christian America* (New York: Oxford University Press, 1984), 42–46, 73–77, 125–127, 172–174, 183–184; Lewis Perry, *Childhood, Marriage, and Reform* (Chicago: University of Chicago Press, 1980), 147–150; Paul Johnson, *A Shopkeeper's Millennium* (New York: Hill and Wang, 1978), 74–75, 83–94, 129; Bertram Wyatt-Brown, "Prelude to Abolitionism," *JAH* 58 (1971): 316–340; John L. Thomas, "Romantic Reform in America, 1815–1865," *AQ* 17 (Winter 1965): 656–681; and Oliver W. Holmes, "Sunday Travel and Sunday Mails," *New York History* 20 (1939): 413–424.

For an interpretation of the Sabbatarian movement over the course of the nineteenth century that differs slightly from the one presented, see Alexis McCrossen, "Sabbatarianism: The Intersection of Church and State in the Orchestration of Everyday Life in Nineteenth-Century America," in *Religious and Secular Reform in America*, ed. David K. Adams and Cornelis A. van Minnen (Edinburgh: Edinburgh University Press, 1999), 133–158. See also Alexis McCrossen, "Holy Day, Holiday: The Rejuvenation of the American Sunday, 1860–1930," (Diss., Harvard University, 1995); John Paul Rossing, "A Cultural History of Nineteenth Century American Sabbath Reform Movements" (Diss., Emory University, 1994); Dennis Lynn Pettibone, "Caesar's Sabbath: The Sunday-Law Controversy in the United States, 1879–1892" (Diss., University of California at Riverside, 1979); J. Thomas Jable, "Sport, Amusements, and Pennsylvania Blue Laws, 1682–1973" (Diss., Pennsylvania State University, 1974); Melvin Hyman, "Sabbatarians and the Sunday Blue Laws Controversy in New York State" (Diss., New York University, 1973); Roy Zebulon Chamlee, "Sabbath Crusade, 1810–1920" (Diss., George Washington University, 1968); Frederick Bronner, "The Observance of the Sabbath in the United States, 1800–1860" (Diss., Harvard University, 1937); and Harold S. Jacoby, "Remember the Sabbath Day?" (Diss., University of Pennsylvania, 1937).

2. John, *Spreading the News,* 170–171; *Statutes at Large* 2 (1810): 595.

3. Will C. Wood, "Historical Sketch," in *Sabbath Essays,* ed. Will C. Wood (Boston: Congregational Publishing Society, 1880), 433; John, *Spreading the News,* 172–174, 177–179. The first and second series of *Early American Imprints,* sponsored by the American Antiquarian Society, has made available numerous primary sources for the study of antebellum Sabbatarianism.

4. [Richard M. Johnson], *Report of the Committee of the Senate . . .* (Baltimore: James Lovegrove, 1829). Johnson, a senator from Kentucky, did not write this report, although his name appears on the title page; Richard R. John has established that a postal clerk named Obadiah Brown was its author. John, *Spreading the News,* 194–199.

5. Lewis Tappan, *The Life of Arthur Tappan* (New York: Hurd and Houghton, 1870), 101.

6. John, *Spreading the News,* 179–189; West, *The Politics of Revelation and Reason,* 166.

7. Lyman Beecher, "Mr. Johnson's Report on Sabbath Mails," *The Spirit of the Pilgrims* 2 (1829), 143–144; Lyman Beecher, "Pre-Eminent Importance of the Christian Sabbath," *National Preacher* 3 (1829), 155–160. Thanks to Richard R. John for sharing these and other antebellum Sabbatarian documents.

8. Wood, "Historical Sketch," 435–443.

Sabbatarian and anti-Sabbatarian convention proceedings published before the Civil War include the following: General Union for Promoting the Observance of the Christian Sabbath, *First Annual Report* (New York: J. Collord, 1829), *Second Annual Report* (New York: Sleight and Robinson, 1830), and *Third Annual Report,* (New York: J. Collord, 1831); Henry M. Parkhurst, ed., *Proceedings of the Anti-Sabbath Convention* (Boston: Andrews and Prentice Printers, 1848), reprinted as *Anti-Sabbath Convention of 1848* (Port Washington, N.Y.: Kennikat Press, 1971); Amos Augustus Phelps, *A Sketch of the Proceedings of the Convention for the Discussion of the Sabbath, the Ministry, and the Church* (New York: American Society for the Promotion of Christian Morals, 1842); *Proceedings of the Sabbath Convention, Held at the City of Rochester, July 20 and 21, 1842* (Rochester, N.Y.: W. Alling, 1842); and *Proceedings of the National Sabbath Convention Held at Saratoga Springs, August 11–13, 1863* (New York: Edward O. Jenkins, 1864).

9. Sunday-School Union, *The Child's Sabbath-Day Book* (New York: Carlton and Philips, 1854), 13.

10. Harriet Beecher Stowe [HBS], *Oldtown Folks,* vol. 1 (1869), reprinted in *The Writings of HBS,* 16 vols. (New York: AMS Press, 1967), 9:50.

11. Alexis de Tocqueville, Letter to Eugène Stoffels (June 28, 1831), reprinted in Roger Boesche, ed., *Alexis de Tocqueville: Selected Letters on Politics and Society,* trans. James Toupin and Roger Boesche (Berkeley: University of California Press, 1985), 44; Anne Boylan, *Sunday School: The Formation of an American Institution, 1790–1880* (New Haven: Yale University Press, 1988), 36.

12. Alexis de Tocqueville, Letter to Louis de Kergorlay (June 29, 1831), reprinted in *Selected Letters,* 48; John L. Thomas, *The Liberator: William Lloyd Garrison* (Boston: Little, Brown, 1963), 224–225.

13. Edmund Quincy, "History of the Church, Ministry and Sabbath Convention," *The Liberator*, March 19, 1841; "Church, Ministry, and Sabbath Convention," *The Liberator*, November 27, 1841; Dean Grodzins, "Theodore Parker and Transcendentalism" (Diss., Harvard University, 1993), 410–415. Thanks to Dean Grodzins for sharing his research concerning this early anti-Sabbatarian gathering.

14. Theodore Parker, "Some Thoughts on the Most Christian Use of the Sunday Delivered January 30, 1848," *The Liberator*, May 12, 1848; "Remarks of the Rev. Theodore Parker at the late Anti-Sabbath Convention in Boston," *The Liberator*, May 12, 1848.

15. Samuel Atkins Eliot, ed., *Heralds of a Liberal Faith: The Pilots* (Boston: Beacon Press, 1952), xxv. Among this group Eliot included several who were prominent in the movement to open Sunday to "Culture" and rational recreation, including Robert Collyer, Moncure Daniel Conway, James de Normandie, William Channing Gannett, Edward Everett Hale, Brooke Herford, and Minot Judson Savage.

16. Henry Whitney Bellows, *The Relation of Public Amusements to Public Morality: Especially of the Theatre to the High Interests of Humanity* (New York: C. S. Francis, 1857), 8; Frederick W. Sawyer, *A Plea for Amusements* (New York: Appleton, 1847); Edward Everett Hale, *Public Amusements for Poor and Rich: A Discourse* (Boston: Phillips, Sampson, 1854), 8. This paragraph is drawn from the essay by Robert Lewis, " 'Rational Recreation': Reforming Leisure in Antebellum America," in *Religious and Secular Reform in America*, 122–132. See also P. Bradley Nutting, " 'We Are Not Amused': Entertainment and Social Values in Worcester, 1780–1860," *New England Journal of History* 51 (1994): 40–48.

17. Frederick Robertson, "The Shadow and the Substance of the Sabbath," in *Sermons Preached at Trinity Chapel, Brighton*, vol. 1 (Boston: Fields, Osgood, 1869), 119, 122. Robertson delivered this sermon in 1849.

18. William Logan Fisher, *The History of the Institution of the Sabbath Day* (Philadelphia: John Penington, 1845); Charles C. Burleigh, *The Sabbath Question* (Philadelphia: Merrihew and Thompson, 1847), 26; *Proceedings of the Anti-Sabbath Convention*, 5–6; Thomas, *The Liberator*, 350.

19. Henry C. Wright, quoted in *Proceedings of the Anti-Sabbath Convention*, 78–81. Wright and the other anti-Sabbatarians' Sabbatarian peers had similar reservations about their childhood Sundays. Arthur Tappan, one of the founders of the Pioneer Line, recalled his youthful Sundays as "tedious" and "gloomy," and noted that his "parents had not acquired the art of making the Lord's day pleasant and profitable to their children" (Tappan, *The Life of Arthur Tappan*, 22–23).

20. *Proceedings of the Anti-Sabbath Convention*, 28–29, 81, 87, 93.

21. Perry, *Childhood, Marriage, and Reform*, 147–152; *Proceedings of the Anti-Sabbath Convention*, 8.

22. *Proceedings of the Anti-Sabbath Convention*, 8, 15, 12–13

23. *Proceedings of the Anti-Sabbath Convention*, 99, 144–145, 34.

24. Appendix, *Proceedings of the Anti-Sabbath Convention*, 142.

25. Robert Ingersoll, "Introduction," in Byron Sunderland and W. A. Croffut, *"The Lord's Day—or Man's?" A Public Discussion* (New York: Truth Seeker Library, 1897). See also L. K. Washburn, *Sunday and "The Sabbath"* (Boston: J. P. Mendum, 1886).

26. "The Civil Sabbath Fallacy," *Liberty* 4 (1909): 33; W. S. Ritchie, "A Vital Difference between Civil and Religious Laws," *Liberty* 28 (1933): 91–92; A. H. Lewis, *Spiritual Sabbathism* (Plainfield, N.J.: ASTS, 1910), 181; "The Papal Theory of Government," *Liberty* 2 (1907): 23.

27. Quote from Lewis, *Spiritual Sabbathism*, 60. See also A. H. Lewis, *The Swift Decadence of Sunday. What Next?* (Plainfield, N.J.: ASTS, 1899).

28. Maurice S. Logan, "The Day of the Sabbath: Origin and Starting Point of the Sabbath," in *Sunday. The World's Rest Day*, ed. Duncan J. McMillan (New York: Doubleday, 1916), 96.

29. Philip Gould, *Covenant and Republic* (Cambridge: Cambridge University Press, 1996), 5, 8, 17, 172–173.

30. Bowdoin regulations quoted in Edwin Haviland Miller, *Salem Is My Dwelling Place* (Iowa City: University of Iowa Press, 1991), 66; Agnes McNeill Donohue, *Hawthorne* (Kent, Ohio: Kent State University Press, 1985), 157. Thanks to Willard Spiegelman for pointing out the autobiographical features of Hawthorne's views concerning Sunday.

31. Nathaniel Hawthorne, "Sunday at Home" (1837), in *Twice-Told Tales*, reprinted in *The Works of Nathaniel Hawthorne*, 15 vols. (Boston: Riverside Press, 1882), 1: 32–40.

32. Joan D. Hedrick, *Harriet Beecher Stowe* (New York: Oxford University Press, 1994), 81–88; HBS, "The Sabbath: Sketches from a Note-Book of an Elderly Gentleman" [1860s], reprinted in *The Writings of HBS*, 15: 273; *Oldtown Folks, vol. 1* (1869), reprinted in *The Writings of HBS*, 9: 51–55 and 66–67.

33. HBS, "The Sabbath: Sketches from a Note-Book of an Elderly Gentleman," 273–275.

34. HBS, "Home Religion," *Household Papers and Stories* (1865), reprinted in vol. 1 of *The Writings of HBS*; "The Sabbath," in *Religious Studies, Sketches, and Poems* (1843), reprinted in vol. 15 of *The Writings of HBS*; "Laughin' in Meetin'," in *Sam Lawson's Oldtown Fireside Stories*, (1872) reprinted in vol. 10 of *The Writings of HBS*; "The Old Meeting-House" (1843), reprinted in vol. 15 of *The Writings of HBS*.

35. For examples of how the Puritan Sabbath was reimagined as beneficent, see Henry M. Brooks, *The Olden Time Series: New England Sunday*, 6 vols. (Boston: Ticknor and Co., 1886), vol. 3; D. L. Lanisors, "A Sunday in the Olden Time," *Magazine of American History* 24 (1890): 214–218; and Alice Morse Earle, *The Sabbath in Puritan New England* (New York: Charles Scribner's Sons, 1891). The reaction against Puritanism in the 1920s extended to the Puritan Sabbath; for a fine example see Gustavus Myers, *Ye Olden Blue Laws* (New York: The Century Company, 1921), 86–245.

36. Winton Solberg, *Redeem the Time: The Puritan Sabbath in Early America* (Cambridge: Harvard University Press, 1977), 281. See also David D. Hall, *Worlds of Wonder, Days of Judgment* (Cambridge: Harvard University Press, 1990), chap. 2.

37. E. A. Spooner, Diary (Kansas State Historical Society), entry dated Sunday, June 10, 1849; William Penn Abrams, Journal (Bancroft Library), entry dated March 11, 1849; E. A. Upton, Diary (Bancroft Library), entry dated January 20, 1850. During the 1950s a folklorist discovered that one of the most popular themes in Kentucky narratives and folklore was the unfortunate consequences of working on Sunday. Herbert Halpert, "The Man in the Moon in Traditional Narratives from the South," *Southern Folklore* 50 (1993): 155–170.

CHAPTER 3. FAR FROM CIVILIZED COUNTRY

1. Mary Parkhurst Warner, Diary (Bancroft Library), entries dated May 1 and 10, 1864. Epigraph from P. F. Castleman, Diary (Bancroft Library), entry dated June 10, 1849.

2. E. A. Spooner, Diary (Kansas State Historical Society), entry dated June 10, 1849.

3. Winton Solberg, "The Sabbath on the Overland Trail to California," *Church History* 59 (1990): 340–355.

4. Frederick Law Olmsted, "A Sunday in Camp," "Sunday Habits," and "The Day of Rest," in *A Journey through Texas* (New York: Dix, Edward and Co., 1857), 83–88.

5. David Hewes, letter dated October 7, 1850, in Wanson Collection (Bancroft Library).

6. For reports about the cited events see *NYT,* February 16, 17, 23, and 24, April 5, June 26, and August 14, 17, 21, 23, 24, and 28, 1852; July 1, 9, and 10, and August 4, 1866.

7. Sidney Ditzion, "Opening the Library on the Lord's Day," in *An American Library History Reader,* ed. John Marshall (Hamden, Conn.: Shoe String Press, 1961), 58; F. Allen Briggs, "The Sunday School Library," in *Reader in American Library History,* ed. Michael H. Harris (Washington, D.C.: Microcard Editions, 1971), 65–66; Doris M. Fletcher, "Read a Book and Sin No More: The Early Y.M.C.A. Libraries," in *Reader in American Library History,* 83–85; C. Howard Hopkins, *History of the Y.M.C.A. in North America* (New York: Association Press, 1951), 383.

8. Anne Boylan, *Sunday School* (New Haven: Yale University Press, 1988); Marilyn Hilley Pettit, "Women, Sunday Schools, and Politics: Early National New York City, 1797–1827" (Diss., New York University, 1991), 34, 75, 78; Brenda G. Haworth, "The Springfield [Guilford County, North Carolina] Schools: 1775–1928," *Southern Friend* 17 (1995): 32–46; Ruth C. Linton, "The Brandywine Manufacturers' Sunday School: An Adventure in Education in the Early Nineteenth Century," *Delaware History* 20 (1983): 168–184; Bettye Gardner, "Ante-Bellum Black Education in Baltimore," *Maryland Historical Magazine* 71 (1976): 360–366; and Joseph R. Rosenbloom, "Rebecca Gratz and the Jewish Sunday School Movement in Philadelphia," *Publications of the American Jewish Historical Society* 48 (1958): 71–77.

9. Amy S. Greenberg, *Cause for Alarm!* (Princeton: Princeton University Press, 1998), 34–39, 52–60, 105.

10. "Free Speech on Sunday," *The Index* 5 (1874): 212–213.

11. Stanley Nadel, *Little Germany* (Urbana.: University of Illinois Press, 1990), 104–116, 132–133; David C. Hammack, *Power and Society* (New York: Russell Sage, 1982), 138, 149–156, 260; Harlow McMillen, "Staten Island's Lager Beer Breweries, 1851–1962," *Staten Island History* 30 (1969): 15–21.

12. Charles Dawson Shanly, "Germany in New York," *AtMo* 19 (1867): 555–565; quotation from page 561.

13. For details about the riots and protests see Nadel, *Little Germany,* 105–116.

14. "The Foreign Movement on the Sunday Question," *Harper's Weekly* 3 (1859): 610.

15. Harriet Beecher Stowe, "Home Religion," *Household Papers and Stories* (1865), reprinted in vol. 1 of *The Writings of Harriet Beecher Stowe* (New York: AMS Press, 1967), 218.

The influence of immigrants on American leisure has yet to be fully explored. One path-breaking essay, by the historian David A. Gerber, traces native-born Protestant appropriation of German ethnic culture, particularly indulgence in drinking and family-centered leisure activities, in a model that may apply to Sunday observance as well: David A. Gerber, " 'The Germans Take Care of Our Celebrations': Middle-Class Americans Appropriate German Ethnic Culture in Buffalo in the 1850s," in *Hard at Play,* ed. Kathryn Grover (Amherst: University of Massachusetts Press, 1992), 39–60. See also Roy Rosenzweig and Elizabeth Blackmar, *The Park and the People* (Ithaca: Cornell University Press, 1992); S. H. Popper, "New Tensions in Old Newark: Germanic Influence and the Sabbath Observance Controversy, 1870–1910," *New Jersey Historical Society Proceedings* 70 (1952): 121–132; William Doane, " 'German-Americans' and the Lord's Day," *Forum* 20 (1895): 733–738; and Shanly, "Germany in New York."

16. "Sketches of People Who Oppose Our Sunday Laws: A Sunday Evening *Sacred Concert,*" *Harper's Weekly* 3 (1859): 642–643; "Sunday Evening in a Beer Garden," *Harper's Weekly* 3 (1859): 657–658; "The Stadt Theatre," *Harper's Weekly* 3 (1859): 673–674; "Sunday in Jones's Woods," *Harper's Weekly* 3 (1859): 701, 708; "Sunday in Chatham Street," *Harper's Weekly* 3 (1859), 754.

17. Wilbur F. Crafts, *The Sabbath for Man* (New York: Funk and Wagnalls, 1885).

18. *Through the Side-Door. By a Working-Woman* (New York: NYSC, [pre-1892]).

Brian Harrison's *Drink and the Victorians* (Pittsburgh: University of Pittsburgh Press, 1971) is indispensable to an understanding of the relationship between Sunday and drinking, Sabbatarianism, and temperance. The following are also useful: Alison M. Parker, *Purifying America* (Urbana: University of Illinois Press, 1997); David W. Conroy, *In Public Houses* (Chapel Hill: University of North Carolina Press, 1995); Susanna Barrows and Robin Rooms, eds., *Drinking Behavior and Belief in Modern History* (Berkeley: University of California Press, 1991); Robert L. Hample, *Temperance and Prohibition in Massachusetts, 1813–1852* (Ann Arbor: University of Michigan Press, 1982); Lewis A. Erenberg, *Steppin' Out* (Westport, Conn.: Greenwood Press, 1981); Elliott West, *The Saloon on the Rocky Mountain Mining Frontier* (Lincoln: University of Nebraska Press, 1979); and Joseph R. Gusfield, *Symbolic Crusade* (Urbana: University of Illinois Press, 1963).

There is still a great deal of research to do about Sunday and saloons. The primary sources are abundant, especially about efforts to close saloons on Sunday. Perry Duis, in *The Saloon* (Urbana: University of Illinois Press, 1983), details the attempts in 1855, 1872, 1907, and 1915 to shut Chicago's saloons on Sundays. About the Sunday-closing movement in Atlantic City, see Charles E. Funnell, *By the Beautiful Sea* (New York: Alfred Knopf, 1975), 103–118; and Martin Paulsson, *The Social Anxieties of Progressive Reform* (New York: New York University Press, 1994).

19. *A Plea for Sabbath in War* (New York: NYSC, 1861), 4, 5, 6.

During the Civil War, the Spanish-American War, and World War I, Americans considered questions relating to Sunday observance during war. Some of the primary sources include: *Plea for the Sabbath in War;* Philip Schaff, *The Anglo-American Sabbath* (N.p. [1863]); Wesley Carroll, *The American Sabbath as a War Day* (Cheyenne Wyo: Sunshine Press, 1899); and *The Sabbath in Army and Navy* (New York: NYSC, 1918).

20. *NYT*, September 8 and 9, 1861; Edward P. Smith, *Incidents of the United States Christian Commission* (Philadelphia: J. B. Lippincott, 1869), 61–62; "Lincoln's Sabbath Edict for Union Troops," *NYT*, November 17, 1862; Gardiner H. Shattuck, *A Shield and a Hiding Place* (Macon, Ga.: Mercer University Press, 1987), 76–77. Lincoln's edict and the incidents leading to it are recounted in *The Soldiers and Sailor's Sabbath* (New York: NYSC, 1918).

21. Quoted in *The Sabbath in Army and Navy*, 4.

22. William J. Johnstone, *Robert E. Lee* (New York: Abingdon, 1933), 94, 128.

23. My thanks to Thomas Brown who shared the quote from Dorothea Dix and provided information about the context in which she expressed such despair. Comments in author's possession.

24. Mildred Throne, ed., *The Civil War Diaries of Cyrus F. Boyd: Fifteenth Iowa Infantry, 1861–1863* (Millwood, Ky.: Kraus Reprint Co., 1977), 23–24, quoted in Shattuck, *A Shield and a Hiding Place*, 74; Robert Howard Winn, "The Diary of Thomas Harwood: A Personal Perspective of the Northern Chaplaincy during the Civil War" (Master's Thesis, Dallas Theological Seminary, 1981), 71; Johnstone, *Robert E. Lee*, 86.

25. Both quotations from Father James Sheehan, Diary, entries dated April 5 and 26, 1863, in *Confederate Chaplain*, ed. Joseph T. Durkin (Milwaukee: Bruce, 1960), 39. See also Charles F. Pitts, *Chaplains in Grey* (Nashville: Broadman, 1957), 13, 60, 303.

26. David Knapp, "The Rodney Church Incident," *Journal of Mississippi History* 32 (1970): 245–249; Sheehan, Diary entries dated August 17 and September 1, 1862, in *Confederate Chaplain*, 7, 18.

27. Letters dated March 15 and May 24, 1863, in *Confederate War Correspondence of James Michael Barr and Wife Rebecca Ann Dowling Barr*, comp. Ruth Barr McDaniel (N.p., 1963), 67–69, 94.

28. Elizabeth Waties Allston Pringle, Journal (Allston-Pringle Collection, from the Collections of the South Carolina Historical Society), entry dated March 12, 1865.

29. *The Sabbath: As It Was and As It Is*, 1, 4, 8. This and the other tracts cited can be found among the 34 documents gathered in *Documents of the NYSC, 1857–1867* (New York: Sabbath Committee Room, 1867).

30. Sabbatarian organizations formed on the local, state, and national levels. Most published tracts, reports, and other papers. The most prominent Sabbatarian organizations included: General Union for Promoting the Observance of the Christian Sabbath (f. 1828); Philadelphia Sabbath Association (f. 1840); Baltimore Sabbath Association (f. 1843); American and Foreign Sabbath Union (f. 1843); New York Sabbath Committee (f. 1857); New Jersey Sabbath Union (f. 1874); Philadelphia Sabbath Alliance (f. 1877); International Sabbath Association (f. 1878); American Sabbath Association (1888–1908); New York State Sabbath Association (f. 1890); Massachusetts Sabbath Union (f. 1891); New England Protective Sabbath League (f. 1895); Women's National Sabbath Alliance (f. 1895); and The Lord's Day Alliance (f. 1908).

31. Roy Zebulon Chamlee, "The Sabbath Crusade, 1810–1920" (Diss., George Washington University, 1968), 250–255; Louis B. Weeks, "Scriptures and Sabbath Observance in the South," *Journal of Presbyterian History* 59 (1981), 270–271; "The Catholic Sunday and Puritan Sabbath," *Catholic World* 23 (1876): 550–565.

32. William Wallace Atterbury, ed., *The Sunday Problem* (New York: Baker and Taylor, 1894); Alexander Jackson, ed. *Sunday Rest in the Twentieth Century* (Cleveland: International Federation of Sunday Rest Associations of America, 1905); Duncan J. McMillan, ed., *Sunday. The World's Rest Day* (New York: Doubleday, 1916).

33. Henry David Thoreau, *The Illustrated "A Week on the Concord and Merrimack Rivers"* (1849; Princeton: Princeton University Press, 1983), 46, 77.

CHAPTER 4. THE SABBATH FOR MAN

1. Frederick Law Olmsted, letter to Frederick John Kingsbury, April 20, 1871, reprinted in *The Papers of Frederick Law Olmsted*, vol. 6, eds. David Schuyler and Jane Turner Censer (Baltimore: Johns Hopkins University Press, 1992), 434–442. My thanks to Richard Bennett for sharing this letter and detailing a few of its opaque points of reference.

2. "The Chicago Lecture Society," *The Index* 8 (1877): 16–17; "Sunday Lectures in Cincinnati," *The Index* 12 (1881): 522–523; "Sunday Evening Lyceums," *The Index* 13 (1882): 381–382.

3. John Q. Bittinger, *A Plea for the Sabbath and for Man* (Boston: CPS, 1892), iii–iv.

4. A survey of addresses printed by various political groups, constitutions adopted by labor unions, and rallies sponsored by a range of groups reveal that many meeting were held Sunday afternoons and evenings. See, for example, John Swinton, *Storm and Stress: Address of John Swinton of New York, Held at the Social Democratic Festival, Ogden's Grove, Chicago, Sunday Afternoon, June 12, 1881* (Chicago: n.p., 1881); and Malden Co-operative Association, *Grand Lecture, National Hall, Sunday, April 19, 2:30 p.m., Six Able Speakers* (Malden, Mass.: n.p. [188–]). See also Monday and Tuesday editions of local newspapers; for instance, a mass meeting reportedly attended by more than one hundred thousand Irishmen in New York City was held on Sunday, March 4, 1866 (*NYT*, March 5, 1866).

5. Kenneth Cauthen, *The Impact of American Religious Liberalism* (Lanham, Md.: University Press of America, 1962), 27. The term "metropolitan gentry" comes from Thomas Bender, *New York Intellect* (New York: Knopf, 1987), 172–202.

Understanding the history of "uplift" in the United States and its relation to sacralization necessitates reading in a range of subfields, starting with the reform of popular culture, and then turning to specific subjects. Historians Richard W. Fox and Jean-Christophe Agnew have written persuasive essays that establish the methodological usefulness and historical context of the term "sacralization." See Richard W. Fox, "The Discipline of Amusement," in *Inventing Times Square*, ed. William R. Taylor (New York: Russell Sage, 1991); Richard W. Fox, "The Culture of Liberal Protestant Progressivism, 1875–1925," *Journal of Interdisciplinary History* 23 (1993): 639–660; and Jean-Christophe Agnew, "Times Square: Secularization and Sacralization," in *Inventing Times Square*. See also Brian Harrison, "Religion and Recreation in Nineteenth-Century England," *Past and Present* 38 (1967): 98–125.

Primary documents that flesh out sacralization and uplift include the following seminal essays: "Should Christians Play on Sunday?" *Literary Digest*, January 30, 1926, 27–28, 57–59; Washington Gladden, "Christianity and Popular Amusements," *The Century* 29 (1885): 384–392; Thomas Wentworth Higginson, "A Plea for Culture," *AtMo* 19 (1867): 29–67; and Parke Godwin, "America for the Americans," in Godwin, *Political Essays* (New York: Dix, Edwards, 1856).

6. Calvin Tomkins, *Merchants and Masterpieces* (New York: Henry Holt, 1989), 25.

The history of museums in the United States reveals a great deal about the relationship between culture and democracy; see: David R. Brigham, *Public Culture in the Early Republic* (Washington, D.C.: Smithsonian Institution Press, 1995); William T. Alderman, *Mermaids, Mummies, and Mastodons* (Washington, D.C.: American Association of Museums, 1992); Joel Orosz, *Curators and Culture* (Tuscaloosa, University of Alabama Press, 1990), 3–9, 210; Sidney Hart and David C. Ward, "The Waning of an Enlightenment Ideal: Charles Wilson Peale's Philadelphia Museum, 1790–1820," *JER* 8 (1988): 389–418; Neil Harris, "Museums, Merchandising, and Popular Taste: The Struggle for Influence," in *Material Culture and the Study of American Life*, ed. Ian Quimby (New York: W. W. Norton, 1978), 141–174; Nathaniel Burt, *Palaces for the People* (Boston: Little, Brown, 1977); Neil Harris, *Humbug: The Art of P. T. Barnum* (Boston: Little, Brown, 1973); and Loyd Haberly, "The American Museum from Baker to Barnum," *The New-York Historical Society Quarterly* 43 (1959): 272–287.

7. About institutions of culture, see: Bender, *New York Intellect*; Kathleen D. McCarthy, "Creating the American Athens: Cities, Cultural Institutions, and the Arts, 1840–1940," *AQ* 3 (1985): 426–439; Joyce Appleby, *Capitalism and a New Social Order* (New York: New York University Press, 1984); Paul DiMaggio and Michael Useem, "Cultural Democracy in a Period of Cultural Expansion: The Social Composition of Arts Audiences in the United States," in *Performers and Performances*, eds. Jack Kamerman and Rosanne Martorella (South Hadley, Mass.: Bergin and Garvey, 1983), 199–225; Neil Harris, "Cultural Institutions and American Modernization," *Journal of Library History* 16 (1981): 28–47; Ronald Story, *The Forging of an Aristocracy* (Middletown, Conn.: Wesleyan University Press, 1980); Helen Horowitz, *Culture and the City* (Lexington: University Press of Kentucky, 1976); and Neil Harris, *The Artist in American Society* (Chicago: University of Chicago Press, 1966).

8. Charles K. Whipple, "Times and Seasons," *The Radical* 2 (1866), 226–227; Whipple, "It Is a Part of the System," *The Radical* 5 (1869), 383–384; William Channing Gannett, "The Working-Man's Sunday," in *How Shall We Keep Sunday? An Answer in Four Parts*, eds. Charles K. Whipple, Minot J. Savage, Charles E. Pratt, and William C. Gannett (Boston: James H. West, 1877).

9. J. Henry Thayer, "The Jewish Sabbath and the Lord's Day," *The Independent* 47 (1895): 2–3; T. Zahn, "Sabbath and Sunday in the Primitive Church," *The Independent* 47 (1895): 3.

10. Minot Judson Savage, "Sunday in Church History," in *How Shall We Keep Sunday?*, 29–42.

11. J. B. Remensynder, "The Foundation of the Sabbath in Social Relations," in *Sunday. The World's Rest Day*, ed. Duncan J. McMillan (New York: Doubleday, 1916), 116.

12. Kerr Boyce Tupper, "Sunday's Social Foundations in the United States," in *Sunday Rest in the Twentieth Century*, ed. Alexander Jackson (Cleveland: International Federation of Sunday Rest Associations of America, 1905), 129.

13. James Freeman Clarke, "Rational Sunday Observance," *NAR* 131 (1880): 497.

14. The text from Colossians 2:16 reads in full: "Let no man therefore judge you in meat, or in drink, or in respect of an holyday, or of the new moon, or of the sabbath days."

15. John Wright Buckham, "The Sacred Day in Social Relations," in *Sunday. The World's Rest-Day*, 123. For views from the 1880s similar to Buckham's, see "Beecher on the Sabbath," *NYT*, November 21, 1881; Russell N. Bellows, "The Uses of Sunday," *New York Tribune*, June 26, 1880; and Robert Collyer, "Sermon," *NYT*, December 25, 1882.

16. "Massachusetts Sunday Laws," *The Index* 16 (1885): 415–416; Frederick May Holland, "Our Sunday Laws," *The Index* 16 (1885): 147–148; J. B. Remensynder, "The Liberal but Not a Lawless Sunday," *The Independent* 47 (1895): 11.

17. Thomas Vickers, "Sunday. Its Uses and Abuses," *The Index* 1 (1870): 5–6; "Sabbath-Breaking," *The Index* 10 (1879): 318–319.

18. Brooke Herford, "On Making the Best Use of Sunday," in *Anchors of the Soul* (London: Philip Green, 1904); J. R. Howard, "The American Sabbath," *The Outlook* 68 (1901): 638–639.

19. "The Sunday Problem," *The Outlook* 61 (1899): 580–581.

20. George U. Wenner, "Holiday or Holy Day," in *Sunday. The World's Rest Day*, 346–347.

21. Harvey D. Ganse, quoted in Robert Cox, *The Literature of the Sabbath Question in Two Volumes* (Edinburgh: MacLachan and Stewart, 1865), 2: 436–437.

22. Herford, "On Making the Best Use of Sunday," 290.

23. Higginson, "A Plea for Culture," 33.

24. Henry Van Dyke, *Holydays and Holidays* (New York: Daniel J. Holden, 1886), 3.

25. Benjamin Warfield, "The Foundation of the Sabbath in the Word of God," in *Sunday. The World's Rest Day*, 65.

26. Frederick Peake, "The Religious Basis of Lord's-Day Observance Historically Justified," in *Sunday Rest*, 171. Peake was the secretary of the Lord's-Day Observance Society (London).

27. E. H. Hughes, "Introductory Speech," in *Sunday. The World's Rest-Day*, 33.

28. Hughes, "Introductory Speech," 33–34.

29. City of Boston, "Report on the Opening of the Public Libraries on Sundays" (City Document No. 80, 1864); Boston Public Library [BPL], *13th Annual Report* (1865), 7–8, 38; City of Boston, "Objection of the Mayor to Opening the Public Library on Sundays" (City Document No. 49, 1865).

30. The newspapers from which I pieced together the progress of the hearings were: *Boston Evening Transcript [BET], Boston Daily Advertiser [BDA], Boston Herald, Boston Daily Evening Traveler, Boston Evening Voice [BEV],* and *Boston Post.* The reports were contained in the July 13, 17, 20, and 23, 1867, issues, except for *BEV*, which printed a satirical report on July 18, 1867.

31. *BDA*, July 13 and 17, 1867; City of Boston, "Report upon Opening the Reading Room of the Public Library on Sundays" (City Document No. 63, 1867), 3; M. Field Fowler, *Protest or Remonstrance of M. Field Fowler, Against Opening the Doors of the Public Library, Boston, on the Lord's Day* (Boston: Rockwell and Rollins, 1867), 5–6.

32. Charles Mayo Ellis, *Argument for Opening the Reading Rooms of the Public Library of the City of Boston on Sunday Afternoons* (Boston: A. Williams, 1867), 23. Ellis's speech was reprinted verbatim in *BET* (July 23, 1867). An edited version was published in pamphlet form that same year (and reprinted in 1872 when Sunday opening came up again).

33. *BET*, July 13, 1867; *BDA*, July 13, 1867; *BDA*, July 20, 1867.

34. "Report upon Opening the Reading Room" (City Document No. 63, 1867), 4; *16th Annual Report of the BPL*, (1868), 24; Ellis, *Argument*, 11–12. See also *15th–28th Annual Reports of the BPL* for discussions about being, or trying to avoid being, "a class institution."

35. The "assignation" quote was in the *Boston Herald*, July 13, 1867; other papers reported the comment in varying degrees of explicitness, culminating with the July 23 issue of the *Voice*, which claimed that it was predicted that courtesans would frequent the reading room. See also *BET*, July 13, 1867; *BDA*, July 13, 1867; *BDA*, July 17, 1867. It is no coincidence that during the 1870s and 1880s library trustees agonized over the propriety of acquiring and circulating fiction, associated at that time with popular culture and lowbrow pursuits. For an example of the debate over fiction in the public library see *29th Annual Report of the Boston Public Library* (1881), 20.

36. Testimony reprinted in *BDA*, July 12, 1867; "Report upon Opening the Reading Room" (City Document No. 63, 1867), 4.

37. City of Boston, "Report on Opening the Reading Rooms of the Public Library on Sundays" (City Document No. 75, 1867).

38. City of Boston, "Report of the Committee on the Opening of the Public Library on Sundays" (City Document No. 97, 1870), 4–5; City of Boston, "Mayor's Message, Giving His Reasons for Not Approving the Order Concerning the Opening of the Boston Public Library on Sunday" (City Document No. 69, 1872), 3.

39. Symposium on Sunday Opening, *Washington Post*, June 25, 1883; Samuel S. Green, "Opening Libraries on Sunday," *Library Journal* 9 (1884): 84–86.

The following sources are useful for thinking about the history of libraries and cultural diffusion: Abigail A. Van Slyck, *Free to All* (Chicago: University of Chicago Press, 1995); Deanna B. Marcum, "The Rural Public Library in America at the Turn of the Century," *Libraries and Culture* 26 (1991): 87–99; Curtis Miner, "The Deserted Parthenon: Class, Culture, and the Carnegie Library of Homestead, 1898–1937," *Pennsylvania History* 57 (1990): 107–135; and Dee Garrison, *Apostles of Culture* (New York: Free Press, 1979).

40. *BET*, February 10, 1873; *21st Annual Report of the BPL* (1873), 8–20; *Bulletin of the BPL* 27 (September 1873): 184.

41. *22nd Annual Report of the BPL* (1874), 10; Cincinnati Public Library, *4th Annual Report* (1871), 17; Cincinnati Public Library, *5th Annual Report* (1872), 25. For a description of a woman entering the Boston Public Library on its first open Sunday see *BET*, February 10, 1873.

42. Most annual reports specify when the library opened on Sunday, and many go into much greater detail. The conclusions expressed in this chapter are based on analysis of annual reports from the public libraries in Boston, Buffalo, Chicago, Cincinnati, Cleveland, Jacksonville (Florida), Los Angeles, Louisville, New Orleans, New York, Philadelphia, Portland (Oregon), St. Paul (Minnesota), San Francisco, and Worcester (Massachusetts).

43. Mary Salome Cutler, "Sunday Opening of Libraries," *Library Journal* 14 (1889), 178–179.

44. Cincinnati Public Library, *Annual Report for the Year Ending July 1, 1896*, 13; Mary Salome Cutler, "Sunday Opening of Libraries," in *Education Reports, 1892–1893* (H.R. Exec. Doc. 1, 53rd Cong., 2d sess., 1894).

45. *22nd Annual Report of the BPL* (1874), 25; *45th Annual Report* (1897), 38; *50th Annual Report* (1902), 24; *46th Annual Report* (1898), 40; *58th Annual Report* (1910), 68; *61st Annual Report* (1913), 56; *66th Annual Report* (1918), 16–17; *77th Annual Report* (1928), 37.

46. Wilbur F. Crafts is quoted in *Library Journal* 32 (1907), 112–113.

CHAPTER 5. OPENING UP SUNDAY

1. "Against Sunday Opening," *NYT,* May 16, 1893; "Not This Sunday, Some Other," *NYT,* May 20, 1893.

2. "The Art Museum to Be Opened Sunday Afternoon," *The Index* 8 (1877): 55–56.

3. "It Was a Grand Success," *NYT,* June 1, 1891.

4. The MFA opened on July 4, 1876; on March 1, 1877, it began Sunday hours. The "Central Park museums" share a similar history concerning Sunday opening, with the American Museum of Natural History opening on Sundays a year after the Met. Walter Muir Whitehill, *Museum of Fine Arts, Boston* (Cambridge: Belknap Press, 1970), 40; Calvin Tomkins, *Merchants and Masterpieces* (1970; New York: Holt, 1989), 59, 75.

5. *NYT,* September 3, 1859.

6. Winifred E. Howe, *A History of the Metropolitan Museum of Art* (New York: n.p., 1913), 239.

7. See *NYT,* March 10, 1886, and March 20 and May 6, 18, and 19, 1891, for reprints of Sunday-opening petitions that circulated throughout the 1880s and into the 1890s.

8. Charles K. Eaton, "The Ideal Sunday," *NAR* 153 (1891), 327–328; Henry Clews quoted in *NYT,* November 22, 1885; Letter reprinted in *NYT,* April 5, 1885. The Sunday-opening advocate Edward Everett Hale gathered letters, testimonials, and articles concerning the salubrious effect of European Sundays in a scrapbook titled "Sundays in Europe" (held by the Bostonian Society). Henry Ward Beecher, *Libraries and Public Reading Rooms: Should They Be Opened on Sunday?* (New York: J.B. Ford, 1872).

9. *NYT,* April 10, 1881; Carlos Martyn, *The American Sunday, the Museums and Libraries, the Public Press, and the Half-Saturday Holiday* (New York: Martin B. Brown, 1886), 5–8, 19; *22nd Annual Report of the Metropolitan Museum of Art* (1891), 501. About efforts similar to those of New York's metropolitan gentry, including a group that called themselves the "Sunday Society," to open museums on Sunday in England, see Diana Frances Maltz, "Lessons in Sensuous Discontent: The Aesthetic Mission to the British Working Classes, 1869–1914" (Diss., Stanford University, 1997).

10. Howe, *History of the Metropolitan,* 236, 238–240; Tomkins, *Merchants and Masterpieces,* 45.

11. *NYT,* April 10, 1881, and April 26, 1885.

12. *NYT,* January 6, 1889.

13. *NYT,* November 18, 1885.

14. Harry Miller Lydenberg, *History of the New York Public Library* (New York: New York Public Library, 1923), 121–122, 337.

15. *NYT,* April 5 and December 15, 1885; February 24, March 2, 3, and 5, 1889.

16. *NYT,* February 25, 1889.

17. *NYT,* January 6, 1889, May 7, 1881, December 9 and 17, 1888.

18. *NYT,* April 19, 1891.

19. *NYT,* January 17, 1886; Eaton, "The Ideal Sunday," 327.

20. Morris K. Jesup, *Sunday Opening of the Museums in the Park* (New York: n.p., [1885]), 5–6; Henry C. Potter, "The Sunday Question," *New Princeton Review* 2 (1886): 41.

21. *NYT,* November 18, 1885.

22. Howe, *History of the Metropolitan,* 243–244.

23. *NYT,* May 24 and June 1, 1891; Howe, *History of the Metropolitan,* 244; *22nd Annual Report of the Metropolitan Museum of Art* (1891), 501.

24. *NYT,* June 8, 1891; Metropolitan Museum's 22nd, 23rd, 24th, and 25th *Annual Reports* (1891–1895).

25. *NYT,* January 20, 1885.

Robert Rydell's *All the World's a Fair* (Chicago: University of Chicago Press, 1984) provides a context for understanding the depth of the passion over opening the expositions on Sunday. See also: Merle Davis, "Sundays at the Fair: Iowa and the Sunday Closing of the 1893 World's Columbian Exposition," *The Palimpset* 74 (1993): 156–159; Benedict Burton, *The Anthropology of World's Fairs* (Berkeley, Calif.: Scolar Press, 1983); Reid Badger, *The Great American Fair* (Chicago: Nelson Hall, 1979); David Burg, *Chicago's White City of 1893* (Lexington: University of Kentucky Press, 1976); and Merle Curti, "America at the World's Fairs, 1851–1893," *AHR* 55 (1950): 833–856.

26. *NYT,* January 20, 1885; *New York Tribune,* April 29, May 1, 8, and 15, and July 8, 1876.

27. *NYT,* July 12, 1892, and May 8, 1893.

28. The roster of those against Sunday opening can be compiled by looking through the *New York Times* between 1891 and 1893. *NYT,* September 2, and October 15 and 16, 1892, May 23 and 30, and June 19, 1893. For reports about extradenominational resistance against Sunday opening see *NYT,* March 7, July 8 and 10, and October 21, 1892, May 14, 16, 17, 20, 22, 23, and 30, June 6, and July 16, 1893.

29. "Several Miles of Petitions," *NYT,* May 3, 1892.

30. *NYT,* May 27, July 10, 12, 14, and 15, and August 7, 1892.

31. *NYT,* May 14, September 13, October 25 and 26, and December 4, 1892, February 27, May 22, and June 4, 1893; *Chicago Tribune,* May 29, 1893; *Washington Post,* May 30, 1893; *New Orleans Times-Picayune,* May 29, 1893; *Detroit News,* May 29, 1893; *St. Louis Dispatch,* May 29, 1893; *Atlanta Constitution,* May 29, 1893.

32. Henry C. Potter, "Sunday and the World's Fair," *Forum* 14 (1892): 194–200; Henry C. Potter, "Some Exposition Uses of Sunday," *Century* 23 (1892): 138–141. For Potter's expression of opposition to Sunday opening see his, "The Sunday Question."

33. J. L. Spalding, "Why the World's Fair Should Be Opened on Sunday," *The Arena* 7 (1892): 47; O. P. Gifford, "Why the World's Fair Should Be Opened on Sunday," *The Arena* 7 (1893): 193–196; James Gorton, *The Sabbath Question and the World's Fair* (Akron, Ohio: Capron and Curtice, 1892), 196; *NYT,* July 14, 1892; "Jesus, the Church, and the World's Fair," *The Arena* 6 (1892): 255, 257.

34. Most of the nation's papers covered the two Sundays the fair was closed in Chicago. For thorough accounts see *NYT,* May 8 and 22, 1893.

35. *NYT,* December 20, 1892, *NYT,* May 14, 17, 21, 24, 26, 28, 29, and 30, June 1, 2, 3, 9, 11, and 17, July 15, 23, and 29, and August 4 and 7 1893. The legal aspects of this controversy are recounted in Edwin Walker, *The Litigation of the Exposition* (Chicago: Bench and Bar of Chicago, 1894).

On December 20, 1892, a businessman who owned stock in the fair had applied for an injunction restraining the fair directors from closing the gates on Sundays. He had based his application on the fact that Jackson Park was public property, and therefore citizens had the right to visit any day of the year. This was not followed up on; presumably the injunction was not filed. After the fair had opened, Charles W. Clingman, a stockholder in the exposition, filed a bill in superior court "praying for an injunction restraining the directors from opening the gates on Sunday." The defendants, in favor of Sunday opening, claimed that Clingman bought his stock before Congress closed the fair on Sundays, that the fair was held on public lands, and that Sunday closing violated the Constitution.

36. *St. Louis Dispatch,* May 29, 1893.

37. See the May 29, 1893, issues of *NYT, Chicago Tribune, Washington Post, New Orleans Times-Picayune, Detroit News, St. Louis Dispatch,* and *Atlanta Constitution* for reports about Sunday at the fair; Harlow N. Higinbotham, *Report of the President to the Board of Directors of the World's Columbian Exposition: Chicago 1892–1893* (Chicago: Rand, McNally, 1898), 239.

38. Some papers carried what appear to be reports lifted from the *Chicago Tribune,* such as the *St. Louis Dispatch.* Other observers recounted similar versions of the story. Higinbotham wrote in his report: "On the first Sunday some of the more enthusiastic patrons emphasized their position on the Sunday question in a very happy manner. The band concert was opened with the music of the hymn 'Nearer, My God, to Thee,' and those in the vicinity caught up the air and sang the hymn" (*Report of the President,* 241).

39. *NYT,* July 24, 1893; *Pan-American Exposition. Some Reasons Why It Should Open on Sundays* (Chicago: Office of the Secretary of American Secular Union and Freethought Federation, 1901), 1–2.

40. Higinbotham, *Report of the President,* 239–243.

The first Sunday the fair was open (May 28, 1893) the paid attendance was 77,212. Attendance on the next three Sundays was between 56,000 and 71,000. Higinbotham reported that Sunday attendance grew smaller and smaller, averaging about 48,000 a Sunday. The last four Sundays of the fair, however, the attendance ranged between 82,000 and 150,000.

41. Letter reprinted in *Pan-American Exposition,* 15; Duncan J. McMillan, ed., *Sunday. The World's Rest Day* (New York: Doubleday, 1916); Bruce J. Evensen, " 'Saving the City's Reputation': Philadelphia's Struggle over Self-Identity, Sabbath-Breaking and Boxing in America's Sesquicentennial Year," *Pennsylvania History* 60 (1993): 6–34.

42. "Gates Open at 11," *NYT,* April 29 and 30, May 1, and July 24, 1939. Incidentally the telecast was a first for a president of the United States.

CHAPTER 6. THE SUNDAY DRIVE

1. Epigraph from William Nast Brodbeck, *The Sunday Bicycle* (New York: Eaton & Mains, 1897), 6. Controversies had erupted in the colonial period when the distance to the local church came to be too great for the settlers living further from the town center than the community's founders. Their wish either to establish their own church or to cease paying church taxes (or both) divided community after community, but these controversies had less to do with traveling on Sunday than with local politics.

2. Oliver Pilat and Jo Ransom, *Sodom by the Sea* (New York: Doubleday, 1941), 17; Norman L. Dunham, "The Bicycle Era in American History" (Diss., Harvard University, 1956), 24–25.

3. John F. Stover, *American Railroads,* 2d ed. (1961; Chicago: University of Chicago Press, 1997), 44, 117–118; *NYT,* August 27, 1852. Starting in 1837 the New York, Providence and Boston Railroad ran one train each Sunday from New York, but it served business travelers rather than day trippers: Franz Anton Ritter von Gerstner, *Early American Railroads,* trans. David J. Diephouse and John C. Decks (1842–1843; Palo Alto: Stanford University Press, 1997), 335.

4. Quote from Carroll D. Wright, *Sunday Labor* (Boston: Wright & Potter, 1885), 45. The history of Sunday streetcars, railroads, and steamships can be found in the archival records of transport companies, especially in the extensive railroad archives found

throughout the nation. I did not do such research, and relied instead on newspapers, periodicals, train schedules, law books, and convention proceedings. Railroad schedules can be found in newspapers from the 1830s, 1840s, and 1850s. During the 1850s travel guides began to publish schedules, but it was not until after the Civil War that a consistent railway guide was published on a monthly basis. This publication, *Travelers' Official Railway Guide*, can be found in the Library of Congress, which holds a run beginning in 1869. See also: von Gerstner, *Early American Railroads; The First Sabbath Excursion, and Its Consequences* (Philadelphia: Presbyterian Board of Publication and Sabbath-School Work, 1856); Edward O. Jenkins, *Railroads and the Sabbath* (New York: NYSC, 1858); Jenkins, *Sunday Railroad Work* (New York: NYSC, 1868); Wright, *Sunday Labor*, 5–24; Harold E. Cox, " 'Daily Except Sunday': Blue Laws and the Operation of Philadelphia Horsecars," *Business History Review* 39 (1965): 228–242; Scott R. Johnson, "The Trolley Car as a Social Factor: Springfield, Massachusetts," *History Journal of Western Massachusetts* 1 (1972): 5–17; and Sarah H. Gordon, *Passage to Union* (Chicago: Ivan R. Dee, 1996).

5. Blanche Linden-Ward, *Silent City on a Hill* (Columbus: Ohio State University Press, 1989), 209, 307–313; Roy Rosenzweig and Elizabeth Blackmar, *The Park and the People* (Ithaca: Cornell University Press, 1992), 254–256.

6. "Sunday Excursions. How the People Go to Harlem and High Bridge—Interesting Scenes on the Route—The Steamers and Other Matters," *NYT*, August 28, 1877.

7. Quoted in Charles E. Funnell, *By the Beautiful Sea* (New York: Knopf, 1975), 14. See also 4–14.

8. W. E. Knox, *Our Sabbaths and Our Morals* (Elmira, N.Y.: Horace A. Brooks, 1873).

9. Vermont railroad order mentioned in Stover, *American Railroads*, 117. Meeting to abolish Sunday traffic reported in *Railway and Engineering Review*, October 22, 1904, 762. See also: Thomas Mellon, *To the Rev. Wm. H. Vincent, Messrs. Jacob Yealey, Wm. Hicks, and Others. Petitioners for the Stoppage of the Sunday Train on the Ligonier Valley Rail Road* (Ligonier, Pa.: Ligonier Valley R.R. Co.'s Office, 1880); and William H. Vincent, *Sunday Trains Demoralizing and Contrary to Laws of God and Man* (Pittsburgh: Nevin Bros., 1880).

10. Stover, *American Railroads*, 44, 118; "Rioters in an Excursion," *NYT*, July 3, 1882.

11. Wright, *Sunday Labor*, 14–24. See also S. G. Buckingham, *The Sabbath and Rail Roads* (Springfield, Mass.: Clark W. Bryan, 1872).

12. Rosenzweig and Blackmar, *The Park and the People*, 309–310 and 384–385; John S. Gilkeson, "The Rise and Decline of the 'Puritan Sunday,' in Providence, Rhode Island, 1810–1926," *New England Quarterly* 54 (1986), 80.

13. For articles and notices about Starin's Glen Island see *NYT*, July 3 and 10, August 21, and September 18, 1882; July 7 and August 4, 1890.

14. Bill Brown, *The Material Unconscious* (Cambridge: Harvard University Press, 1996), 4, 13. See also Michael Oriard, *Sporting with the Gods* (New York: Cambridge University Press, 1991).

15. Jenkins, *Railroads and the Sabbath*, 11.

16. Mitchell was quoted in "The Sabbath: How the Day Was Spent by Various Classes of People," *NYT*, August 7, 1871.

17. Harris, *A Treatise on Sunday Laws*, 185, 188, 193–199. The case concerning the drowned man is *Opsahl v. Judd*, 30 Minn. 126. Tourism, vacations, and resorts provide other contexts for understanding the history of Sunday. See: William Irwin, *The New Niagara* (University Park: Pennsylvania State University Press, 1996) and John F. Sears, *Sacred Places* (New York: Oxford University Press, 1989).

18. Funnell, *By the Beautiful Sea*, 76–83.

19. Glenn Uminowicz, "Recreation in Christian America: Ocean Grove and Asbury Park, New Jersey, 1869–1914," in *Hard at Play*, ed. Kathryn Grover (Amherst: Univer-

sity of Massachusetts Press, 1992), 29–35. Brown addresses the relationship between Stephen Crane, Asbury Park, and Ocean Grove in *The Material Unconscious,* chap. 2.

20. NYT, August 6 and 8 1897; August 22, 1898; Dorothy Daniels Birk, *The World Came to St. Louis* (St. Louis: Bethany Press, 1979). About visits to soliders' homes, see Patrick J. Kelly, *Creating a National Home* (Cambridge: Harvard University Press, 1997), 169–172, 183–191.

21. "Queries and Answers," *The Bicycle World,* March 20, 1880, 152; D. W. Barker, "Is It Right to Ride on the Sabbath?", *The Bicycle World,* October 25, 1889, 690; Frances E. Willard, *A Wheel within a Wheel: How I Learned to Ride the Bicycle* (1895; Sunnyvale, Calif.: Fair Oaks, 1991); J. R. Wilson Jr., "Is It Right to Ride on the Sabbath?", *The Bicycle World,* November 8, 1889, 35. See also Robert A. Smith, *A Social History of the Bicycle* (New York: American Heritage Press, 1972); Richard Harmond, "Progress and Flight: An Interpretation of the American Cycle Craze of the 1890s," *JSH* 5 (1971–1972): 235–257; and Dunham, "The Bicycle Era in American History." In addition to city newspapers, firsthand reports about Sunday rides can be found in *The Bicycle World* and *The Wheel.*

22. *The Bicycle World,* July 15, 1881, 113–114.

23. Donald L. Miller, *City of the Century* (New York: Simon and Schuster, 1996), 297.

24. "Mission of the Bicycle," *Wheel and Cycling Trade Review,* May 5, 1893, 30, cited in Harmond, "Progress and Flight," 247.

25. Brodbeck, *The Sunday Bicycle,* 7; Edward Everett Hale, "The Sunday Laws," in Hale, *June to May: Sermons of a Year Preached at the South Congregational Church in Boston, in 1880 and 1881* (Boston: Roberts Brothers, 1881).

26. United Lutheran Church in America Committee on Moral and Social Welfare, *The Sunday Problem: A Study Book for Groups and Individuals* (Philadelphia: The United Lutheran Publication House, 1923), 48–49; Robert Lynd and Helen Lynd, *Middletown* (New York: Harcourt, Brace, 1929), 259; *Watchman-Examiner* 10 (1922): 519, cited in Michael L. Berger, *The Devil Wagon in God's Country* (Hamden, Conn.: Archon Books, 1979), 136.

27. Lester Evans, "Should a Christian Drive His Car on Sunday?—Pulpit Editorial," *The Homiletic Review* 91 (1926), 206.

The history of the Sunday drive is part of the larger social and cultural history of the automobile, which can be explored in the following sources: Michael L. Berger, "The Car's Impact on the American Family," in *The Car and the City,* eds. Martin Wachs and Margaret Crawford (Ann Arbor: University of Michigan Press, 1992), 14; Renold M. Wik, "The Early American Auto and the American Farmer," in *The Auto and American Culture,* eds. David L. Lewis and Laurence Goldstein (1980; Ann Arbor: University of Michigan Press, 1983), 47; Berger, *The Devil Wagon,* 114, 133–135; and Norman T. Moline, *Mobility and the Small Town, 1900–1930* (Chicago: University of Chicago, Department of Geography, Research Paper No. 132, 1971), 53, 95, 97, 101.

28. See volume 126 (1924) of *The Annals of the American Academy of Political and Social Science,* which concerns the impact of the automobile on religion.

CHAPTER 7. PUTTING THE DOLLAR MARK ON IT

1. After the Civil War, the literature on Sunday laws multiplied, along with the laws themselves. Primary sources on Sunday laws are abundant, and include: D. W. Bond, *The Power of the Legislature to Enact Sunday Laws* (Northampton, Mass.: Metcalf and Company, 1870); Will C. Wood, *Five Problems of State and Religion* (Boston: H. Hoyt, 1877); Edward E. Hale, *The Sunday Laws* (Boston: George H. Ellis, 1880); Henry E. Young, "Sunday Laws," in *Report of the Third Annual Meeting of the American Bar*

Association (Philadelphia: E. C. Markley and Sons, 1880): 109–147; Leonard Woolsey Bacon, *The Sabbath Question* (New York: G. P. Putnam's Sons, 1882); William Addison Blakey, ed., *American State Papers Bearing on Sunday Legislation* (New York: National Religious Liberty Association, 1891); George E. Harris, *A Treatise on Sunday Laws* (Rochester, N.Y.: The Lawyers' Co-operative, 1892); *A Compilation of the Labor Laws of the Various States and Territories and the District of Columbia* (Washington, D.C.: G.P.O., 1892); and *Second Special Report of the Commissioner of Labor. Labor Laws of the United States* (Washington, D.C.: G.P.O., 1896).

The history of Sunday laws in the United States has yet to be synthesized. The number of local, state, and federal cases concerning violation of Sunday laws is mind-boggling. The best starting—and possibly ending—point is *McGowan v. Maryland*, 366 U.S. 420 (1961). The following are helpful secondary sources: Peter Wallenstein, "Never on Sunday: Blue Laws and Roanoke, Virginia," *Virginia Cavalcade* 43 (1994): 132–143; Barbara J. Redman, "Sabbatarian Accommodation in the Supreme Court," *Journal of Church and State* 33 (1991): 495–523; David N. Laband and Deborah H. Heinbuch, *Blue Laws* (Lexington, Mass.: Lexington Books, 1987); James Kushner, "Toward the Central Meaning of Religious Liberty: Non-Sunday Sabbatarians and Sunday Closing Cases Revisited," *Southwestern Law Journal* 35 (1981): 557–584; Michael Bologna, "A Critical History of Connecticut Sunday Closing Legislation since 1955," *Connecticut Law Review* 12 (1980): 539–570; Charles Vincent, "Lousiana's Black Legislators and Their Efforts to Pass a Blue Law during Reconstruction," *Journal of Black Studies* 7 (1976): 47–56; William G. Harper, *The Texas Blue Laws* (Hicksville, N.Y.: Exposition Press, 1974); Arnold Roth, "Sunday 'Blue Laws' and the California State Supreme Court," *Southern California Quarterly* 55 (1973): 43–47; Jerome A. Barron, "Sunday in North America," *Harvard Law Review* 79 (1965): 42–54; J. E. Erickson and James McCrocklin, "From Religion to Commerce: The Evolution and Enforcement of Blue Laws in Texas," *Southwestern Social Science Quarterly* 45 (1964): 50–58; and Candida Lund, "The Sunday Closing Laws and the Law" (Diss., University of Chicago, 1963).

2. About amusements in general see Foster Rhea Dulles, *America Learns to Play* (New York: Appleton-Century, 1940). Concerning amusement parks see Robert Cartmell, *The Incredible Scream Machine* (Bowling Green, Ohio: Bowling Green State University Press, 1987); John Kasson *Amusing the Million* (New York: Hill and Wang, 1978); and William F. Mangels, *The Outdoor Amusement Industry* (New York: Vantage Press, 1952).

Dating and measuring participation in public recreation and amusements are difficult, but several historians have studied the working classes' patronization of commercial amusements; see Kathy Peiss, *Cheap Amusements* (Philadelphia: Temple University Press, 1986), 34–55, 115–138; and Roy Rosenzweig, *Eight Hours for What We Will* (Cambridge: Cambridge University Press, 1983), 171–207.

Recently historians have begun to consider the intersection of religion, leisure, and the consumer culture; see: Lynne Mark, *Revivals and Roller Rinks* (Toronto: University of Toronto Press, 1996); Leigh Eric Schmidt, *Consumer Rites* (Princeton: Princeton University Press, 1995); R. Laurence Moore, *Selling God* (New York: Oxford University Press, 1994); William Taylor, ed., *Inventing Times Square* (New York: Russell Sage Foundation, 1991); Susan Curtis, *A Consuming Faith* (Baltimore: Johns Hopkins University Press, 1991); Andrew Heinze, *Adapting to Abundance* (New York: Columbia University Press, 1990); and Richard W. Fox and T. Jackson Lears, eds., *The Culture of Consumption* (New York: Pantheon, 1983).

Celebrations, holidays, and festivals have become topics of historical inquiry during the 1980s and 1990s. The theoretical literature on commemoration is extensive; see especially Paul Connerton, *How Societies Remember* (New York: Cambridge University

Press, 1989). Pertaining to the American context, see: David Waldstreicher, *In the Midst of Perpetual Fetes* (Chapel Hill: University of North Carolina Press, 1997); Stephen Nissenbaum, *The Battle for Christmas* (New York: Knopf, 1997); and Len Travers, *Celebrating the Fourth* (Amherst: University of Massachusetts Press, 1997).

3. Jay Stewart Bergman, "Theodore Roosevelt as Police Commissioner of New York" (Diss., Rutgers University, 1985); Jeffry Wert, "Theodore Roosevelt: Patron Saint of Dry Sundays," *American History Illustrated* 17 (1982): 30–35; Charles E. Funnell, *By the Beautiful Sea* (New York: Knopf, 1975), 103–118; Perry Duis, *The Saloon* (Urbana: University of Illinois Press, 1983), 233–234, 282, 286–287. For background concerning the conflict over closing Chicago's saloons, see Maureen A. Flanagan, "The Ethnic Entry into Chicago Politics: The United Societies for Local Self-Government and the Reform Charter of 1907," *Journal of the Illinois State Historical Society* 75 (1982): 2–14.

4. Kasson, *Amusing the Million*, 3–9, 41, 50.

5. *NYT*, April 10, 1852; New York State Library, "Compilation of the Laws," 20, 44; Edwin M. Gagey, *The San Francisco Stage* (New York: Columbia University Press, 1950), 100; "Light Blue Sunday Laws," *Public Opinion* 40 (1906): 406.

There are no secondary sources that directly address theater on Sunday. To understand Sunday and the theater, it is best to start with general histories of theater and theater-going in the United States, and then turn to local histories of theater, which are abundant, especially for the nineteenth century. Several reference sources have been helpful to me. See Bruce A. McConachie, *Melodramatic Formations* (Iowa City: Iowa State University Press, 1992); Rosemarie K. Bank, *Theatre Culture in America, 1825–1860* (New York: Cambridge University Press, 1997); Judith L. Fisher and Stephen Watt, eds., *When They Weren't Doing Shakespeare* (Athens: University of Georgia Press, 1989); Lawrence W. Levine, *Highbrow/Lowbrow* (Cambridge: Harvard University Press, 1988); Walter J. Meserve, *Heralds of Promise* (New York: Greenwood Press, 1986), and especially Milton Epstein, *The New York Hippodrome: A Complete Chronology of Performances from 1905 to 1939* (New York: Theatre Library Association, 1993). Epstein's chronology includes the names of the performers, the titles of the pieces performed, the organizations that sponsored events, and the days of the week and dates of each performance, as well as other relevant information.

6. "Light Blue Sunday Laws," 406; *NYT*, July 5, 13, and 14, and August 4, 1890.

7. *NYT*, January 27, 1895; advertisement in *Missouri Republican*, November 18, 1883; Playbill, Wallace's Comedy Theatre (Chicago), January 13, 1890; Foster Coates, "Popular Amusements in New York," *The Chautauquan* 24 (1897): 708.

8. "Light Blue Sunday Laws," 406; *Public Shows on Sunday Whether Admission Is Charged or Not Violate the Law and Judicial Decisions* (New York: Interdenominational Committee of Clergy of Greater New York for the Suppression of Sunday Vaudeville, [1907]); *Report of the Committee of Ladies Regarding the Closing of Theaters on Sunday* (St. Paul, Minn.: William L. Banning, 1891).

9. Jane Elder, "Interstate Theatres, Vaudeville, and Sunday Laws in Dallas," *Legacies* 10 (1998). Thanks to Jane Elder for sharing this article with me when it was still in draft form.

10. Boston District Police, *Law Relative to the Observance of the Lord's Day* (Boston: Wright and Potter, 1915); Boston District Police, *Law Relative to the Observance of the Lord's Day* (Boston: Wright and Potter, 1916); New York State Library, "Compilation of the Laws," 9–10. See also Daniel Czitrom, "The Politics of Performance: From Theater Licensing to Movie Censorship in Turn-of-the-Century New York," *AQ* 44 (1992): 525–553.

There are several excellent local histories about screening movies on Sunday; see: Donald Schneider, "The Controversy over Sunday Movies in Hastings, 1913–1929," *Nebraska History* 69 (1988): 60–72; Joe E. Smith, "Early Movies and Their Impact on Columbia," *Missouri Historical Review* 74 (1979): 72–85; and Orville Zabel, *God and Caesar in Nebraska* (Lincoln: University of Nebraska Press, 1955), 66–84.

11. Christian Reisner, "Special Sunday Night Attractions," in W. B. Ashley, compiler, *Church Advertising: Its Why and How* (Philadelphia: J. B. Lippincott, 1917), 53–70.

12. New York State Library, "Compilation of Laws," 15, 22, 23, 44, 48, 53.

13. *Bulletin of the NYSC* 4 (February–March 1917): 5–15; Roy Zebulon Chamlee, "The Sabbath Crusade, 1810-1920" (Diss., George Washington University, 1968) 347–348.

14. John S. Gilkeson, "Rise and Decline of the 'Puritan Sunday' in Providence, Rhode Island, 1810–1926," *New England Quarterly* 54 (1986), 89–90; Forrest L. Marion, "Blue Laws, Knoxville, and the Second World War," *Journal of East Tennessee History* 68 (1996): 41–62.

15. Schneider, "The Controversy over Sunday Movies in Hastings," 62, 69.

16. Chamlee, "The Sabbath Crusade," 342–350; Steven Riess, "Professional Sunday Baseball: A Study in Social Reform, 1892–1934," *The Maryland Historian* 4 (1973): 102–103; John A. Lucas, "The Unholy Experiment—Professional Baseball's Struggle against Pennsylvania's Sunday Blue Law, 1926–1934," *Pennsylvania History* 38 (1971): 163–175; Jeffrey A. Kroessler, "Baseball and the Blue Laws," *Long Island Historical Journal* 5 (1993): 168–177.

Helpful works about the history of sports in the United States include: Nancy Struna, *People of Prowess* (Urbana: University of Illinois Press, 1996); Steven Riess, *City Games* (Urbana: University of Illinois Press, 1989); Melvin Adelman, *A Sporting Time* (Urbana: University of Illinois Press, 1986); Donald J. Mrozek, *Sport and American Mentality, 1880–1910* (Knoxville: University of Tennessee Press, 1983); Stephen Hardy, *How Boston Played* (Boston: Beacon Press, 1982); and Dale Somers, *The Rise of Sports in New Orleans, 1850–1900* (Baton Rouge: Louisiana State University Press, 1972).

17. Reisner, "Special Sunday Night Attractions," 56; Riess, "Professional Sunday Baseball," 95–105; Thomas Jable, "Sports, Amusements, and Pennsylvania Blue Laws, 1682–1973" (Diss., Pennsylvania State University, 1974), 117–123, 137–138.

18. Keith McClellan, *The Sunday Game* (Akron, Ohio: University of Akron Press, 1998); A. M. Weyland, *American Football* (New York: D. Appleton, 1926); Howard Roberts, *The Story of Pro Football* (New York: Rand McNally, 1953; Ray Nitschke, *Mean on Sunday* (Garden City, N.Y.: Doubleday, 1973); "Get Stoned," *The Met* (Dallas), April 7–April 14, 1999. Other commemorations of professional football with Sunday in the title include Irving Fryar, *Sunday Is My Day* (Sister, Ore.: Multnomah, 1997); Reggie White, "Never on a Sunday?" in *First and Goal,* ed. Dave Branon (Chicago: Moody, 1996); *Six Days to Sunday* (New York: National Football League Films, 1995); Richard Whittingham, *Sunday Mayhem* (Dallas: Taylor, 1987); Art Holst, *Sunday Zebras* (Lake Forest, Ill.: Forest Books, 1980); Jim Klobuchar, *Sunday at the Met* (Minneapolis: Twin Cities Federal Savings and Loan Association, 1971); Jack Fleischer, *My Sunday Best* (New York: Grosset and Dunlap, 1971); Mike Holovak, *Violence Every Sunday* (New York: Coward-McCann, 1967); Bobby Layne, *Always on Sunday* (Englewood Cliffs, N.J.: Prentice Hall, 1962).

19. Testimony of D. H. Overton at New York State Hearings concerning Mooney and McCue Bill, reprinted in NYSC, *Public Opinion on Sunday Baseball* (New York: NYSC, 1907), 5–6; Presbyterian Church, U.S.A., *Fourth Annual Report of the Permanent Committee on Sabbath Observance* (New York: n.p., 1923), 1; "The Love of Money," *The Reform Bulletin* 6 (February–March 1919): 5–6.

20. *Bulletin of the New York Sabbath Committee* 6 (August–September 1919): 5; W. T. Manning, "Should Christians Play on Sunday?" *Literary Digest* 88 (1926): 27–28, 57–59.

21. Schneider, "The Controversy over Sunday Movies in Hastings," 62; House of Representatives, *Sunday Observance: Hearings,* Testimony of William Sheafe Chase, 69th Congress, 1st sess. (Washington, D.C.: GPO, 1926), 28; *Bulletin of the Bulletin of the New York Sabbath Committee* 7 (October–November 1920): 11; Reisner, "Special Sunday Night Attractions," 67.

22. The quotations are from a retired person living in Washington, D.C., interviewed for Sunday observance hearings; an exchange between a congressman and a minister in 1926 on the Sunday observance bill; and the testimony of labor representative Marx Lewis. All are in *Sunday Observance: Hearings,* 175, 184, 110.

23. *Sunday Observance: Hearings,* 1–2.

24. *Sunday Observance: Hearings.* For comparisons between various types of recreations and church activities see 7–10, 19, 28–29, 44–53, 81, 150–152, 184. For examples of the contrasts made between seeking pleasure and worshiping in church see 55, 176–177, 184. For references to Sunday in America's cities see 14–16, 94–95, 187, 216. Through the first four decades of the twentieth century New York City's Hippodrome—"America's National Theater"—was used on Sundays for public celebrations, meetings, political rallies, benefits, concerts, motion picture screening, and basketball games: Epstein, *The New York Hippodrome,* 1–2, 141–144, 397–444.

25. Joe D. Willis and Richard G. Welton, "Religion and Sport in America: The Case for the Sports Bay in the Cathedral Church of Saint John the Divine," *Journal of Sports History* 4 (1977): 189–207. See also Robert J. Higgs, *God in the Stadium* (Lexington: University of Kentucky Press, 1995).

26. Benjamin Kline Hunnicutt, *Work without End: Abandoning Shorter Hours for the Right to Work* (Philadelphia: Temple University Press, 1988), 159–190. See also Lawrence B. Glickman, *A Living Wage: American Workers and the Making of Consumer Society* (Ithaca: Cornell University Press, 1997).

27. Prohibitions against Sunday stock-car races fell under state statutes prohibiting games and sports; see *Worly v. State,* 79 Ga. App. 594 (1949), *Brown v. Akin,* 206 Ga. 153 (1949), and *Bishop v. Hanna,* 218 SC 474, 63 SE2d 308 (1951). States revising their codes around 1960 include Pennsylvania (1959) and Maine (1961).

28. *McGowan v. Maryland,* 366 U.S. 420 (1961); *Two Guys from Harrison v. McGinley,* 366 U.S. 582 (1961); *Braufeld v. Brown,* 366 U.S. 599 (1961); *Gallagher v. Crown Kosher Market,* 366 U.S. 617 (1961). For more discussion about the social and cultural context within which these cases were decided, see Alexis McCrossen, "Neither Holy Day, Nor Holiday: Sunday in the Sixties," *Southwest Review* 82 (1997): 336–381.

29. *Commonwealth v. Chamberlain* 343 Mass. 49, 175 SE2d 486 (1961).

30. *State ex. Rel. McNary v. Levitz Furniture Co. of Missouri, Inc.,* 502 SW2d 370 (1973).

31. *Bulletin of the New York Sabbath Committee* 15 (September–August 1928): 533–534. Quote concerning Marshall Field and Company found in *Literary Digest* 96 (1928): 29–30.

32. The history of how state legislatures and courts defined "necessity and charity" deserves further study. Since "luxury" is the antonym of necessity, such research might start with the history of luxury in Western thought: Werner Sombart, *Luxury and Capitalism,* trans. W. R. Dittmar (1913; Ann Arbor: University of Michigan Press, 1967); John Sekora, *Luxury: The Concept in Western Thought* (Baltimore: Johns Hopkins University Press, 1977); and Christopher J. Berry, *The Idea of Luxury* (New York: Cambridge University Press, 1994). It might also include a history of the idea of "comfort." As standards of comfort changed, so did those of necessity. Historian John E.

Crowley's arguments about the emergence of a "language of comfort" in Anglo-American society during the seventeenth and eighteenth centuries are important to understanding the constant reevaluation of necessity during the nineteenth and twentieth centuries: John E. Crowley, "The Sensibility of Comfort," *AHR* 104 (1999): 749–782, quotation from p. 752. Theoretical works concerning the production of "needs" may help untangle the history; see: Jean Baudrillard, *For a Critique of the Political Economy of the Sign*, trans. Charles Levin (St. Louis: Telos, 1981); and Edmond Préteceille and Jean-Pierre Terrail, *Capitalism, Consumption, and Needs*, trans. Sarah Matthews (Oxford: Basil Blackwell, 1985).

33. Noelle Oxenhandler, "Fall from Grace," *New Yorker*, June 16, 1997, 65.

34. For "social" definitions of necessity, see *State of Missouri v. Katz Drug Co.* 352 SW2d 678; and *State of South Carolina v. Solomon*, 141 SE2d 818 (1965). For representative Texas cases defining necessity in individualistic terms, see *A.M. Servicing Corp. of Dallas v. State of Texas*, 380 SW2d 747 (1964); *Atlantic Mills Thrift Center of San Antonio, Inc. v. State of Texas*, 385 SW2d 487 (1965).

35. For a court decision based on the desire to "preserve an atmosphere," see *City of Bismarck, South Dakota, v. Materi*, 177 NW2d 530 (1970). The decision contains the following phrase: "Extreme complexity of needs is evident in Sunday legislation because one of the prime objectives of legislation is preservation of atmosphere . . . numerous compromises must be made." For an overview of the effect of Sunday closing laws between 1960 and 1985, see Alan Raucher, "Sunday Business and the Decline of Sunday Closing Laws: A Historical Overview," *Journal of Church and State* 36 (1994): 13–33.

36. E. B. Weiss, *"Never* on Sunday?" (typewritten manuscript; New York: Doyle Dane Bernbach Inc., 1962), 70. Weiss was director of the advertising firm Doyle Dane Bernbach's Special Merchandising Service.

CHAPTER 8. DADDY'S DAY WITH BABY

1. Joseph Lee, *Sunday Play* (New York: American Playground Association, 1910), 7.

2. Undated note in undated file of sermons and notes from the papers of Jeremiah Burke Sanderson (1821–1875), (Bancroft Library).

Sources that directly address the history of Sunday in the home include Stephen Frank, *Life with Father* (Chapel Hill: University of North Carolina Press, 1997); Colleen McDannell, *The Christian Home in Victorian America, 1840–1900* (Bloomington: Indiana University Press, 1986); and Ann Taves, *The Household of Faith* (Notre Dame, Ind.: University of Notre Dame Press, 1986). Concerning Presbyterian devotional practices in the home, see James H. Smylie, " 'Of Secret and Family Worship': Historical Meditations, 1875–1975," *Journal of Presbyterian History* 58 (Summer 1980): 95–115.

3. Margaret Sangster, *The Art of Home-Making* (New York: Christian Herald Bible House, 1898), 169.

4. Gwendolyn Wright, *Moralism and the Model Home* (Chicago: University of Chicago Press, 1980), 9, 12, 80–81.

A major source on the nineteenth-century home and family life is Catherine Beecher and Harriet Beecher Stowe's *The American Woman's Home* (New York: J. B. Ford, 1869). See also: John R. Gillis, *A World of Their Own Making* (New York: Basic Books, 1996); Jane C. Nylander, *Our Own Snug Fireside* (New Haven: Yale University Press, 1993); Donna R. Braden, " 'The Family that Plays Together Stays Together': Family Pastimes and Indoor Amusements, 1890–1930," in *American Home Life, 1880–1930*, eds. Jessica H. Foy and Thomas J. Schlereth (Knoxville: University of Tennessee Press,

1992), 145–161; Elizabeth Donaghy Garrett, *At Home* (New York: Abrams, 1990); Karen Halttunen, "From Parlor to Living Room: Domestic Space, Interior Decoration, and the Culture of Personality," in *Consuming Visions*, ed. Simon Bronner (New York: Norton, 1989), 157–190; Sally McMurray, *Families and Farmhouses in Nineteenth Century America* (New York: Oxford University Press, 1988); Katherine C. Grier, *Culture and Comfort* (Rochester, N.Y.: Strong Museum, 1988); Clifford Clark, Jr., *The American Home, 1800–1960* (Chapel Hill: University of North Carolina Press, 1986); and Harvey Green, *The Light of the Home* (New York: Pantheon, 1983).

5. Griffing Bancroft, Diaries (Bancroft Library), entries dated June 19, August 14, October 2, and August 21, 1887; "Philip Bancroft, Sr. Recollections of Hubert Howe Bancroft, 1971" (University of California, Regional Oral History Office); Henry R. Wagner, "Albert Little Bancroft: His Diaries, Account Books, Card String of Events, and Other Papers," *California Historical Society Quarterly* 29 (1950), 98.

Numerous articles and dissertations have been written about Sunday school, but Anne Boylan's *Sunday School* (New Haven: Yale University Press, 1988) remains authoritative.

6. Griffing Bancroft, diary entries dated May 26, June 23, August 11, September 8, 22, and 29, and October 6, 13, 20, and 27, 1889; June 22 and July 13, 1890; January 25, February 8, March 8, and June 14, 1891.

7. Griffing Bancroft, diary entries dated November 20, 1892; February 11, April 23, March 14, May 28, June 25, July 2, August 27, and October 29, 1893; January 7, March 11, April 22, June 23, September 9 and 16, and October 7, 1894; September 29 and November 10, 1895.

8. Henry M. King, "The Sabbath and the Family," in *Sabbath Essays*, ed. Will C. Wood (Boston: Congregational Publishing Society, 1880), 74–76; *How to Make Sabbath Afternoons Profitable and Pleasant for Your Children* (N.p. 1894), 10–19; *The Sabbath at Home*, 1 (Boston: ATS, 1867): 3.

9. Mrs. Child, *The Mother's Book* (Boston: Carter and Hendee, 1831), 72.

10. Harriet Beecher Stowe, "Sketches from the Note-Book of an Elderly Gentleman," (1843), reprinted in *The Writings of Harriet Beecher Stowe*, 16 vols. New York: AMS Press, 1967), 15:277.

11. Ida M. Gardner, "Sunday Occupations for Children," *Outlook* 60 (1898), 673–675; McDannell, *The Christian Home*, 135–136.

12. Gillis, *A World of Their Own Making*, 87.

13. *Aunt Louisa's Picture Book* (London: Frederick Warner, 1867); Mary Blake, *Twenty-Six Hours a Day* (Boston: D. Lothrop, 1883), 178.

14. George E. Sweazey, *The Keeper of the Door* (St. Louis: Bethany Press, 1946), 18.

15. Sunday-School Union, *The Child's Sabbath-Day Book* (New York: Carlton and Philips, 1854).

16. Roy Zebulon Chamlee, "The Sabbath Crusade, 1810–1920" (Diss., George Washington University, 1968), 322; David James Burrell, *Woman and the Sabbath* (N.p., 1895).

17. Blake, *Twenty-Six Hours a Day*, 180–181.

18. Anne W. Booth, Diary (Bancroft Library), entry dated August 19, 1849; "Reverend Levi Rhutt," Interview (1939), in the Works Progress Administration's "American Life Histories: Manuscripts from the Federal Writers' Project, 1936–1940" (http://lcweb2.loc.gov/ammem/wpaintro/wpahome.html); James Agee and Walker Evans, *Let Us Now Praise Famous Men* (Boston: Houghton Mifflin, 1939), 257–265, 276–286.

Scholars in various fields have approached the issue of Sunday clothes with a great deal of imagination and sensitivity, including: Nylander, *Our Own Snug Fireside*, chap. 6; Meredith Wright, *Put on Thy Beautiful Garments* (East Montpelier, Vt.:

Clothes Press, 1990); Leigh Eric Schmidt, " 'A Church-Going People Are a Dress-Loving People': Clothes, Communication, and Religious Culture in Early America," *Church History* 58 (1989): 36–51.

19. Schmidt, "A Church-Going People," 46; Philip Curtiss, "Sunday," *AtMo* 151 (1933), 573; Booth, diary entry dated August 26, 1849; Texas woman quoted in *The News from Brownsville*, ed. Caleb Coker (Austin: Texas State Historical Association, 1992), 37.

20. Charles Parson Bigelow, Diaries (Bancroft Library), entries dated April 13, 1870, and January 29, 1871.

21. Journals of James Beith (b. 1832) covering the years between 1862 and 1888 (Bancroft Library), entries dated September 21 and December 7, 1862; January 4, 1863; February 4 and June 3, 1866, and May 26, 1867.

22. Mrs. J. H. Knowles, "Sunday Rest in the Home and Family Life," in *The Sunday Problem*, ed. W. W. Atterbury (New York: Baker and Taylor, 1894), 161.

23. *The Diaries of Margaret Scholl Hood, 1851–1861*, eds. Rose Barquist, Mary Frear Keeler, and Ann Lebherz (Camden, Me.: Pictor Press, 1992). See the entries dated January 26, 1851; January 2, June 26, and November 27, 1853; October 8, 1854; January 28 and June 10, 1855; and March 25, June 17, and August 19, 1860.

24. Georgiana L. Vail, Diary. Courtesy, The Winterthur Library: Joseph Downs Collection of Manuscripts and Printed Ephemera.

25. "Old Josh Dover," Interview (1939), in the Works Progress Administration's "American Life Histories."

26. *Diaries of Margaret Scholl Hood*, entries dated January 26, 1851; January 2, June 26, and November 27, 1853; October 8, 1854; January 28 and June 10, 1855; March 25, June 17, and August 19, 1860.

27. Lucy S. Jones, Diary (Bancroft Library), entries dated October 11 and December 13 and 20, 1874; January 3, February 7, April 11, June 13, and August 22, 1875.

28. Edward Robbins Howe, Diary (Bancroft Library), entry dated January 8, 1871. Howe was born in Cincinnati in 1843, graduated from Harvard in the class of 1864, and then studied mining and engineering in Germany and France for four years. He arrived in San Francisco in 1869.

29. Nylander, *Our Own Snug Fireside*, 240–241; Gillis, *A World of Their Own Making*, 89–94.

Social and cultural histories of meal preparation and mealtimes include: Harvey Levenstein, *Paradox of Plenty* (New York: Oxford University Press, 1993); Nylander, *Our Own Snug Fireside*, chap. 8; Margaret Visser, *The Ritual of Dinner* (New York: Grove and Weidenfeld, 1991); Barbara Carson, *Ambitious Appetites* (Washington, D.C.: American Institute of Architects Press, 1990); Kathryn Grover, ed., *Dining in America, 1850–1900* (Amherst: University of Massachusetts Press, 1987); Susan Williams, *Savory Suppers and Fashionable Feasts* (New York: Pantheon, 1985); and Louise Conway Belden, *The Festive Tradition* (New York: W. W. Norton, 1983).

30. First two quotes in paragraph from Curtiss, "Sunday," 575; Olive Hyde Foster, "Easing Up Sunday Housekeeping," *Ladies Home Journal* 29 (1912), 82; Caroline Burrell, "The Child's Sunday," in *The Mother's Book*, ed. Caroline Burrell (New York: The University Society, 1907), 180. See also John Steele Garden, "The Chicken Story," *American Heritage* 47 (1996): 52–56, 58, 60, 62.

31. Margaret F. Byington, *Homestead* (New York: Russell Sage, 1910), 65; Anatole Broyard, "Sunday Dinner in Brooklyn," in *The Brooklyn Reader*, eds. A. W. Sexton et al. (1954; New York: Harmony Books, 1994), 19; Gillis, *A World of Their Own Making*, 97; Poll conducted in 1998 by the Gallup Organization for MCI, quoted in *MCI Tracker* 1 (June 1998); Frederick Wirt, interviewer, "Growing Up in the Cities: Oral History Interviews, 1977–1979," (Donated Oral History Collection, Bancroft Library).

32. Karen V. Hansen, *A Very Social Time* (Berkeley: University of California Press, 1994); *The Sunday Problem: A Study Book for Groups and Individuals* (Philadelphia: United Lutheran Publication House, 1923), 10–11.

33. Alexander Mackay-Smith, *The Sunday Newspaper* (New York: WNSA, [1897]), 2–3, 10; Herrick Johnson, quoted in *Our Day*, reprinted in *Public Opinion* 6 (1889): 396.

34. David James Burrell, *The Sunday Newspaper* (New York: WNSA Tract, n.d.); Renwick Harper Martin, *Six Studies on the Day* (Pittsburgh: NRA, 1934), 45–46.

35. Frank Luther Mott, *American Journalism* (New York: Macmillan, 1941), 318, 397, 480–481, 584–585; Frank Luther Mott, *A History of American Magazines* 5 vols. (Cambridge: Harvard University Press, 1938), 2:34–38; *The Sunday Newspaper* (New York: American Church Press, n.d.), 8.

For information about the size, circulation, and history of Sunday newspapers, see also: Ian Lewis, "Envisioning Consumer Culture: Comic Strips, Comic Books, and Advertising in America, 1890–1945" (Diss., University of Rochester, 1993); Michael J. Dillon, " 'A Smart Live Journal': E. H. Butler's *Buffalo News* and the Rise and Decline of an Open Public Forum, 1873–1914" (Diss., Pennsylvania State University, 1995); *Daily and Sunday Newspaper Audience* (New York: Newspaper Advertising Bureau, 1988); Michael Schudson, *Discovering the News* (New York: Basic Books, 1978); Glen W. Peters, "The American Weekly," *Journalism Quarterly* 48 (1971): 466–471; William A. Hachten, "The Metropolitan Sunday Newspaper in the United States: A Study of Trends in Content and Practices" (Diss., University of Minnesota, 1961); John A. Haney, "A History of the Nationally Syndicated Sunday Magazine Supplements" (Diss., University of Missouri–Columbia, 1953); Alfred Lee, *The Daily Newspaper in America* (New York: Macmillan, 1937); James M. Lee, *History of American Journalism* (Boston: Houghton and Mifflin, 1923), 309–379; "The Man Who Invented the Sunday Newspaper," *Review of Reviews* 22 (1900): 619; and Robert Donald, "Sunday Newspapers in the United States," *The Universal Review* 8 (1890): 78–89.

36. *Sunday Newspapers: A List Giving Full Descriptions* (New York: John F. Phillips, 1888). The list includes circulation numbers for each paper.

37. Donald, "Sunday Newspapers in the United States," 82; Martin, *Six Studies on the Day*, 45–46. The Sunday papers of the 1890s usually contained from twenty to fifty pages (compared to the eight-page dailies).

38. *New York Herald*, reprinted in *Public Opinion* 6 (1889): 396; "Concerning Sunday," *New York Tribune*, December 7, 1879; "Sermons for Sunday Papers," *Public Opinion* 19 (1895): 309.

39. Ray Barfield, *Listening to Radio, 1920–1950* (Westport, Conn.: Praeger, 1996), 3, 6, 89–91, 171; George C. Ericson, "Swedish Radio Services in Chicago," *Swedish Pioneer Historical Quarterly* 24 (1973): 157–162; Jon D. Swartz and Robert C. Reiner, *Handbook of Old Time Radio* (Metuchen, N.J.: Scarecrow Press, 1993).

40. J. Elwin Wright, *The Old Fashioned Revival Hour and the Broadcasters* (Boston: Fellowship Press, 1988). About Fuller, see also Philip Goff, " 'We Have Heard the Joyful Sound': Charles E. Fuller's Radio Broadcast and the Rise of Modern Evangelism," in *Religion and American Culture* 9 (1999). About the design of radios see Barfield, *Listening to Radio*, 15.

41. Barfield, *Listening to Radio*, 128–129; Swartz and Reiner, *Handbook of Old Time Radio*, 259, 271, 280, 305, 376, 384, 387.

42. Barfield, *Listening to Radio*, 33–35, 39, 70–73; Lizabeth Cohen, *Making a New Deal* (Cambridge: Cambridge University Press, 1990), 132–143; Swartz and Reiner, *Handbook of Old Time Radio*, 305.

43. Prime-time fall schedules for NBC, ABC, and CBS between 1948 and 1980, found in Alex McNeil, *Total Television* (New York: Penguin Books, 1980), 850–882.

For information about radio and television programming and listening and viewing practices, see: Michele Hilmes, *Radio Voices* (Minneapolis: University of Minnesota Press, 1997); Ronald Hager, "Television Viewing and Physical Activity in Children" (Diss., Arizona State University, 1997); Barfield, *Listening to Radio;* Swartz and Reiner, *Handbook of Old Time Radio;* Jim Spring, "Seven Days of Play," *American Demographics* 15 (1993): 50–54; J. Fred MacDonald, *Don't Touch That Dial!* (Chicago: Nelson Hall, 1991); Mitchell Shapiro, *Television Network Daytime and Late-Night Programming, 1959–1989* (Jefferson, N.C.: McFarland, 1991); Stephen Pullum, "A Rhetorical Profile of Pentecostal Televangelists" (Diss., Indiana University, 1988); Gregory Stemen, "Patterns of Television Viewing in the United States" (Diss., Ohio State University, 1983); and Wright, *The Old Fashioned Revival Hour.*

44. Wirt, "Growing Up in the Cities."

CHAPTER 9. WHAT IS REST?

1. Quotation from G. Stanley Hall, Introduction to John Robert Floody, *Scientific Basis of Sabbath and Sunday: A New Investigation After the Manner and Methods of Modern Science, Revealing the True Origin and Evolution of the Jewish Sabbath and the Lord's Day* (1901; Boston: Turner, 1906), vi. See also G. Stanley Hall, "Philosophy in the United States," *Mind* (1879): 89–105.

2. See Juliet Schor, *The Overworked American* (New York: Basic Books, 1991).

3. MCI, *The Sunday Tracker* 1 (June 1998). *The Sunday Tracker* is "a comprehensive, monthly research initiative aimed at recent trends in the Sunday activities of Americans." A national survey conducted by the Gallup Organization for MCI in mid 1998 found that 79 percent of Americans considered Sunday the most enjoyable day of the week.

4. Quotation from "The Sunday Problem," *The Outlook* 61 (1899): 581.

The meaning of rest is an elusive subject, but a number of primary and secondary sources are suggestive. During the last decade a few dissertations have been prepared concerning the theological aspects of rest: Judith Hoch Wray, "Rest as a Theological Metaphor in the Epistle to the Hebrews and the Gospel of Truth: Early Christian Homiletics of Rest" (Diss., Union Theological Seminary, 1997); Edward Allen, "Rest as a Spiritual Discipline: The Meaning and Manner of Sabbath Observance" (D. Min., Fuller Theological Seminary, 1991); Barry Casey, "Hope, Suffering, and Solidarity: The Power of the Sabbath Experience" (Diss., Claremont Graduate School, 1988).

5. P. T. Barnum, *Struggles and Triumphs* (1871; New York: Penguin, 1981).

6. Annie Payson Call, *Power through Repose* (Boston: Roberts Brothers, 1891).

7. John P. Hylan, "Public Worship: A Study in the Psychology of Religion" (Diss., Clark University, 1899). Quotations are from reprint with the same title (Chicago: Open Court, 1901), 9–10, 28–29, 30–33.

8. William A. Hammond, "How to Rest," *NAR* 153 (August 1891): 215–219.

9. Michael Oriard, *Sporting with the Gods* (New York: Cambridge University Press, 1991), 356–380. See also Tony Ladd and James A. Mathiesen, *Muscular Christianity* (Grand Rapids, Mich.: Baker Books, 1999); Clifford Putney, "Men and Religion: Aspects of the Church Brotherhood Movement, 1880–1920," *Anglican and Episcopal History* (63) 1994: 450–467; and William E. Winn, " 'Tom Brown's Schooldays' and the Development of 'Muscular Christianity,' " *Church History* 29 (1960): 64–73.

10. Benjamin Kline Hunnicutt, *Work without End* (Philadelphia: Temple University Press, 1988), chap. 4. See also "Sunday Use of Public Playgrounds," *The Survey* 44 (1925): 4.

About recreation and fitness there is a growing literature: Mark Dyerson, "Regulating the Body and the Body Politic: American Sport, Bourgeois Culture, and the Language of Progress, 1880–1920," in *Sport and Society*, ed. Benjamin G. Rader and Randy Roberts (Urbana: University of Illinois Press, 1997); Joan Burbick, *Healing the Republic* (New York: Cambridge University Press, 1994); Kathryn Grover, ed., *Fitness in American Culture* (Amherst: University of Massachusetts Press, 1989); Harvey Green, *Fit for America* (Baltimore: Johns Hopkins University Press, 1988); David Nasaw, *Children of the City* (New York: Basic Books, 1985); James Whorton, *Crusaders for Fitness* (Princeton: Princeton University Press, 1982); and Dominick Cavallo, *Muscles and Morals* (Philadelphia: Temple University Press, 1981).

11. Marvin Vincent, *The Pleasure-Sunday a Labor-Sunday. A Sermon* (New York: Rufus Adams, [1886]), 4; Wilbur F. Crafts, *Sabbath for Man* (New York: Funk and Wagnalls, 1885), 490, 513–514; Charles Hodge, *Conference Papers or Analyses of Discourses, Doctrinal and Practical* (New York: Charles Scribner's Sons, 1879), 301–302; Samuel B. Lyon, "The Physiological Basis of Sunday Rest," in *The Sunday Problem*, ed. W. W. Atterbury (New York: Baker and Taylor, 1894), 21–39.

12. Robert Patterson, *The Sabbath: Scientific, Republican, and Christian* (Cincinnati: Western Tract Society, [1870]), 17–22, 9.

13. Floody, *Scientific Basis of Sabbath and Sunday*.

14. Haegler's chart is reprinted in the following texts, all of which use it to stress the centrality of Sunday: W. W. Atterbury, "The Natural Law of Weekly Rest," in *Sabbath Essays*, ed. Will C. Wood (Boston: Congregational Publishing Society, 1880), 34; Wilbur F. Crafts, "What Are Innocent Sunday Recreations?" in *The Sunday Problem*, 120; Theodore Gilman, "The Day Which Divine Love Established and Human Love Must Preserve," in *Sunday. The World's Rest Day*, ed. Duncan J. McMillan (New York: Doubleday, 1915), 289; Duncan J. McMillan, "The Necessity of the Day of Rest, Pictorially Illustrated," in *Sunday. The World's Rest Day*, 203; and Duncan J. McMillan, *The Influence of the Weekly Rest-Day on Human Welfare: A Scientific Research* (New York: NYSC, 1927), 36.

15. Quotes are from addresses delivered by William Allen Butler, A. Spaeth, and W. W. Atterbury reprinted in *The Sunday Problem*, 179, 252, 256.

16. E. G. Martin, "Variations in the Sensory Threshold of Faradic Stimulation in Normal Human Subjects," *American Journal of Physiology* (April 1914); E. G. Martin, "The 'Day of Rest' and Human Efficiency," *Journal of the American Medical Association* (June 1914); "Science Speaks Again on the Need of the Day of Rest," *The Bulletin of the New York Sabbath Committee* (December 1914–January 1915); E. G. Martin, "The Scientific View of a Weekly Rest Day," *The Lord's Day Leader* (April–May, 1916): 15–19.

17. "The Scientific Research into the Influence of the Sabbath upon Human Welfare," *The Bulletin of the New York Sabbath Committee* (October–November, 1914): 7–16.

18. A. D. Emmett and Katherine R. Coleman, "Studies of the Physiological Influence of the Weekly Day of Rest: Effects on General Nutrition," *The Bulletin of the New York Sabbath Committee* (December 1915–January 1916).

Gies and Martin each delivered papers to a panel titled "The Day of Rest in Nature and Human Nature" at the 14th International Lord's Day Congress held in October 1915. W. J. Gies and E. G. Martin, "Scientific Research, Laboratory Experiments," in *Sunday. The World's Rest Day*, 168–197.

In 1927, the NYSC published *Influence of the Weekly Rest-Day on Human Welfare: A Scientific Research*, by its secretary, Duncan J. McMillan. The inability of even the most committed Sabbatarian to marshal evidence that Sunday should be the day of rest is clear from the opening pages, where eminent physicians and clergymen praised the effort, but did not stress the benefits of Sunday rest as opposed to a weekly day of rest. (Dr. Chittenden, dean of Yale's Sheffield School; Dr. Allen J. Smith, dean of the medical faculty of the University of Pennsylvania; Dr. William H. Howell and Dr. Howard Kelly, of the medical faculty of Johns Hopkins University; and Dr. W. J. Gies of Columbia University's College of Physicians and Surgeons praised the effort.)

19. Chapter 45, Section 1883 in *Arkansas Digest of 1884*, reprinted in *A Compilation of the Labor Laws of the Various States and Territories and the District of Columbia* (Washington, D.C.: GPO, 1892), 62. The definition of the Sabbath is from Chapter 202, Section 4315 of Vermont's 1880 laws reprinted in the same volume, 487. The definition of labor is from the 1877 revision of New Jersey's codes, reprinted there also, 318.

20. New Hampshire General Laws of 1878, Chapter 273, Section 10, reprinted in *A Compilation of the Labor Laws* (1892), 309.

21. Charles Worcester Clark, "The Day of Rest," *AtMo* 64 (1889): 369–371; Charles M. Sheldon, "Slaves of Civilization," *The Independent* 53 (1901): 2029–2032.

22. Clinton Xavier, *Sunday Laws: Constitutional?* (Boston: Mudge, 1899).

23. Arnold Roth, "Sunday 'Blue Laws' and the California State Supreme Court," *Southern California Quarterly* 55 (1973): 43–47.

24. Wilbur F. Crafts, "The Civil Sabbath the Friend, Not the Foe, of Liberty," in Wilbur F. Crafts, ed., *Addresses on the Civil Sabbath* (Washington, D.C.: The Reform Bureau, 1890), 19–21.

25. Vincent, *The Pleasure-Sunday a Labor-Sunday*, 10.

26. There were fourteen international conferences on Sunday rest in all, held in Geneva (1876), Bern (1879), Paris (1881), Brussels (1885), Paris (1889), Stuttgart (1892), Chicago (1893), Brussels (1897), Paris (1900), St. Louis (1904), Milan (1906), Frankfurt (1907), Edinburgh (1908), and San Francisco (1915). Some of the proceedings are in print.

27. Crafts, "Labor's Right to the Weekly Rest Day," in *Addresses on the Civil Sabbath*, 31–34. He delivered this address in Scranton, Pennsylvania, on October 20, 1889. Xavier, *Sunday Laws*, 72; *Chicago Tribune*, July 8, 1904; Charles Sheldon, *Robert Hardy's Seven Days* (Philadelphia: Littleton, 1897); "Sunday Labor," *Forum* 23 (1902): 338–401.

28. Letters to the Editor, *The Railway Age*, May 10, 1883—June 21, 1883; "Sunday Rest in Railway Traffic," in *The Sunday Problem*, 63–102.

29. Margaret F. Byington, *Homestead* (New York: Russell Sage, 1910), 173, 176, 236; Henry F. May, *Protestant Churches in Industrial America* (New York: Harper Brothers, 1949), 129; David Brody, *Steelworkers in America* (Cambridge: Harvard University Press, 1960), 117; Ken Fones-Wolf, *Trade Union Gospel* (Philadelphia: Temple University Press, 1989), 51–52.

30. 49th Congress, 1st sess. *CR* 17 (1886): 3401; 49th Congress, 2d sess. *CR* 18 (1887): 15, 386, 710, 747, 1306, 1334, 1657; 50th Congress, 1st sess. *CR* 19 (1888): 1170, 2243, 2327, 2679, 2823, 2824, 3381, 3497, 3673, 3767, 3799, 4741, 4455.

31. For a text of the Blair Bill see S.2983, 50th Congress, 1st sess., *CR* 19 (1888). For petitions in favor of the Blair Bill see: 50th Congress, 2d sess., *CR* 20 (1889); 50th Congress, 2d sess., *Senate Miscellaneous Document 43* (1889); 51st Congress, 1st sess., *CR* 21 (1889); 51st Congress, 2d sess., *CR* 22 (1891); 52d Congress, 1st sess., *CR* 23 (1892). For petitions against the Blair Bill see: 50th Congress, 2d sess., *CR* 20 (1889); 51st Congress, 1st sess., *CR* 21 (1889); 51st Congress, 2d sess., *CR* 22 (1891). See the *Index to the CR* for the numerous page numbers.

32. S. 4695 and H.R. 12752, 51st Congress, 2d sess., *CR* 22 (1891): 673, 705; 52d Congress, 1st sess., *CR* 23 (1892): 352, 3074, 4077.

33. Quoted in Alonzo T. Jones, *The Captivity of the Republic* (New York: International Religious Liberty Association, 1893), 27.

34. Ferdinand C. Iglehart, "The Saloon and the Sabbath," *NAR* 161 (1895): 467–475.

35. "The Sunday Saloon," reprinted from the *Toledo Blade* in *Public Opinion* 2 (1887): 308.

36. S. 1628, S. 1890, and H.R. 6592, 53d Congress, 2d sess., *CR* 24 (1894): 221, 3688, 3490; S. 1441 and S. 3136, 54th Congress, 1st sess., *CR* 28 (1896): 526, 5154.

37. Quotations are from "One Day of Rest in Seven for District of Columbia Workers," *American Labor Legislation Review* (*ALLR*) 10 (1920): 256. See also: John A. Fitch, "One Day of Rest in Seven," *The Survey* 22 (1909): 134; William Sheafe Chase, "One Day of Rest," *The Survey* 22 (1912): 1999–2000; "One Day of Rest in Seven," *ALLR* 2 (1912), entire issue; *The Importance of One Day of Rest in Seven* (New York: Federal Council of Churches, 1912); John A. Fitch, "One Day of Rest in Seven by State and Federal Legislation," *ALLR* 3 (1917): 168–174; Solon De Leon, "Progress in One-Day-of-Rest-in-Seven Legislation," *ALLR* 10 (1920): 129–130; John B. Andrews, "One-Day-of-Rest-in-Seven Legislation," *ALLR* 13 (1923): 175–176; and Louise Y. Gottschall, "One Day Rest in Seven," *ALLR* 18 (1928): 320–323.

38. David Roediger and Philip Foner, *Our Own Time* (New York: Verso, 1989), 227–229; Crafts, *Sabbath for Man*, 172, 183, 263, 400, 418; Henry Van Dyke, *Holydays and Holidays: A Human View of the Sunday Question* (New York: Daniel J. Holden, 1886), 15–17; Vincent, *The Pleasure-Sunday a Labor-Sunday*, 15; Alice Woodbridge, "Sunday Rest for Women and Children in Factories, Stores, and Domestic Service," in *The Sunday Problem*, 149.

For more information on the movements for shorter hours, see: Benjamin Kline Hunnicutt, *Kellogg's Six-Hour Day* (Philadelphia: Temple University Press, 1996); William Mirola, "Fighting in the Pews and Fighting in the Streets: Protestantism, Consciousness, and the Eight-Hour Movement in Chicago, 1867–1912" (Diss., Indiana University, 1995); Teresa Anne Murphy, *Ten Hours Labor* (Ithaca: Cornell University Press, 1992); Schor, *The Overworked American*; Roediger and Foner, *Our Own Time*, 26–27; Hunnicutt, *Work without End*; Ronnie Steinberg, *Wages and Hours* (New Brunswick, N.J.: Rutgers University Press, 1982); R. M. Miller, "American Protestantism and the 12-Hour Day and the Steel Strike of 1919–1923," *Social Science Quarterly* 37 (1956): 137–150; May, *Protestant Churches in Industrial America*; Marion Cotter Cahill, *Shorter Hours* (New York: Columbia University Press, 1934); Louise Y. Gottschall, "The Five Day Week?", *ALLR* 20 (1930): 89–93; Solon De Leon, "The Five-Day Week," *The Labor Age* (1927): 11–12; William B. Dickson, "Eight-Hour Day and Six-Day Week in the Continuous Industries," *ALLR* 3 (1917): 155–167; and "Sunday and the Trades-Unions," *Outlook* 55 (1899): 337–338.

39. See Roediger and Foner, *Our Own Time*, 184, 236–242; Hunnicutt, *Work without End*, 70–78; Roy Rosenzweig, *Eight Hours for What We Will* (Cambridge: Cambridge University Press, 1983), 1–8; and Lawrence Glickman, *A Living Wage* (Ithaca: Cornell University Press, 1997).

40. *ALLR* 2 (1912): 528–529; Cahill, *Shorter Hours*, 275–276; John A. Fitch, "Sunday Rest," *The Survey* 22 (1909): 134; Roy Zebulon Chamlee, "The Sabbath Crusade, 1810–1920" (Diss., George Washington University, 1968), 351; and Roediger and Foner, *Our Own Time*, 215.

41. Section 3 of "A Bill to Secure Sunday as a Day of Rest in the District of Columbia" [H.R. 7179], reprinted in *Sunday Observance: Hearings*, 69th Congress, 1st sess., (Washington, D.C.: GPO, 1926), 1.

42. Jointly endorsed position of the Massachusetts Council of Churches and the Massachusetts Commission on Christian Unity (1977), reprinted in *Labor and Leisure: A Look at Contemporary Values* (Boston: Massachusetts Council of Churches, 1994), 40.

43. R. C. Gordon-McCutchan, *The Taos Indians and the Battle for Blue Lake* (Santa Fe: Red Crane Books, 1991). About sacred space see especially Marc Auge, *Non-Places: Introduction to an Anthropology of Supermodernity,* trans. John Howe (1992; New York: Verso, 1995), and David Chidester and Edward T. Linenthal, eds., *American Sacred Space* (Bloomington: Indiana University Press, 1995).

EPILOGUE: CRAZY SUNDAY

1. NBC, "Wide, Wide World, Parts I and II," broadcast October 16 and 23, 1955. The entire tape of the first Sunday's show and a small part of the second show are available for viewing at the Museum of Radio and Television Broadcasting (New York City), T79:0486 and T79:0487.

2. Harvey Newcomb, *The Young Lady's Guide to the Harmonious Development of Christian Character* (Boston: James B. Dow, 1841), 137.

3. Philip Curtiss, "Sunday," *AtMo* 151 (1933) 573.

Selected Bibliography
of Primary Sources

Note: The selected bibliography of primary sources is offered as a supplement to the chapter notes. Sources cited in the notes may not appear in the bibiography, which was prepared in order to suggest the breadth and variety of sources, not their extent or number.

1600–1800

Dorington, Theophilus. *Family Devotions for Sunday Evenings Throughout the Year*. London: Printed for John Wyat, 1693.
Mather, Cotton. *A Good Evening for the Best of Dayes; An Essay To Manage an Action of Trespass, Against Those Who Mispend the Lord's-day Evening*. Boston: B. Green, 1708.
Pynchon, William. *Holy Time, or, The True Limits of the Lord's Day*. London: R. I., 1654.
Shepard, Thomas. *Theses Sabbaticae, or, The Doctrine of the Sabbath*. 1649, London: John Rothwell, 1650.

1800–1829

Beecher, Lyman. "Pre-Eminent Importance of the Christian Sabbath." *The National Preacher* 3 (1829): 155–160.
——. "Mr. Johnson's Report on Sabbath Mails." *The Spirit of the Pilgrims* 2 (1829): 143–144.
Considerations on the Foundation, Ends, and Duties of the Christian Sabbath. Utica, N.Y.: Northway and Porter, 1829.
Dickinson, Pliny. *A Discourse on the Institution, Observance, and Profanation of the Sabbath*. Walpole, N.H.: n.p., 1813.

Evarts, Jeremiah, ed. *An Account of Memorials Presented to Congress, Respecting Sabbath Mails*. Boston: n.p., 1829.

Field, David. *The Sabbath: A Sermon Preached at Hartford*. Hartford, Conn.: Benjamin L. Hamlen, 1816.

Hervey, James. *Considering the Prevailing Custom of Visiting on the Sabbath*. Boston: Lincoln and Edwards, 1809.

Hughes, Mary. *Family Dialogues, or Sunday Well-Spent*. Philadelphia: Society of the Evangelical Church of St. John, 1828.

Irving, Washington. "Sunday in London." In *The Sketch-Book of Geoffrey Crayon, Gent*. New York: C. S. Van Winkle, 1819–1820.

Johnson, Richard. *Report of the Committee of the Senate. . . .* Baltimore: James Lovegrove, 1829.

Leland, John. *Remarks on Holy Time*. Pittsfield, Mass.: Phineas Allen, 1815.

A Sunday's Excursion. Philadelphia: Philadelphia Female Tract Society, 1816.

1830–1849

Andrews, Silas W. *The Sabbath at Home*. Philadelphia: Presbyterian Tract and Sunday School Society, 1837.

Browne, John W. *Sunday Law Neither Christian Nor American*. Boston: Committee of the Anti-Sabbath Convention, 1849.

Burleigh, Charles C. *The Sabbath Question*. Philadelphia: Merrihew and Thompson, 1847.

Child, Mrs. *The Mother's Book*. Boston: Carter and Hendee, 1831.

"Church, Ministry, and Sabbath Convention." *The Liberator*, November 27, 1841.

Duffield, George, and Albert Barnes. *Discourses on the Sabbath*. Philadelphia: George W. Donohue, 1836.

Everett, A. H. "Sunday Mails." *NAR* 31 (1830): 154–167.

First Annual Report of the American and Foreign Sabbath Union. Boston: T. R. Marrin, 1844.

Fisher, William Logan. *The History of the Institution of the Sabbath Day, Its Uses and Abuses*. Philadelphia: John Penington, 1845.

Hall, Willard. *A Plea for the Sabbath*. Baltimore: Baltimore Sabbath Association, 1845.

Huntington, Frederick D. *The Lord's Day*. Boston: American Unitarian Association, 1848.

Kingsbury, Harmon. *Petition Praying a Repeal of that Part of an Act of Congress, Regulating the Post Office Department*. Cleveland: n.p., 1838.

———. *The Sabbath: A Brief History*. New York: R. Carter, 1840.

Mitchell, A. W. *Conversations of a Father with His Children*. Philadelphia: PBP, 1849.

Parker, Theodore. "Some Thoughts on the Most Christian Use of the Sunday." *The Liberator*, May 12, 1848.

Parkhurst, Henry M., ed. *Proceedings of the Anti-Sabbath Convention*. 1848; Port Washington, N.Y.: Kennikat Press, 1971.

Phelps, Amos Augustus. *The Sabbath*. New York: American Society for the Promotion of Christian Values, 1842.

——. *A Sketch of the Proceedings of the Convention for the Discussion of the Sabbath, the Ministry, and the Church.* New York: American Society for the Promotion of Christian Morals, 1848.

Poe, Edgar Allan. "Three Sundays a Week." *Broadway Journal* 1 (1845): 293–296.

Report on Sabbath Desecration Adopted by the Franklin County Conference of Churches. Greenfield, Mass.: C. A. Minck, 1848.

"The Sabbath in Lowell." *The Lowell Offering and Magazine* 3 (1843): 239–240.

Sedgwick, Catharine Maria. *Home.* Boston: James Munroe, 1835.

"Sunday Mails." *American Quarterly and Review* 8 (1830): 175–197.

Sunday Whaling: or, Is It Right to Take Whales on the Sabbath? Honolulu: Hawaiian Tract Society, [1844].

Tappan, Lewis. *Letter to Eleazer Lord, Esq. In Defense of Measures for Promoting the Observance of the Christian Sabbath.* New York: John P. Haven, 1831.

Wells, Lucy. *A Mother's Plea for the Sabbath: In a Series of Letters to an Absent Son.* 1843; Portland, Me.: Hyde, Lord, and Dureb, 1845.

Whipple, Charles. *Sunday Occupations.* Boston: Committee on the Anti-Sabbath Convention, 1849.

The Young Lady's Sunday Book. Philadelphia: Desliver, Thomas, 1836.

1850–1869

Bacon, George B. *The Sabbath Question: Sermons Preached to the Valley Church.* Orange, N.J.: n.p., 1868.

Beecher, Henry Ward. *Norwood.* 1867; New York: Fords, Howard, and Hulbert, 1887.

Blagden, G. W. *The Duty of More Strict Observance of the Sabbath.* Boston: Nichols and Noyes, 1866.

Boardman, H. A. *A Plea for Sunday Afternoon.* Philadelphia: n.p., 1850.

Brace, Charles Loring. "Keeping the Sunday." In *Short Sermons to News Boys.* New York: Charles Scribner, 1866.

Brown, Thomas B. *Thoughts Suggested by the Perusal of Gilfillan and Other Authors on the Sabbath.* New York: New York Tract Society, 1869.

Cook, Russell. *The Sabbath in Europe: The Holy Day of Freedom—The Holiday of Despotism.* New York: Robert Craighead, 1858.

Corner, Julia. *Sabbath Day Readings, or, Children's Own Sabbath Book.* Philadelphia: PBP, 1853.

Cox, Robert. *The Literature of the Sabbath Question in Two Volumes.* Edinburgh: MacLachan and Stewart, 1865.

Crosby, Howard. *Remember the Sabbath.* New York: E. French, 1865.

Cutler, Benjamin. *Half-Day Worship.* Brooklyn, N.Y.: E. B. Spooner, 1861.

Edwards, Justin. *The Sabbath Manual.* New York: ATS, [1844], 1845, 1850, 1860.

Elliott, Charles. *The Sabbath.* Philadelphia: PBP, 1867.

Ellis, Charles Mayo. *Argument for Opening the Reading Rooms of the Public Library of the City of Boston on Sunday Afternoons.* Boston: A. Williams, 1867.

"A Foreign Movement on the Sunday Question." *Harper's Weekly* 3 (1859): 610.

Fowler, M. Field. *Protest or Remonstrance of M. Field Fowler, Against Opening the Doors of the Public Library, Boston, on the Lord's Day.* Boston: Rockwell and Rollins, 1867.

General Order Respecting the Observance of the Sabbath Day in the Army and Navy. Washington, D.C.: GPO, 1862.

Hill, Micaiah. *The Sabbath Made for Man.* London: John Farquhar, 1857.

Hopkins, Mark. *The Sabbath and Free Institutions.* New York: Edward O. Jenkins, 1863.

J.F.W.W., "The Sunday at Home." *Monthly Religious Magazine* 26 (1861): 86–104.

Nash, Nathaniel C. *The Sunday Law Unconstitutional and Unscriptural.* Boston: n.p., 1868.

Nelson, Henry A. *Benefits of the Sabbath.* Philadelphia: PBP, 1867.

NYSC. *The Civil Sabbath Restored.* New York: Edward O. Jenkins, 1861.

——. *Plea for the Sabbath in War.* New York: NYSC, [1861].

——. *Railroads and the Sabbath.* New York: Edward O. Jenkins, 1858.

——. *The Sabbath: As It Was and As It Is.* New York: NYSC, 1857.

——. *Sunday Theatres, "Sacred Concerts," and Beer Gardens.* New York: NYSC, 1860.

Opinion of Hon. John M. Read, of the Supreme Court of Pennsylvania in Favor of the Passenger Railway Cars Running on Every Day of the Week, Including Sunday. Philadelphia: Sherman, 1867.

Parker, James. *The Operative's Friend, and Defense.* Boston: Charles H. Pierce, 1850.

Presbyterian Church in U.S.A. Presbytery of Utica, N.Y. *Sunday Cheese-Making.* Utica: Roberts, 1865.

Rice, N. L. *The Christian Sabbath.* New York: Robert Carter and Brothers, 1862.

The Sabbath at Home, vol. 1. Boston: ATS, 1867.

"The Stadt Theatre." *Harper's Weekly* 3 (1859): 673–674.

Stoughton, L. Ellsworth. *Railroad Excursion.* Warehouse Point, Conn.: L. E. Stoughton, 1864.

"Sunday Evening in a Beer Garden." *Harper's Weekly* 3 (1859): 657–658.

"A Sunday Evening *Sacred* Concert." *Harper's Weekly* 3 (1859): 642–643.

"Sunday in Chatham Street." *Harper's Weekly* 3 (1859): 739.

"Sunday in Jones' Woods." *Harper's Weekly* 3 (1859): 701, 708.

"Sunday Law." *American Law Review* 2 (1868): 226–239.

"The Sunday Question and Its Witnesses." *The Christian Examiner* 83 (1867): 208–220.

Sunday-School Union. *The Child's Sabbath-Day Book.* New York: Carlton and Philips, 1854.

Whipple, Charles K. "Efforts for Sunday Sabbatism." *The Radical* 2 (1867): 677–679.

——. "It is a Part of the System." *The Radical* 5 (1869): 378–384.

——. "Times and Seasons." *The Radical* 2 (1866): 225–229.

——. *The Truth Shall Make You Free.* Boston: Mudge, 1850.

1870–1879

Beecher, Henry Ward. *Libraries and Public Reading Rooms: Should They Be Opened on Sunday?* New York: J. B. Ford, 1872.

Bellows, Henry. "The Use of Sunday." *Old and New* 7 (1873): 368–372.

Buckingham, Samuel. *The Sabbath and Rail Roads.* Springfield, Mass.: Clark W. Bryan, 1872.

Chadwick, John. *The Best Use of Sunday. A Sermon.* New York: n.p., 1876.

Charles Atwell; or, The Ruinous Effects of Sabbath Recreations. New York: ATS, [187–].

Fowler, M. Field. *Essay on the Sunday Library and Horse Car Question.* Boston: Alfred Mudge and Son, 1872.

Hall, G. Stanley. "Philosophy in the United States." *Mind* 4 (1879): 89–105.

Herford, Brooke. "The Sunday Question." *Unitarian Review* 8 (1877): 396–407.

Knox, W. E. *Our Sabbaths and Our Morals.* Elmira, N.Y.: Horace A. Brooks, 1873.

McKay, J. J. *The Claims of the Sabbath Against the Assumptions of Rev. Henry Ward Beecher.* New York: n.p., 1872.

Patterson, Robert. *The Sabbath: Scientific, Republican, and Christian.* Cincinnati: Western Tract Society, [1870].

Porter, Noah. "Religious Books and Sunday Reading." *Books and Reading; or, What Books Shall I Read and How Shall I Read Them?* New York: Charles Scribner, 1871, chap. 20.

Robinson, Stuart. "Sabbath Laws in the United States." *Catholic Presbyterian* 2 (1879): 87–96.

Sabbath Bells Chimed by the Poets. Philadelphia: Hubbard Brothers, 1873.

Schmucker, S. S. *Appeal in Behalf of the Christian Sabbath.* New York: ATS, [187–].

Spring, Gardiner. *The Sabbath: A Blessing to Mankind.* New York: ATS, [187–].

Stacy, James. *The Holy Sabbath.* Richmond, Va.: Presbyterian Committee of Publication, 1877.

Whipple, Charles K. "Free Speech on Sunday." *The Index* 5 (1874): 212–213.

Whipple, Charles K., Minot J. Savage, Charles E. Pratt, and William C. Gannett, eds. *How Shall We Keep the Sunday? An Answer in Four Parts.* 1877; Boston: James H. West, 1898.

1880–1889

Atticus, pseud. "Vacation Sundays in Town." 8-part series in *The Index* 13 (1881): 57, 64–65, 76–77, 89, 100–101, 110, 123, 140–141.

Bacon, Leonard Woolsey. *The Sabbath Question: Sunday Observance and Sunday Laws.* New York: G. P. Putnam's Sons, 1882.

Beach, Edwin. *Recent Progress of Sabbath Reform Among Railroads.* Columbus, Ohio: n.p., 1889.

Blake, Mary. *Twenty-Six Hours a Day.* Boston: D. Lothrop, 1883.

Brooks, Henry M. *The Olden Time Series: New England Sunday.* Boston: Ticknor, 1886.

Brown, George W. *Historical and Critical Review of the Sunday Question.* Rockford, Ill.: n.p., 1882.

Cheever, George Barrell. *God's Timepiece for Man's Eternity.* 1883; New York: A. C. Armstrong and Son, 1888.

Church, Ella Rodman. *Sunday Evenings at Elmridge.* Philadelphia: Presbyterian Board of Publication and Sabbath-School Work, 1887.

Clark, Charles Worcester. "The Day of Rest." *AtMo* 64 (1889): 366–375.

Clarke, James Freeman. "Rational Sunday Observance." *NAR* 131 (1880): 496–506.

Clarke, E. P. "Sunday Laws." *Overland Monthly* 12 (1888): 317–321.

Crafts, Wilbur F. *The Sabbath for Man.* New York: Funk and Wagnalls, 1885.

Cutler, Mary Salome. "Sunday Opening of Libraries." *Library Journal* 14 (1889): 176–191.

Fellows, George H. *Sunday and the Workingman.* New York: NYSC., [1880s].

Gardiner, George. "Shall We Have a Sabbath and How?" *Baptist Review* 2 (1880): 584–593.

Green, Samuel S. "Opening Libraries on Sunday." *Library Journal* 9 (1884): 85–86.

Hale, Edward E. *Sunday Afternoon Stories for Home and School, Volumes 1 and 2.* Boston: Roberts Brothers, 1888.

——. *The Sunday Laws.* Boston: George H. Ellis, 1880.

Hayman, Henry. "Sabbath Observance and Sunday Recreation." *The Modern Review* 5 (1884): 238–258.

Hertwig, John George. *Sunday Laws.* Washington, D.C.: Eckler, 1883.

Holland, Frederick May. "Our Sunday Laws." *The Index* 16 (1885): 147–148.

Jesup, Moris K. *Sunday Opening of the Museums in the Park.* New York: n.p., [1885].

Jones, Jesse H. "Sunday Labor." *The Chautauquan* 9 (1889): 398–401.

"Keeping Sunday." *The Railroad Gazette* 15 (1883): 329.

Kennedy, William Sloan. "Sunday in Boston." *The Index* 15 (1884): 411–412.

Larcom, Lucy. *A New-England Girlhood.* 1889; Gloucester, Mass.: Peter Smith, 1973.

Lewis, A. H. *A Critical History of Sunday Legislation from 321 to 1888 A.D.* Alfred Center, N.Y.: ASTS, 1886.

Linklater, R. *Sunday and Recreation: A Symposium.* London: Griffith, Farrar, Okeden, and Welsh, 1889.

Martyn, Carlos. *The American Sunday, The Museums and Libraries, the Public Press, and the Half-Saturday Holiday.* New York: Martin B. Brown, 1886.

NYSC. *The Right of the People to Their Sunday Rest.* New York: NYSC, 1880.

Nisbet, E. *Our Sunday; Whence and What.* Santa Barbara, Calif.: Independent Job Printing Office, 1885.

Potter, Henry C. "The Sunday Question." *New Princeton Review* 2 (1886): 37–47.

Rossiter, William. "The Continental Sunday." *Nineteenth Century* 15 (1884): 933–944.

Schenck, E. H. Mrs. *The Lord's Day.* Bridgeport, Conn.: Standard Print, 1880.

Stanton, Elizabeth Cady. "Our Boys on Sunday." *Forum* 1 (1886): 191–198.

Stuart, Reed. "The Gospel of Culture and the Gospel of Christ." *The Unitarian* 3 (1888): 260–261.

Sumptuary Laws and Sunday Laws Are Unconstitutional and Void. New York: Bonfort and Leoser, 1887.

Sunday as a Civil Institution. The Laws of the State of New York. Syracuse, N.Y.: Syracuse Sabbath Association, 1882.

Sunday as a Civil Institution. Under the Laws of Illinois and the Ordinance of the City of Chicago. Chicago: Chicago Sabbath Association, 1881.

"Sunday Morning at Asbury Park, New Jersey." *Harper's Weekly* 26 (1882): 242.

Sunday Newspapers: A List Giving Full Descriptions. New York: John F. Phillips, 1888.

Sunday Railway Work: Opinions of Prominent Railway Managers. N.p., [1883].

"Sunday Trains in Massachusetts." *The Railroad Gazette* 15 (1883): 493.

Through the Side Door, By a Working-Woman. New York: NYSC, [188–].

Whipple, Charles K. "For and Against Sabbatism." *The Index* 17 (1886): 412.

Work and Rest. New York: Concord Co-operative Printing, [188–].

Van Dyke, Henry. *Holydays and Holidays: A Humane View of the Sunday Question.* New York: Daniel J. Holden, 1886.

Vincent, Marvin. *The Pleasure-Sunday a Labor-Sunday. A Sermon.* New York: Rufus Adams, [1886].

Ward, Julius H. "The New Sunday." *AtMo* 47 (1881): 526–537.

Washburn, L. K. *Sunday and "The Sabbath."* Boston: J. P. Mendum, 1886.

1890–1899

Atterbury, William Wallace. *Sunday Rest: The New Movement for Its Legal Protection.* New York: n.p., [1890].

Bittinger, John Q. *A Plea for the Sabbath and for Man.* Boston: CSP, 1892.

Burrell, David. *The Sunday Newspaper.* New York: WNSA, [1897].

———. *Woman and the Sabbath.* N.p. 1895.

Carroll, Wesley Philemon. *The Sabbath as an American War Day: "The Carroll Theory."* Cheyenne, Wyo.: Sun-Leader Printing House, 1899.

Congress and Sunday Laws. New York: Truth Seeker Library, 1891.

Conway, Moncure. "Civilising the Sabbath." *Open Court* 6 (1892): 3495–3500.

Crafts, Wilbur F., ed. *Addresses on the Civil Sabbath.* Washington, D.C.: The Reform Bureau, 1890.

De Normandie, James. *Sunday at the Columbian Fair.* Boston: n.p., 1892.

Doane, William. " 'German-Americans' and the Lord's Day." *Forum* 20 (1895): 733–738.

Donald, E. W. "Observance of Sunday." In *Some Things that Trouble Young Manhood.* New York: Styles and Cash, 1899.

Donald, Robert. "Sunday Newspapers in the United States." *The Universal Review* 8 (1890): 78–89.

Doyle, Alexander. "The Catholic Church and the Sunday Saloon." *Independent* 47 (1895): 10.

Earle, Alice Morse. *The Sabbath in Puritan New England.* New York: Charles Scribner's Sons, 1891.

Eaton, Charles K. "The Ideal Sunday." *NAR* 153 (1891): 322–328.

Evans, F. W. *Russian Famine: A Shaker Protest against Closing the World's Fair on Sunday.* Mt. Lebanon, N.Y.: n.p., 1891.

Fairly, John S. *Answer to Bishop H. C. Potter on Sunday Opening of the Columbian Exposition.* Charleston, S.C.: Daggert, 1893.

Gannett, William Channing. *The Sunday I Would Keep.* Boston: James H. West, 1898.

Gardner, Ida M. "Sunday Occupations for Children." *Outlook* 60 (1898): 673–675.

Gibbons, James Cardinal. "The Dangers of Sunday Desecration." *Independent* 47 (1895): 1.

Gifford, O. P. "Why the World's Fair Should Be Opened on Sunday." *The Arena* 7 (1893): 193–196.

Gorton, James. *The Sabbath Question and the World's Fair.* Akron, Ohio: Capron and Curtice, 1892.

Hammond, William. "How to Rest." *NAR* 153 (1891): 215–219.

Harris, George E. *A Treatise on Sunday Laws.* Rochester, N.Y.: The Lawyers' Co-operative, 1892.

Hawley, Joseph. *Closing on Sundays: The Columbian Exhibition.* Washington, D.C.: G. R. Gray, 1892.

Hooker, Charles E. *In Defense of the South, and In Favor of Closing the World's Fair on Sunday.* Washington, D.C.: n.p., 1892.

How to Make Sabbath Afternoons Profitable and Pleasant for Your Children. Boston: n.p., 1894.

Huntington, William Reed. *Ought Cities to Make Sunday-Laws?* New York: NYSC, 1895.

Iglehart, Ferdinand C. "The Saloon and the Sabbath." *NAR* 161 (1895): 467–475.

"In Praise of Leisure: A Summer Symposium." *AtMo* 66 (1890): 137–139.

"Jesus, the Church, and the World's Fair." *The Arena* 6 (1892): 250–260.

Jones, Alonzo T. *The Captivity of the Republic.* New York: International Religious Liberty Association, 1893.

——. *The National Sunday Law.* New York: American Sentinel, 1892.

——. *The Union of Church and State in the United States.* Oakland, Calif.: Pacific Press, 1892.

Kinney, Henry C. *Why the Columbian Exposition Should Be Opened on Sunday.* Chicago: Rand, McNally, 1892.

Lanisors, D. L. "A Sunday of the Olden Time, Manchester, Massachusetts." *Magazine of American History* 24 (1890): 214–218.

Lewis, A. H. *The Swift Decadence of Sunday. What Next?* Plainfield, N.J.: ASTS, 1899.

MacKay-Smith, Alexander. *The Sunday Newspaper.* New York: WNSA, [1897].

NYSC. *Sunday Observance in the United States As a Civil Institution.* New York: NYSC, 1897.

Olcott, Euphenia M. *The Sabbath a Delight.* New York: WNSA, 1898.

Oswald, F. L. "An Expensive Delusion." *NAR* 162 (1896): 125–128.

Parkhurst, Charles H. *The Lord's Day.* New York: WNSA, [1896].

Potter, Henry C. "Some Exposition Uses of Sunday." *Century* 23 (1892): 138–141.

——. "Sunday and the World's Fair." *Forum* 14 (1892): 194–200.

Protestant Episcopal Church, 1899 Church Congress. *Papers, Addresses and Discussions.* New York: Thomas Whitacker, [1899].

Ramage, J. "Sunday Legislation." *Sewanee Review* 4 (1895): 116–123.

Remensynder, J. B. "The Liberal but Not a Lawless Sunday." *Independent* 47 (1895): 11.

Report of the Committee of Ladies Regarding the Closing of Theaters on Sunday. St. Paul, Minn.: William L. Banning, 1891.

Ringgold, James Trapier. *The Legal Sunday: Its History and Character.* Battle Creek, Mich.: International Religious Liberty Association, 1899.

——. *The Sunday: The Legal Aspects of the First Day of the Week.* Jersey City, N.J.: F. D. Linn, 1891.

"Shall We Obey God's Commandment? or Shall We Open the Columbian Exposition Sunday?" *The Independent* 43 (1891): 37–41.

Sheldon, Charles M. *Robert Hardy's Seven Days: A Dream and Its Consequences.* Boston: CSP, 1893.

Solved; or The Sunday Evening Problem. New York: Riley Brothers, 1895.

Spalding, J. L. "Why the World's Fair Should Be Opened on Sunday," *The Arena* 7 (1892): 45–47.

Stevenson, Robert Louis. *A Lowden Sabbath Morning.* New York: Scribner's, 1898.

"Sunday at Chicago Next Year." *Nation* 55 (1892): 236.

Sunday. Is Not Its Religious Observance a Blot on Bible Christianity Which Ought to Be Removed? Plainfield, N.J.: Buell, 1895.

The Sunday Newspaper. New York: American Church Press, [189–].

"The Sunday Question," *Independent* (special issue) 47 (November 7, 1895).

Sunderland, Byron, and W. A. Croffut. *"The Lord's Day—Or Man's?" A Public Discussion.* New York: Truth Seeker Library, 1897.

Swing, David. "What the American Sunday Should Be." *Forum* 13 (1892): 120–127.

"We Must Live." Interesting Narratives: Showing the Absurdity of this Excuse for Sabbath Breaking and Other Violations of the Word of God. New York: ATS, [189–].

1900–1919

Abbott, Lyman. "Letters to an Unknown Friend." *Outlook* 103 (1913): 158–160.

Ashley, W. B., compiler. *Church Advertising: Its Why and How.* Philadelphia: J. B. Lippincott, 1917.

Blewitt, C. J. "The First Sabbath." *The Gospel Trumpet* 34 (1914): 5–6.

Burrell, Caroline, ed. *The Mother's Book.* 1907; New York: University Society, 1909.

The Child Welfare Manual, vol. 2. New York: University Society, 1915.

"The Civil Sabbath Fallacy." *Liberty* 4 (1909): 33.

Dana, William B. *A Day for Rest and Worship.* New York: Fleming H. Revell, 1911.

Draper, W. R. "Sunday Closing in Kansas City." *Independent* 64 (1908): 254–255.

"Easing Up Sunday Housekeeping." *Ladies Home Journal* 29 (1912): 82.

Esser, Joseph Henry. *Should a Letter-Carrier Have a Free Sunday?* New York: WSNA, [1909].

Ferris, Carrie. *The Sunday Kindergarten.* Chicago: University of Chicago Press, 1909.

Fitch, John A. "Sunday Rest." *The Survey* 22 (1909): 134.

Floody, John Robert. *Scientific Basis of Sabbath and Sunday.* 1901; Boston: Turner, 1906.

Friedenberg, Albert. *The Jews and the American Sunday Laws.* New York: n.p., 1903.

Hall, G. Stanley. "Sunday Observance." *The Pedagogical Seminary* 15 (1908): 217–229.

Harland, Marion. "What Is the Matter with Sunday?" *Independent* 72 (1912): 876.

Harris, Elmer Blaney. "The Day of Rest at Coney Island." *Everybody's Magazine* 19 (1908): 24–34.

Herrick, Christine T. *Sunday Night Suppers.* Boston: D. Estes, 1907.

Hill, James L. *Seven Sorts of Successful Services: Suggestive Solutions of the Sunday Evening Problem.* New York: E. B. Treat, 1904.

Hinrichs, Frederic W. *Sunday in New York.* New York: n.p., 1904.

Hodgson, James, compiler. "Digest of Laws Prohibiting Sport of Baseball on Sunday." Typewritten manuscript, Albany: New York State Library, February 1917.

Horsman, O. C. *One Rest-Day in Seven.* Philadelphia: Baptist Publication Service, 1912.

Howard, J. R. "The American Sabbath." *The Outlook* 68 (1901): 638–639.

Hylan, John P. *Public Worship: A Study in the Psychology of Religion.* Chicago: Open Court, 1901.

Independent Citizens' Union of Maryland. *The Sabbath Question.* Baltimore: Independent Citizens' Union, 1902.

Jerome, William. *The Liquor Tax in New York: A Plea for the Opening of Saloons on Sunday.* New York: G. P. Putnam's, 1905.

Lampman, Rosamond. "The Sunday Supper." *Harper's Bazaar* 46 (1912): 141.

Lee, Frederic S. *The Human Machine and Industrial Efficiency.* New York: Longmans, 1919.

Lee, Gerald Stanley. "Making the Crowd Beautiful." *AtMo* 87 (1901): 240–253.

Lee, Joseph. *Sunday Play.* New York: National Recreation Association, [1910].

Leonard, A. H. "The Passing of the Sunday Evening Service." *Methodist Review* 93 (1911): 431–439.

Lewis, Abram Herbert. *Spiritual Sabbathism.* Plainfield, N.J.: ASTS, 1910.

——. *The Evolution and Future of Sunday Legislation.* Plainfield, N.J.: ASTS, 1905.

"New York's Demoralizing Sunday." *Literary Digest* 46 (1913): 1129–1130.

NYSC. *Legislative Hearings at Albany.* New York: NYSC, 1909.

——. *Public Opinion on Sunday Baseball.* New York: NYSC, 1907.

Pan-American Exposition. Some Reasons Why It Should Open on Sundays. Chicago: Office of the Secretary of American Secular Union and Freethought Federation, 1901.

Peabody, Francis Greenwood. *Sunday Evenings in the College Chapel.* Boston: Houghton Mifflin, 1911.

Porter, Roscoe. *The World's Fair: Sunday Closing and the Transference of the Sabbath as Viewed by Eminent Men, and Presented by the Word of God.* Oakland, Calif.: Pacific Press, 1903.

Plumb, Albert Hale. *Sunday Golf.* Boston: New England Sabbath Protective League, 1900.

Rainsford, W. S. *The Rest Day.* N.p., [1902].

"Report of the Sunday Recreation Commission." *Worcester Magazine* 17 (1914): 201.

Sangster, Margaret E. *Social Sabbath Breaking.* New York: n.p., 1902.

Sheldon, Charles M. "Some Slaves of Civilization." *Independent* 53 (1901): 2029–2032.

Soule, Ella Frances. *Sunday Afternoons for the Children: A Mother's Book.* New York: Fords, Howard, and Hubert, 1900.

"Sunday Games." *Independent* 53 (1901): 1391–1392.

"Sunday in the City." *Outlook* 87 (1907): 836–837.

Sunday in the Home. New York: Abingdon Press, 1914.

Sunday in the Home. Philadelphia: American Institute of Child Life, 1914.

"Sunday Opening." *Library Journal* 32 (1907): 112–113.

"Sunday Trains." *The Railway and Engineering Review*, August 6, 1904, 568, 762.

"Sunday Tabu." Editorial. *New Republic* 25 (1920): 62–63.

Taylor, Joseph Judson. *The Sabbatic Question*. New York: F. H. Revell, 1914.

United States Congress. Committee on the District of Columbia. *Closing Certain Places of Business in District of Columbia on Sunday*. Washington, D.C.: GPO, 1908.

Washington, Booker T. *Character Building: Being Addresses Delivered on Sunday Evenings to the Students of Tuskegee Institute*. New York: Doubleday, Page, 1902.

What Are We Going to Do about Sunday Theater? Minneapolis: C. W. Arnold, 1911.

"Why Are Sunday Amusements Prohibited?" *Case and Comment* 22 (1915): 553–557.

Wylie, Richard C. *Sabbath Laws in the United States*. Pittsburgh: NRA, 1905.

1920–1949

"At Home Sunday," *Good Housekeeping* 82 (1926), 78.

Carver, William Owen. *Sabbath Observance: The Lord's Day in Our Day*. Nashville: Broadman Press, 1940.

"The Cotter's Sunday at Home." *The Bulletin of the NYSC* 15 (1929): 666–670.

Cotton, John Paul. *From Sabbath to Sunday*. Bethlehem, Pa.: Times Publishing, 1933.

Curtiss, Philip. "Sunday." *AtMo* 151 (1933): 571–578.

Davis, William Walters, ed. *The Day of Worship*. New York: Macmillan, 1932.

Deseo, Lydia May. *Nason, the Blind Disciple: A Sermon Drama with Suggestions for a Sunday Evening's Worship Service*. New York: Abingdon Press, 1927.

Dreifuss, Arthur, dir. *Sunday Sinners*. Colonnade Pictures, 1940.

Emmons, C. A. "Shall Play and Recreation Centers Be Operated on Sunday?" *The American City* 44 (1931): 135.

Evans, Lester. "Should a Christian Drive His Car on Sunday? " *The Homiletic Review* 91 (1926): 206.

Fitzgerald, F. Scott. "Crazy Sunday." 1932; In *Babylon Revisited and Other Stories*. New York: Charles Scribner's Sons, 1960.

Franke, Elmer E., ed. *Anti-Blue Law Magazine*. New York: People's Christian Bulletin, [1921].

Githens, Harry. "Modern Pagans: A Playlet." *Bulletin of the NYSC* 15 (1928): 537–540.

Haldeman, I. M. *Truth about the Sabbath and the Lord's Day*. New York: H. L. Day, [1921].

"How Henry Ward Beecher Would Redeem the Sabbath with Music." *Étude* 41 (1923): 865–866.

"How to Rest." *Literary Digest* 86 (1925): 21–22.

"How to Spend Sunday." *Journal of Religion* 1 (1921): 311–312.

"How to Spend Sunday: A Symposium." *Independent* 105 (1921): 8–10, 22–24.

Jones, Herbert. *The Menace of Blue Laws; or, Why I Champion the Sunday The-atre.* Huntington Park, Calif.: n.p., 1921.

Kaye, Joseph. "You *Still* Can't Dance on Sunday!" *The Dance Magazine of Stage and Screen* 15 (1931): 30, 59, 64.

LaBarre, George B. *History of the Observance of Sunday.* Trenton, N.J.: Trenton Evening Times, 1923.

"The Lord's Day in the Bible Belt." *Christian Century* 47 (1930): 43–44.

Lynd, Robert, and Helen Lynd. *Middletown.* New York: Harcourt, Brace, 1929.

——. *Middletown Revisited.* New York: Harcourt, Brace, 1937.

Manning, W. T. "Should Christians Play on Sunday?" *Literary Digest* 88 (1926): 27–28, 57–59.

Martin, Renwick Harper. *The Day: A Manual on the Christian Sabbath.* Pitts-burgh: NRA, 1933.

——. *The Movie Barons and Sunday Movies.* Pittsburgh: NRA, 1936.

——. *Six Studies of the Day.* Pittsburgh: NRA, 1934.

McMillan, James Duncan. *Influence of the Weekly Rest-Day on Human Wel-fare: A Scientific Research.* New York: NYSC, 1927.

Motion Pictures on Sunday: A Collection of Facts and Figures. Cincinnati: Bill-board, 1920.

Myers, Gustavus. *Ye Olden Blue Laws.* New York: The Century Co., 1921.

Nelson, Janet Fowler. *Leisure-Time Interests and Activities of Business Girls.* New York: The Women's Press, 1934.

NYSC. *Bulletin of the NYSC for the Years 1914–1922.* New York: NYSC, 1923.

"The Only Day I Have: A One-Act Sabbath Observance Play." Franklin, R.I.: n.p., 1927. Held in the Harris Collection at Brown University.

"Our Sunday and Anti-Sunday Laws." *Literary Digest* 86 (1925): 32–33.

Peabody, Francis Greenwood. *Sundays in College Chapels since the War; Ser-mons and Addresses.* Boston: Houghton Mifflin, 1921.

"Polo as Prayer," *Literary Digest* 88 (1926): 32.

Porter, Eliot, and Arthur C. Wickenden. *The Sabbath for Man.* Philadelphia: Presbyterian Church in the USA, 1936.

Porter, Henry Alford. *The Question of Sunday.* Charlottesville, Va.: First Baptist Church of Charlottesville, 1936.

Schelling, Felix E. "A Sabbatarian," In Schelling, *Summer Ghosts and Winter Topics.* Philadelphia: J. B. Lippincott, 1924, 152–156.

Schulman, Samuel. *The Many-Sided Question of Sunday Observance.* New York: n.p., 1920.

Shafer, Charles. "Good Old Day: It Ain't What It Used to Be." *American Monthly* 109 (1930): 48–49.

"Should Christians Play on Sunday?" *Literary Digest* 88 (1926): 27–28, 57–59.

"Should Sunday Be Kept or Spent?" *Independent* 105 (1921): 180–181.

Smith, William C. *Blue Law Ballads: A Purge for Puritans.* Cincinnati: The Sin-ners Club, 1922.

Sunday Evenings with Jesus. Kansas City, Mo.: Beacon Hill Press, 1946.

"Sunday Use of Public Playgrounds." *Literary Digest* 84 (1925): 32.

Sweazey, George. *The Keeper of the Door.* St. Louis: Bethany Press, 1946.

Terrell, John Upton. *Sunday Is the Day You Rest.* New York: Coward-McCann, 1939.

United States Congress, House. *Sunday Observance: Hearings.* 69th Congress, 1st sess. Washington, D.C.: GPO, 1926.

Van Ness, I. J. "The Day and the Home," in *The Day of Worship,* ed. William Walter Davis. New York: Macmillan, 1932.

Von Keppler, Paul Wilhelm. "Sunday in Very Truth." *The Catholic World* 124 (1927): 829.

Weld, John. *The Sabbath Has No End: A Novel of Negro Slavery.* New York: Scribner's, 1942.

White, William C. "Bye, Bye, Blue Laws." *Scribner's* 94 (August 1933): 108.

" 'Y' Swimming on Sunday." *Literary Digest* 103 (1929): 25.

1950–2000

Andreasen, Niels-Erik. *Rest and Redemption: A Study of the Biblical Sabbath.* Berrien Springs, Mich.: Andrews University Press, 1978.

Asinof, Eliot. *Seven Days to Sunday.* New York: Simon and Schuster, 1968.

Breasted, Mary. "City's Pulse Is Langorous on Final Sunday in August." *NYT,* August 27, 1973.

Chaplin, Sid. *The Smell of Sunday Dinner.* Newcastle upon Tyne: Graham, 1971.

Cohen, Richard. *Sunday in the Sixties.* New York: New York Public Affairs Committee, 1962.

Come Sunday: Photographs by Thomas Roma. New York: Museum of Modern Art, 1996.

Directory of Sabbath-Observing Groups. Fairview, Okla.: Bible Sabbath Association, 1974.

Edwards, Tilden. *Sabbath Time: Understanding and Practice for Contemporary Christians.* New York: Seabury Press, 1982.

Galligan, Phil, dir. *The Blue Laws.* Boston: WBZ-TV, 1961.

Gamman, Lorraine. "Sunday Visits." *Critical Quarterly* 34 (1992): 59–67.

Harris, Thomas. *Black Sunday.* New York: Putnam, 1975.

Heo, Yumi. *One Sunday Morning.* New York: Orchard Books, 1999.

Krasna, Norman. *Sunday in New York.* New York: Dramatists Play Service, 1962.

Labor and Leisure: A Look at Contemporary Values. Boston: Massachusetts Council of Churches, 1994.

Lantry, Eileen. *A Family Guide to Sabbath Nature Activities.* Mountain View, Calif.: Pacific Press, 1980.

Marden, Norman. *Sunday Dinner: Essays and Anecdotes.* New York: Exposition Press, 1972.

Nossiter, Jonathan, dir. *Sunday.* New York: Cinepix Film Properties, 1997.

Oates, Joyce Carol. *Sunday Dinner.* New York: American Place Theatre, 1970.

Odom, Robert Leo. *The Lord's Day on a Round World.* Nashville: Southern Publishing Association, 1970.

Parrott, Lora Lee. *Sunday Dinner: Meals from Family Kitchens.* Kansas City, Mo.: Beacon Hill Press, 1979.

Porter, H. B. *The Day of Light: The Biblical and Liturgical Meaning of Sunday.* 1960; Washington, D.C.: The Pastoral Press, 1987.

Schaper, Donna. *Sabbath Sense: A Spiritual Antidote for the Overworked.* Philadelphia: Innisfree Press, 1997.

Schulter, Michael. *Keeping Sunday Special.* Basingstoke: Marshall Pickering, 1988.

Scott-Goodman, Barbara. *Sunday Dinner: Seasonal Menus to Enjoy with Family and Friends.* San Francisco: Chronicle Books, 1998.

Stewart, E. J. "Sunday Family Dinner." *Jump Up and Say! A Collection of Black Storytelling,* ed. Linda Goss and Clay Goss. New York: Simon and Schuster, 1995.

Strand, Kenneth A. *The Early Christian Sabbath: Selected Essays and a Source Collection.* Worthington, Ohio: Ann Arbor Publishers, 1979.

Strum, Charles. "On 7th Day, a Town of Malls Repents." *NYT,* December 7, 1992.

Sunday Closing Laws Revisited: A Biblical, Ethical, and Sociological Study of a Common Day of Rest. Boston: Massachusetts Council of Churches, 1993.

The Sunday Dinner. Atlanta: Peachtree Baptist Church, 1975.

Tentler, Leslie Woodcock. "One Historian's Sundays." In *Religious Advocacy and American History,* eds. Bruce Kuklick and D. G. Hart. Grand Rapids, Mich.: Eerdmans, 1997.

"A Typical Sunday in Autumn: NBC's Wide Wide World." Parts I and II. New York: National Broadcast Corporation, 1955 (aired October 1955). Held by the Museum of Radio and Television Broadcasting. T79:0486 and T79:0487.

Ward, Hiley H. *Space-Age Sunday.* New York: Macmillan, 1960.

Weilerstein, Sadie. *Dick, the Horse that Kept the Sabbath.* New York: Bloch, 1955.

Weiss, E. B. *Never On Sunday?: A Study of Sunday Retailing.* Typewritten manuscript. New York: Doyle Dane Bernbach, Inc., 1962.

Williams, Tennessee. *A Lovely Sunday for Creve Coeur.* New York: New Directions, 1980.

Index